Export Procedures and Documentation

AED-01

For
BA, B.Com., BSc.
[Application Oriented Course]

Sudhir Kochhar
B.Com. (H), M.Com., JAIIB, CAIIB, CITF, ICSI,
CA Foundation, Diploma in Management

Useful For

IGNOU, KSOU (Karnataka), Bihar University (Muzaffarpur), Nalanda University, Jamia Millia Islamia, Vardhman Mahaveer Open University (Kota), Uttarakhand Open University, Kurukshetra University, Himachal Pradesh University, Seva Sadan's College of Education (Maharashtra), Lalit Narayan Mithila University, Andhra University, Pt. Sunderlal Sharma (Open) University (Bilaspur), Annamalai University, Bangalore University, Bharathiar University, Bharathidasan University, Centre for distance and open learning, Kakatiya University (Andhra Pradesh), KOU (Rajasthan), MPBOU (MP), MDU (Haryana), Punjab University, Tamilnadu Open University, Sri Padmavati Mahila Visvavidyalayam (Andhra Pradesh), Sri Venkateswara University (Andhra Pradesh), UCSDE (Kerala), University of Jammu, YCMOU, Rajasthan University, UPRTOU, Kalyani University, Banaras Hindu University (BHU) and all other Indian Universities.

Closer to Nature   We use Recycled Paper

GULLYBABA PUBLISHING HOUSE (P) LTD.

ISO 9001 & ISO 14001 CERTIFIED CO.

Published by:

GullyBaba Publishing House Pvt. Ltd.

Regd. Office:	**Branch Office:**
2525/193, 1ˢᵗ Floor, Onkar Nagar-A, Tri Nagar, Delhi-110035 (From Kanhaiya Nagar Metro Station Towards Old Bus Stand) Call: 9991112299, 9312235086 WhatsApp: 9350849407	1A/2A, 20, Hari Sadan, Ansari Road, Daryaganj, New Delhi-110002 Ph.011-45794768 Call & WhatsApp: 8130521616,8130511234

E-mail: hello@gullybaba.com, **Website:**GullyBaba.com

New Edition

ISBN: 978-93-81970-81-2

Copyright© with Publisher

HOME DELIVERY of GPH Books

You can get GPH books by VPP/COD/Speed Post/Courier.
You can order books by Email/SMS/WhatsApp/Call.
For more details, visit gullybaba.com/faq-books.html
Our packaging department usually dispatches the books within 2 days after receiving your order and it takes nearly 5-6 days in postal/courier services to reach your destination.

In the ever-changing world of complex international rules, laws, and regulations, even seasoned export/import professionals may find themselves in unfamiliar situations. As we all know we are living in a global village and there is hardly anything that doesn't shift between borders be it rations, home items, chemical goods and even automobile. Export-import trade is a regular practice for several manufacturing industries, and the basis for living for others.

A common saying is that exporting and importing has nothing much to do with products and a lot to do with documentation! It sounds completely odd but it is true! The significance of correct paperwork can't be underplayed in accurately organizing exporting and importing. Export-import credentials are the keystone of global trade and make the process easy to understand.

This GPH book *"Export Procedures and Documentation (AED-01)"* deals with various procedures and documentation of export.

The book is written specially in question & answer format to provide students the instant gratification of a correct answer. In this book, I have tried to solve all possible questions from the exams' point of view. Solutions of previous years' question papers have also been included to help students to understand the unique examination structure.

I hope that this book would not only be a favourite study material for the students but also can be a nice resource for teaching.

An attempt has been carefully made to present this book more useful and meet the requirement and challenges of the course prescribed by Indian Universities.

I wish you a successful and rewarding career ahead. Feedback in this regard is solicited.

– Sudhir Kochhar

Acknowledgement

My compliments go to the **GullyBaba Publishing House (P) Ltd.,** and its meticulous team who have been enthusiastically working towards the perfection of the book.

Their teamwork, initiative and research have been very encouraging. Had it not been for their unflagging support, this work wouldn't have been possible. The creative freedom provided by them along with their aim of presenting the best to the reader has been a major source of inspiration in this work. Hope that this book would be successful.

— Sudhir Kochhar

Publisher's Note

The present book AED-01 is targeted for examination purpose as well as enrichment. With the advent of technology and the Internet, there has been no dearth of information available to all; however, finding the relevant and qualitative information, which is focused, is an uphill task.

We at **GullyBaba Publishing House (P) Ltd.,** have taken this step to provide quality material which can accentuate in-depth knowledge about the subject. GPH books are a pioneer in the effort of providing unique and quality material to its readers. With our books, you are sure to attain success by making use of this powerful study material. Provided book is just a reference book based on the syllabus of particular University/Board. For a profound information, see the textbooks recommended by the University/Board.

Our site **gullybaba.com** is a vital resource for your examination. The publisher wishes to acknowledge the significant contribution of the Team Members and our experts in bringing out this publication and highly thankful to Almighty God, without His blessings, this endeavor wouldn't have been successful.

— Publisher

Topics Covered

CONTENTS

QUESTION PAPERS

1 Fundamentals of Export Business

An Overview

A function of international trade whereby goods produced in one country are shipped to another country for future sale or trade is known as export business. The sale of such goods adds to the producing nation's gross output. It allows us to purchase items made in other countries. People around the world would not have the opportunity to enjoy goods and services made in foreign. It includes all business activities needed to create, ship and sell goods and services across national borders.

Export business is important for many reasons. It provides a source of raw materials and parts and demand for foreign products. Global business allows for new market and investment opportunities. It can help in improving the political relations too. Government policy for exports aims at promoting exports to the maximum extent to earn foreign exchange.

Q1. **Explain the meaning and importance of International Trade.**

Or

What is the importance of International Trade?

Ans. International trade refers to the exchange of capital, goods and services across international borders or territories. In most countries, such trade represents a significant share of gross domestic product (GDP).

Industrialisation, advanced transportation, globalisation, multinational corporations and outsourcing are all having a major impact on the international trade system. Increasing international trade is crucial to the continuance of globalisation. Without international trade, nations would be limited to the goods and services produced within their own borders.

The basis of international trade is to be found in the diversity of economic resources in different countries. Not all countries have been endowed by nature with the same production facilities. There are differences in climatic condition and geological deposits as also in the supply of labour and capital. Due to these differences, each country finds it advantageous to specialise in the production of some specific commodities. Such specialisation is facilitated by the exchange of surplus production through international trade. International trade takes place when buyers find foreign markets cheaper to buy in and sellers find them more profitable to dispose of their products than the domestic market. Thus, a more effective use of world's resources is made possible through international trade.

Importance of International Trade

Economics deals with the proper allocation and efficient use of scarce resources. International Trade is also concerned with allocation of economic resources among countries. Such allocation is done in the world markets by means of international trade under the concept of free trade, the best products are produced and sold in competitive market, and benefits of efficient production like better quality and lower price are available to all people of the world. The importance of foreign trade has been discussed as follows:

(1) **Better use of Country's Resources:** International trade helps in the utilisation of country's resources in the best possible manner. In many cases, domestic industries depend upon foreign markets for the disposal of their production. For example, the jute and tea industries of India are mainly dependent upon export markets. Japanese industry depends upon exports for its prosperity. In many cases, the existence of an export market enables the producers to increase their production and thus avail themselves of the economies of large-scale production. Some domestic industries depend upon foreign countries for the supply of the capital goods and equipment as also for their supply of raw materials and components.

(2) **Stability of Prices:** Foreign trade could also be utilised to control the nefarious activities of monopolists. It helps to control the prices in a country. Whenever the price of some commodity tends to increase, it can increase the level of its imports of that commodity to check the rise in prices. Similarly, whenever the price of a commodity falls due to a glut in its supply, the trend may be checked by exporting the same. This, in turn, leads to more or less uniform price throughout the world.

(3) **Harmonious Relationship between various Countries:** It decreases the distance of countries, now people are more aware of other countries' tradition, fashion, trends, etc. It promotes harmonious and cordial relationship between all of them. It can lead to world economic integration. This in turn leads to political peace and greater cooperation in countries regarding socio-cultural development. Growth of trade can thus reduce the likelihood of war. International trade makes the term "Globalisation" more meaningful.

(4) **Greater availability of Goods:** Only international trade made it possible for a country to obtain those goods, which it cannot produce (or cannot produce as cheaply as other countries). Thus, a country's well being is determined largely by the extent to which it participates in international trade. Consumers benefit from international trade as much as they can purchase from the cheapest source. India depends upon foreign countries for a substantial portion of her supplies of edible oils. US consumers depend upon imports for the supply of coffee and sugar while the UK consumers obtain the major portion of their foodstuffs and the entire supply of tea from foreign countries.

(5) **Reduction in Cost of Production:** As international trade helps to get capital goods and raw materials from the cheapest sources, the overall cost of production goes down leading to lower prices of commodities.

(6) **High Rate of Economic Development:** Reduction in costs of production, stability of prices and greater employment opportunities; all these benefits of foreign trade lead to rapid economic development and higher rate of growth in national income. In fact, foreign trade was considered as an engine of growth. Many developed countries like UK, USA and Japan owe their prosperity to their exports of manufactured products. In recent years, many developing countries like Korea, Taiwan, Thailand, Singapore and Hongkong have benefited from international trade.

(7) **Greater Employment Opportunities:** Foreign trade leads to an increase in domestic agricultural and industrial production, which in turn generates more employment in the country.

(8) Contribution to Government Revenues: Most governments impose duties on imports and sometimes on exports too. These duties generate substantial revenues for the state exchequer. Read GPH books and score excellent marks.

Q2. What are the factors that motivate a firm to export? Explain giving suitable illustrations in support of your answer.

Ans. There are some basic economic reasons, which might influence a firm decision regarding export business. These are as follows:

- **Insufficiency of Domestic Demand**: If the domestic demand of a commodity is insufficient for utilising the installed capacity, it can lead to export that commodity. Export business offers a suitable mechanism for utilising the unused capacity. This will reduce costs and improve the overall profitability of the firm. Recession in the domestic market often serves as a stimulus to export ventures.

- **Obtaining Imported Inputs**: Nations have to pay for imports of materials, technology or processes not available within their national boundaries. Therefore, governments may be compelled to impose export obligations on the firms, especially those in need of imported inputs. In other words, in order to import, the firms will have to export.

- **Increased Productivity**: Increased productivity is necessary for ultimate survival of a firm. This will lead the firm to increase production and then move to export business. To meet the increased costs of research and development (R&D), larger markets become a necessity and exports become unavoidable.

- **Legal Restrictions**: Sometimes, governments impose certain restrictions on further growth and capacity expansion of some firms within the domestic market in order to achieve certain social objectives. But there may not be any such restrictions, if the additional capacity is utilised for exports. Then the firm may be tempted to export its products abroad.

- **Technological Improvement**: Entry to export market may enable a firm to pick up new product ideas and to add to product line, improve its products, reduce costs and discover new applications for its products.

- **Relative Profitability:** The rate of profit to be earned from export business may be higher than the corresponding rate on the domestic sales. The price realised in export markets may be relatively higher than that realised in the home market. This is so, for example, in the case of readymade garments and jewellery. In other cases, export incentives provided by the government may make exporting relatively more profitable than selling in the domestic market.

- **Social Responsibility**: Sometimes businessmen themselves feel a sense of responsibility and contribute towards the national exchequer by increasing their exports. They also build up their image in domestic marketing by their export activities. They also look at exporting to attain status and prestige.

- **Reducing Business Risks**: When a firm is selling its products in a number of markets then the downward fluctuations in sales in one market, may be the domestic market, is fully or partly counter balanced by a rise in the sales in other markets. On the other hand, geographic diversification also provides the momentum to growth in as much as a single or few markets will have only limited absorbing capacity.

Q3. **Discuss the broad trends in India's exports in recent years. What are the major products exported from India?**

Or

What are the important items in India's export trade? Discuss.

Ans. Exports have played an increasingly important role in India's economic growth in the last two decades. Exports recorded a growth of 40.49 per cent during April-March 2010-11. Export target and achievement from 2004-05 to 2010-11 and 2011-12 (Apr-Dec) is given in Fig. 1.1:

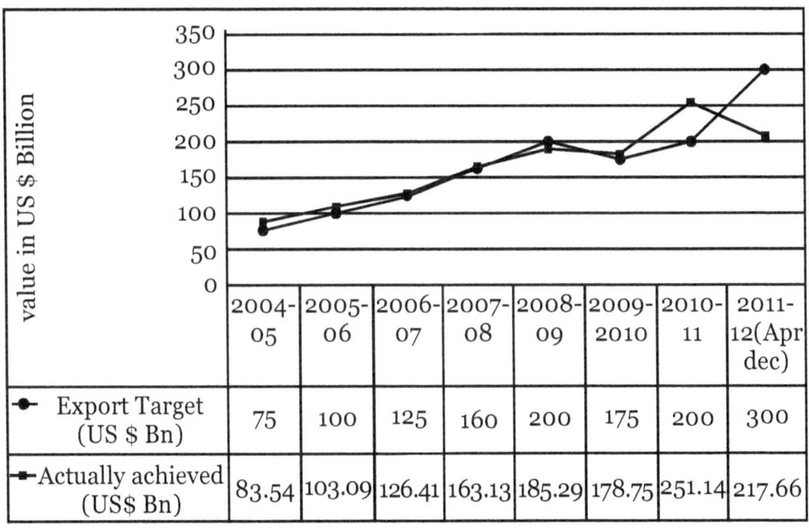

	2004-05	2005-06	2006-07	2007-08	2008-09	2009-2010	2010-11	2011-12(Apr dec)
Export Target (US $ Bn)	75	100	125	160	200	175	200	300
Actually achieved (US$ Bn)	83.54	103.09	126.41	163.13	185.29	178.75	251.14	217.66

Fig. 1.1: Export Target and Achievement

Trade Balance

The trade deficit in 2011-12 (April-October) was estimated at US $133.27 billion which was higher than the deficit of US $96.21 billion during 2010-11 (April-October). Performance of exports, imports and trade balance during 2004-05 to 2011-12 is given in Table 1.1:

Table 1.1: Performance of Exports, Imports and Trade balance

(Value in ` crore)

Year	Exports	% Growth	Imports	% Growth	Trade Balance
2004-2005	3,75,340	27.94	5,01,065	39.53	-1,25,725
2005-2006	4,56,418	21.60	6,60,409	31.80	-2,03,991
2006-2007	5,71,779	25.28	8,40,506	27.27	-2,68,727
2007-2008	6,55,864	14.71	10,12,312	20.44	-3,56,448
2008-2009	8,40,755	28.19	13,74,436	35.77	-5,33,680
2009-2010	8,45,534	00.57	13,63,736	-00.78	-5,18,202
2010-2011 (Apr-Dec)	7,89,069	—	12,28,074	—	-4,39,006
2011-2012 (Apr-Dec)	10,24,707	29.86	16,51,240	34.46	-6,26,533

Major Products Exported from India

Disaggregated data on exports by Principal Commodities is available for the period 2011-12 (April-October) as compared with the corresponding period of the previous year given in Table 1.1. Exports of the top five commodities during the period 2011-12 (April-October) registered a share of 53.1 per cent mainly due to significant contribution in the exports of petroleum (crude & products), gems & jewellery, transport equipments, machinery and instruments, drugs and pharmaceuticals & fine chemicals. The share of top five principal commodity groups in India's total exports during 2011-12 (April-October) is given below in Fig. 1.2:

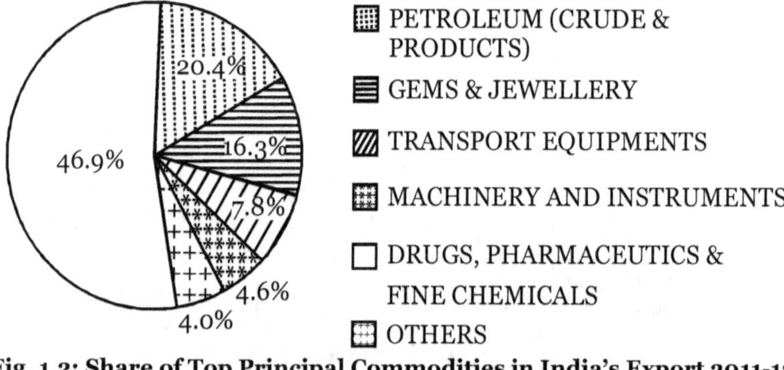

Fig. 1.2: Share of Top Principal Commodities in India's Export 2011-12 (April-October)

- **Plantation Crops:** Export of plantation crops during 2011-12 (April-October), increased by 39.29 per cent in US$ terms compared with the corresponding period of the previous year. Export of coffee registered a growth of 77.50 per cent, the value increasing from US $313.53 million to US $556.52 million. Export of tea also increased by 9.34 per cent.

- **Agriculture and Allied Products:** Agriculture and allied products as a group include cereals, pulses, tobacco, spices, nuts and seeds, oil meals, guar gum meals, castor oil, shellac, sugar and molasses, processed food, meat and meat products, etc. During 2011-12 (April-October), exports of commodities under this group registered a growth of 62.90 per cent with the value of exports increasing from US $8165.03 million in the previous year to US $13300.63 million during the current year.

- **Ores and Minerals:** Exports of Ores and Minerals were estimated at US $4700.29 million during 2011-12 (April-October) registering a negative growth of 8.32 per cent over the same period of the previous year. Sub groups, viz. processed minerals and iron ore have recorded a negative growth of 17.22 per cent and 23.29 per cent. Coal registered a growth of 35.76 per cent and other ores & minerals 78.37 per cent respectively. Mica has registered a growth of 5.74 per cent.

- **Leather and Leather Manufactures:** Export of leather and leather manufactures recorded a growth of 27.64 per cent during 2011-12 (April-October). The value of exports increased to US $2704.51 million from US $2118.86 million during the same period of the previous year. Exports of leather and manufactures have registered a growth of 30.19 per cent and leather footwear also registered a growth of 24.55 per cent.

- **Gems and Jewellery:** The export of gems and jewellery during 2011-12 (April-October) increased to US $27664.09 million from US $16770.33 million during the corresponding period of last year showing a growth of 64.96 per cent.

- **Chemicals and Related Products:** During the period 2011-12 (April-October), the value of exports of chemicals and allied products increased to US $21977.24 million from US $16276.94 million during the same period of the previous year registering a growth of 35.02 per cent. Rubber, glass and other products, residual chemicals and allied products, basic chemicals, pharmaceuticals and cosmetics and plastic and linoleum have also registered a positive growth.

- **Engineering Goods:** Items under this group consist of machinery, iron, steel, and other engineering items. Export from this sector during the period 2011-12 (April-October) stood at US $36694.23 million compared with US $27098.96 million during the same period of the previous year, registering a growth of 35.41 per cent. The growth in export of iron and steel bar rod stood at 51.86 per cent, transport equipments 39.38 per cent, primary and semi-finished iron and steel 23.20 per cent, non-ferrous metals 13.59 per cent and machine tools at 10.99 per cent.

- **Electronic Goods:** During the period 2011-12 (April-October), exports of electronic goods as a group was estimated at US $5024.92 million compared with US $4299.36 million during the corresponding period of last year, registering a growth of 16.88 per cent.

- **Textiles:** During the period 2011-12 (April-October), the value of textiles exports was estimated at US $15101.96 million compared with US $11987.38 million in the corresponding period of the previous year, recording a growth of 25.98 per cent. The export of readymade garments registered a growth of 28.60 per cent, cotton yarn/fabrics/made-ups, etc. registered a growth of 23.06 per cent; wool and woolen manufactures 54.21 per cent; coir and coir manufactures 38.85 per cent; manmade textiles and made ups has shown a growth of 30.25 per cent; natural silk textiles and jute manufactures registered a negative growth of 35.15 per cent and 4.67 per cent respectively.

- **Handicrafts and Carpets:** Exports of handicrafts declined to US $101.67 million during 2011-12 (April–October), from US $128.24 million during the corresponding period of the previous year registering a negative growth of 20.72 per cent. Export of carpets decreased to US $439.66 million from US $536.98 million during the same period last year registering a negative growth of 18.12 per cent.

- **Project Goods:** During 2011-12 (April–October), the export of project goods were estimated at US $29.05 million compared with US $38.18 million during the corresponding period of last year registering a negative growth of 23.91 per cent.

- **Petroleum Products:** Export of petroleum products increased to US $34667.02 million during 2011-12 (April–October), as compared with US $21135.13 million during the same period of last year recording a growth of 64.03 per cent.

- **Cotton Raw including Waste:** There was a growth in the exports of cotton raw including waste by 178.63 per cent from US $389.52 million in 2010-11 (April–October) to US $1085.30 million during 2011-12 (April–October).

Q4. Discuss major markets for Indian products.

Or

What are important destinations for exports from India? Discuss.

Ans. In the financial year 2007, the US was India's leading export destination and also it accounted for as much as 14.9 per cent of the total merchandise exports worth an estimated US $18.9 billion. Even though the US share in India's merchandise exports dwindled from 20.7 per cent in FY 2003 to 14.9 per cent in FY 2007, in value terms it increased from US $10.9 billion to US $18.9 billion. This was also an indication of India's growing preference for trading with other emerging markets by diversifying its product group and improving its quality, etc. The UAE which is India's second largest export market, accounted for 9.5 per cent of its total exports in FY 2007 (in FY 2003, UAE accounted for 6.3 per cent). The spurt in exports to the UAE can be largely attributed to rise in exports of mineral fuels, mineral oils and products (Under the HS Code 27), which constituted almost 30.4 per cent of the total exports to the UAE. It is to be noted that UAE is an important market for re-export in the entire middle east region and in 2005, its total re-export was as high as US $26.4 billion.

India's exports to China have also seen rapid growth from just 3.7 per cent in FY 2003 to 6.6 per cent in FY 2007. Similarly, India's export share to Singapore has gone up from around 2.0 per cent in FY 2001 to 4.8 per cent in FY 2007. This underscores India's growing export focus on Asian countries.

Table 1.2: Top Ten Exporting Countries (2003-2007)

(In US$ mn)

Country	FY03	FY04	FY05	FY06	FY07	% share to total exports in FY07
USA	10,895.8	11,490.1	13,765.8	17,353.1	18,866.2	14.9
UAE	3,327.5	5,125.6	7,347.9	8,591.8	12,032.2	9.5
China	1,975.5	2,955.1	5,615.9	6,759.1	8,294.0	6.6
Singapore	1,421.6	2,124.8	4,000.6	5,425.3	6,068.9	4.8
UK	2,496.4	3,023.3	3,681.1	5,059.3	5,618.0	4.4
Hong Kong	2,613.3	3,261.8	3,691.8	4,471.3	4,680.6	3.7
Germany	2,106.7	2,544.6	2,826.3	3,586.1	3,979.5	3.2
Italy	1,357.1	1,729.4	2,286.0	2,519.0	3,582.9	2.8
Belgium	1,661.8	1,805.7	2,509.7	2,871.2	3,474.5	2.8
Japan	1,864.03	1,709.3	2,127.9	2,481.3	2,860.5	2.3
Total Exports	52,719.0	63,843.0	83,536.0	103,091.0	126,331.1	55.0

D & B Research
Source: DGFT

In 2012–2013, India's top five trading partners were United Arab Emirates, United States, Singapore, China and Hong Kong. But it was changed during 2013-2014. During this FY, USA again regain his leading place in India's export with China ranked 3rd while Hong Kong slide down on 4th rank; Germany remains on his 9th place in both FYs.

Q5. What are the methods for promoting products in international trade?

Ans. Companies no longer limit themselves to local markets. The need and desire of profit make them to go further beyond their boundaries to access more profit, popularity and prestige. For that, there is a need of promotion of products in the international market. Methods of promotion are as follows:

    (1) Advertising: It is a usual way to bring the products to be sold to the notice of foreign customers. The advertisement campaign has very often to be adapted to the specific requirements of the target market. Hence, advertising in foreign markets becomes an expensive affair. Availability of media may also be different from country to country. In a country where literacy rate is low, the effectiveness of a printed advertising copy obviously becomes low. Social networking sites are the proper medium in such a marketing situation.

(2) **Direct Mailing:** This method of promotion costs much less than advertising. In addition, it is selective and more personal. It is selective because approach is made directly to those who have been identified as the target audience. It is personal because the letter and other publicity materials are mailed either by name or by designation of the identified receiver. Mailing lists can be prepared on the basis of names and addresses given in the trade directories or they can be purchased from merchandising service companies. By and large, direct mailing is the most effective method of promoting products abroad provided sufficient care is taken to design the product brochures, catalogues, etc.

(3) **Trade Fairs and Exhibitions:** They constitute the means of presenting goods and services in an attractive manner with the aid of colour, light and motion. These catch the imagination of the visitors, attract their attentions and get them interested in the objects displayed. Participation in a trade fair will help the exporter to have following ideas about their product: (a) what is available in the market concerned, (b) who would be his competitors, (c) to what extent would the product have to be adapted, (d) prevailing prices in world markets and (e) strengths and weaknesses of competing products. In addition, he would be able to know the new developments and technological trends in his industry.

Q6. **What are sources of information to know about the market conditions and business practices in foreign countries?**

Or

Write a short note on Indian Trade Promotion Organisation.

[Dec-2013, Q.No.-7(b)]

Ans. Following sources are the major sources of information, which provide the exporter with a lot of useful information:

(1) **Export Statistics of India:** These will enable the exporter to know where his product is being exported, to what extent and what is the value realisation per unit. Export statistics is provided in monthly bulletin of Foreign Trade Statistics, Volume-I.

(2) **Import Statistics of Foreign Countries:** The exporter can find out the overall size of a particular foreign market for his product, which are the competing countries and what are approximate unit value paid to each individual country.

(3) **Import Promotion Centres:** These centres which are established in most developed countries provide a lot of valuable information to the exporters of developing countries including India. The information provided by these centres include: (a) Statistical information on the market concerned, (b) Information on marketing techniques and business practices, (c) Information on import regulations and practices,

(d) List of importers, wholesalers, agents and distributors, and

(e) Dates of various trade fairs and exhibitions.

(4) Country's Commercial Representatives Abroad: They can inform the exporters about the export potential of their products in their respective countries, tariff and non-tariff barriers facing them and the government procedures in the importing countries.

(5) Export Promotion Councils and Commodity Boards: These councils and commodity boards can provide information about where and to what extent your product can be sold in different countries. They also provide information about export incentives, availability of shipping services and freight rates, approximate prices which can be realised for the products and also provide overall guidance in your export operations.

(6) Indian Trade Promotion Organisation (ITPO): It came into effect from 1 January 1992 with the main objective of promoting exports and imports, upgradation of technology through the medium of fairs to be held in India and abroad, to undertake publicity through the print and electronic media, to assist Indian companies in product development, to organise programmes, buyer seller meets, contact promotion programmes for specific products in specific markets. The Indian Trade Promotion Organisation provides information and market intelligence to the business community in India. It also organises visits of buyers and trade delegations to industry and trade establishment in India with a view to promote business contacts.

The Indian Trade Promotion Organisation is a service organisation and had close and periodical interaction with the trade, industry and government. It serves the industry by entering into comparatively less explored markets, provides information and support for participation in fairs for developing exports of new items, and gathers and disseminates improved trade related services.

Q7. What do you mean by EXIM Policy?

Ans. Export-Import Policy or EXIM Policy, which is also known as Foreign Trade Policy, is a set of guidelines and instructions related to the import and export of goods by an individual firm or any organisation. In other words, Export-Import (EXIM) Policy frames rules and regulations for exports and imports of a country. It provides policy and strategy of the government to be followed for promoting exports and regulating imports. This policy is periodically reviewed to incorporate necessary changes as per changing domestic and international environment. In this policy, approach of government towards various types of exports-imports is conveyed to different exporters-importers. Export-Import policy regulated exports and imports of a country. Now in the era of globalisation, no economy in the world remains cut-off from rest of the world. Export and import play a significant role in the economic development of all the developed and developing economies. With the growth in international organisations like WTO, UNCTAD, ASEAN, etc. world trade is growing at a very fast rate.

To regulate import and export in the desired direction, it is very essential that government frame some rules and regulations for exports and imports. A developing country like India has to import capital goods, modern technology and other essential items. For making payments of these essential imports, exports have to be promoted, so as to maintain balance between exports and imports. If imports are more than exports, then need for foreign debt will arise, which is not desirable. For boosting exports, government gives various incentives to exporters by offering export promotion schemes.

Government of India used various restrictions on imports in the form of import licensing, import quotas, import duties and in some cases, even banning imports of some specific goods.

The purpose of restrictions on imports is to curb unnecessary imports. However, government has given concessions on imports of capital goods, technology, raw materials and essential goods. On the export side, various export promotion schemes are launched for increasing exports like relaxing export controls, reducing export duties and providing incentives (like concessional loans) to exporters.

In the year 1985 for the first time, a joint Export-Import Policy (EXIM) was announced. Before this, government used to announce separate policy for imports and separate policy for exports. But in 1985, a single policy was announced incorporating both export-import policy. After that, various EXIM policies were announced. The main EXIM policies government expanded list of import items under Open General Licence (OGL). OGL list refers to items, which can be freely imported. Government promoted import of raw materials, technology, capital goods, etc. and gave various concessions to exporters for promoting exports.

Q8. Discuss various objectives and features of Export-Import Policy (1997-2002) of India. Also, explain its highlights.

Or

What are the salient features of Indian Export Import Policy 1997-2002? Suggest necessary changes in the policy to restore equilibrium in the country balance of payments.

[June-2014, Q.No.-1]

Or

Write a short note on EPCG Scheme.[June-2015, Q.No.-7(a)]

Ans. The new Export-Import Policy for 1997-2002 was unveiled by the Union Commerce Minister (Dr. B.B. Ramaiah) on 31 March, 1997. This EXIM Policy ran concurrent with the Ninth Plan period commenced on 1 April 1997.

The Policy had set "an ambitious target", as pinpointed in the preface of the policy book, "of attaining an export level of US $90-100 billion by the year 2002 and achieving 1 per cent share in world trade". The target is indeed ambitious. The Policy continued the process of trade liberalisation and procedural simplification.

Objectives of EXIM Policy 1997-2002: The principal objectives of the Export Import Policy (1997-2002) of India were:

- to accelerate the economy from low level of economic activities to high level of economic activities by making it a globally oriented vibrant economy and to derive maximum benefits from expanding global market opportunities.
- to motivate sustained economic growth by providing access to essential raw materials, intermediates, components, consumables and capital goods required for augmenting production.
- to improve the technological strength and efficiency of Indian agriculture, industry and services, thereby, improving their competitiveness.
- to create new employment opportunities and encourage the attainment of internationally accepted standards of quality.
- to give quality consumer products at practical prices.

Features of EXIM Policy: The features of the EXIM policy (1997-2002) were:

- The new Duty Entitlement Passbook Scheme was started.
- The scope of Export Promotion Capital Goods (EPCG) scheme was widened.
- Special incentives to agricultural products were given.
- Special incentives to software exports were provided.
- Custom duties were reduced.
- A number of restricted items were made freely importable.
- Procedures of exports and imports were further simplified.
- EOUs and EPZs were given more incentives and facilities. (EOU stands for Export Oriented Units and EPZ for Export Processing Zones).

Highlights of the EXIM Policy 1997-2002

The new EXIM Policy 1997-2002 aims at giving a major thrust to acceleration of India's exports through restructuring and revamping of various export promotion schemes. The procedures have been simplified and streamlined with a view to making them more transparent and easy to administer. The policy aims at continuing the trade reforms and trade liberalisation with a view to achieving a higher rate of export growth. The policy encourages the industry to enhance its competitiveness in the global market and to achieve its full potential in the areas of its strength. The major changes are as follows:

(1) **Simplification of Schemes:** EXIM Policy for the year 1997-2002 has simplified the procedures and educed the interface between exporters and the Director General of Foreign Trade (DGFT) by reducing the number of documents required for export by half. Import has been further liberalised and better efforts have been made to promote Indian exports in international trade. In order to facilitate easy access to inputs required for export production this policy has only two schemes.

They are Advance Licensing Scheme and Duty Entitlement Pass Book (DEPB) scheme.

(2) Liberalisation of Imports: A very important feature of the policy is liberalisation. It has substantially eliminated licensing, quantitative restrictions and other regulatory and discretionary controls. All goods, except those coming under negative list, may be freely imported or exported.

(3) EPCG Scheme: Duty on capital goods has been reduced from 15 per cent to 10 per cent under the Export Promotion Capital Goods (EPCG) scheme. Under the zero duty EPCG scheme, the threshold limit for zero duty imports has been reduced from ₹20 crores to ₹5 crores for agricultural and allied sectors. Special Imprest Licence facility is being extended to domestic capital goods suppliers for supply under the zero duty EPCG scheme.

(4) Gold and Jewellery Scheme: For the promotion of export of gold and jewellery, the number of nominated agencies permitted to stock gold has been increased. Earlier it was done by MMT, STC, SBI, etc. Under the gems and Jewellery Replenishment (RP) scheme, third party exports have been allowed so that small exporters are able to sell their products in the international markets. They can claim REP Licence based on disclaimer certificate from the third party. Bulk Licence for import of rough diamonds has been further liberalised. Further, EOU, EPZ units in the gems and jewellery sector are being permitted to sell 10 per cent of the output in the DTA on payment of duty.

(5) Agricultural Sector: The changes in this sector to boost agro-export include:

(a) Allowed import of equipments of ₹5 crore and above under zero duty EPCG scheme.

(b) Double weightage will be given for agro export in calculating eligibility of export house, trading house, etc. On total value of exports, 1 per cent additional special Import Licence will be given if export of fruits, vegetables, floriculture and horticulture produce/products, constitute 10 per cent or more of the total exports.

(c) EOU/EPZ units will be permitted to sell 5 per cent of their output in the DTA on payment of duty without stipulation of any value addition condition.

(6) Software: For export promotion of software, following facilities have been provided:

(a) Software units can undertake exports using data communication link in the form of physical exports through the courier service also. Software units have been permitted on-line data communication for DTA sales.

    (b)   Software units can use the computer system for commercial training as well.

    (c)   Software units can also import goods on loan from client for a specified period.

(7) Deemed Exports: Deemed exports facilities have been extended to oil and gas sectors in addition to power sector. In a bid to encourage domestic sourcing of inputs, domestic manufacturers supplying against EPCG, Licences will be entitled now for deemed export drawback facility. In case of supply to zero duty EPCG Licence holder, the domestic supplier will be entitled to import raw materials duty-free under the special Imprest Licence.

(8) Special Incentives for Export of SSI Produce/Products from North Eastern States/New Markets: Following facilities have been provided for export of SSI produce from North Eastern States/New Markets.

    (a)   Additional Special Import Licence of 1 per cent on total value of exports will be given to export houses/trading houses, etc. where such export of products from North Eastern States constitute 10 per cent or more of the total exports.

    (b)   Double weightage on such exports is being given for recognition as EH/TH/STH/SSTH.

    (c)   Additional SIL will be given for exploration of new markets.

    (d)   SIL on export of SSI products has been increased from 1 per cent to 2 per cent.

(9) Export House/Trading House/Star Trading House/Super Star Trading House: Existing eligibility criterion for the recognition of EH/TH/STH/SSTH based on average annual export performance of preceding 3 licensing years was ₹10 crores, ₹50 crores, ₹250 crores and ₹750 crores. This has been revised to ₹20 crores, ₹100 crores, ₹500 crores and ₹1500 crores respectively. It has been targeted to contribute nearly 60 per cent to 70 per cent of the country's total exports by EH/TH/STH/SSTH by the turn of the century.

(10) Incentive to Improve Quality of Export Products: The SIL entitlement of exporters holding ISO 9000 series or IS/ISO 9000 series has been increased from 2 per cent of FOB to 5 per cent of FOB. The book you can believe most—GPH book.

Q9. Describe the general provisions for exports and imports in India.

Ans. General Provisions for exports in India

- **Exports and Imports free unless Regulated:** Exports and Imports shall be free, except in cases where they are regulated by the provisions of this policy or any other law for the time being in force. The item wise export and import policy shall be, as specified in ITC (HS) published and notified by Director General of Foreign Trade, as amended from time to time.

- **Compliance with Laws:** Every exporter or importer shall comply with the provisions of the Foreign Trade (Development and Regulation) Act, 1992, the Rules and Orders made thereunder, the provisions of this policy and the terms and conditions of any licence/certificate/permission granted to him, as well as provisions of any other law for the time being in force.

- **Exemption from Policy/Procedure:** Any request for relaxation of the provisions of this policy or of any procedure, on the ground that there is genuine hardship to the applicant or that a strict application of the policy or the procedure is likely to have an adverse impact on trade, may be made to the Director General of Foreign Trade for such relief as may be necessary. The Director General of Foreign Trade may pass such orders or grant such relaxation or relief, as he may deem fit and proper.

- **Importer-Exporter Code Number:** No export or import shall be made by any person without an Importer-Exporter Code (IEC) number unless specifically exempted. An Importer-Exporter Code (IEC) number shall be granted on application by the competent authority in accordance with the procedure specified in the Handbook (Vol.1).

- **Trade with Neighbouring Countries:** The Director General of Foreign Trade may issue, from time to time, such instructions or frame such schemes as may be required to promote trade and strengthen economic ties with neighbouring countries.

- **Transit Facility:** Transit of goods through India from or to countries adjacent to India shall be regulated in accordance with the bilateral treaties between India and those countries and will be subjected to such restrictions as may be specified by DGFT in accordance with International Conventions.

- **Trade with Russia under Debt-Repayment Agreement:** In the case of trade with Russia under the Debt Repayment Agreement, the Director General of Foreign Trade may issue, from time to time, such instructions or frame such schemes as may be required, and anything contained in this policy, in so far as it is inconsistent with such instructions or schemes, shall not apply.

- **Free Exports:** All goods may be exported without any restriction except to the extent such exports are regulated by ITC (HS) or any other provision of this policy or any other law for the time being in force. The Director General of Foreign Trade may, however, specify through a public notice such terms and conditions according to which any goods, not included in the ITC (HS), may be exported without a licence/certificate/permission.

- **Export of Samples:** Export of samples and Free of charge goods shall be governed by the provisions given in Handbook (Vol.1).

- **Export of Passenger Baggage:** Bonafide personal baggage may be exported either along with the passenger or, if unaccompanied, within one year before or after the passenger's departure from India. However, items mentioned as Restricted in ITC (HS) shall require a licence/certificate/permission.

- **Export of Gifts:** Goods, including edible items, of value not exceeding ₹5,00,000/- in a licensing year, may be exported as a gift. However, items mentioned as restricted for exports in ITC (HS) shall not be exported as a gift, without a licence/certificate/permission.

- **Export of Spares:** Warranty spares, whether indigenous or imported, of plant, equipment, machinery, automobiles or any other goods, except those restricted under ITC (HS), may be exported along with the main equipment or subsequently but within the contracted warranty period of such goods subject to approval of RBI.

- **Export of Imported Goods:** Goods imported, in accordance with this policy, may be exported in the same or substantially the same form without a licence/certificate/permission provided that the item to be imported or exported is not mentioned as restricted for import or export in the ITC (HS).

  Exports of such goods imported against payment in freely convertible currency would be permitted against payment in freely convertible currency. Goods, including those mentioned as restricted item for import (except prohibited items) may be imported under Customs Bond for export in freely convertible currency without a licence/certificate/permission provided that the item is freely exportable without any conditionality/requirement of licence/permission as may be required under ITC (HS) Schedule II.

- **Export of Replacement Goods:** Goods or parts thereof on being exported and found defective/damaged or otherwise unfit for use may be replaced free of charge by the exporter and such goods shall be allowed clearance by the customs authorities provided that the replacement goods are not mentioned as restricted items for exports in ITC (HS).

- **Export of Repaired Goods:** Goods or parts, except restricted under ITC (HS), thereof on being exported and found defective, damaged or otherwise unfit for use may be imported for repair and subsequent re-export. Such goods shall be allowed clearance without a licence/certificate/permission and in accordance with customs notification issued in this behalf.

- **Private Bonded Warehouses for Exports:** Private bonded warehouses exclusively for exports may be set up in DTA as per the terms and conditions of the notifications issued by Department of Revenue. Such warehouses shall be entitled to procure the goods from domestic manufacturers without payment of duty. The supplies made by a domestic supplier to the notified warehouses shall be treated as physical exports provided the payments for the same are made in free foreign exchange.

- **Denomination of Export Contracts:** All export contracts and invoices shall be denominated either in freely convertible currency or Indian rupees but the export proceeds shall be realised in freely convertible currency. However, export proceeds against specific exports may also be realised in rupees provided it is through a freely convertible Vostro account of a non-resident bank situated in any country other than a member country of ACU or Nepal or Bhutan. Additionally, the rupee payment through the Vostro account must be against payment in free foreign currency by the buyer in his non-resident bank account. The free foreign exchange remitted by the buyer to his non-resident bank (after deducting the bank service charges) on account of this transaction would be taken as the export realisation under the export promotion schemes of this policy. Contracts for which payments are received through the Asian Clearing Union (ACU) shall be denominated in ACU Dollar. The Central Government may relax the provisions of this paragraph in appropriate cases. Export contracts and invoices can be denominated in Indian rupees against EXIM Bank/Government of India line of credit.

- **Realisation of Export Proceeds:** If an exporter fails to realise the export proceeds within the time specified by the Reserve Bank of India, he shall, without prejudice to any liability or penalty under any law for the time being in force, be liable to action in accordance with the provisions of the Act, the Rules and Orders made there under and the provisions of this policy.

- **Free Movement of Export Goods:** Consignments of items meant for exports shall not be withheld/delayed for any reason by any agency of the Central/State Government. In case of any doubt, the authorities concerned may ask for an undertaking from the exporter.

General provisions regarding imports in India

- **Second Hand Goods:** All second hand goods, excepting second hand capital goods, shall be restricted for imports and may be imported only in accordance with the provisions of this policy, ITC (HS), Handbook (Vol.1), Public Notice or a licence/certificate/permission issued in this behalf.

  Import of second hand capital goods, including refurbished/reconditioned spares, shall be allowed freely.

- **Import of Samples:** Import of samples shall be governed by the provisions given in Handbook (Vol.1).

- **Import of Gifts** Import of gifts shall be permitted where such goods are otherwise freely importable under this policy. In other cases, a Customs Clearance Permit (CCP) shall be required from the DGFT.

- **Passenger Baggage:** Bonafide household goods and personal effects may be imported as part of passenger baggage as per the limits, terms and conditions thereof in the Baggage Rules notified by the Ministry of Finance. Samples of such items that are otherwise freely importable under this policy may also be imported as part of passenger baggage without a licence/certificate/permission.

  Exporters coming from abroad are also allowed to import drawings, patterns, labels, price tags, buttons, belts, trimming and embellishments required for export, as part of their passenger baggage without a licence/certificate/permission.

- **Import on Export Basis:** New or second hand capital goods, equipments, components, parts and accessories, containers meant for packing of goods for exports, jigs, fixtures, dies and moulds may be imported for export without a licence/certificate/permission on execution of Legal Undertaking/Bank Guarantee with the Customs Authorities provided that the item is freely exportable without any conditionality/requirement of licence/permission as may be required under ITC (HS) Schedule II.

- **Re-import of Goods Repaired Abroad:** Capital goods, equipments, components, parts and accessories, whether imported or indigenous, except those restricted under ITC (HS) may be sent abroad for repairs, testing, quality improvement or upgradation or standardisation of technology and re-imported without a licence/certificate/permission.

- **Import of Goods used in Projects Abroad:** After completion of the projects abroad, project contractors may import, without a licence/certificate/permission, used goods including capital goods, provided, they have been used for at least one year.

- **Sale on High Seas:** Sale of goods on high seas for import into India may be made subject to this policy or any other law for the time being in force.

- **Import under Lease Financing:** Permission of licensing authority is not required for import of new capital goods under lease financing.

- **Clearance of Goods from Customs:** The goods already imported/shipped/arrived, in advance, but not cleared from customs may also be cleared against the licence/certificate/permission issued subsequently.

- **Execution of BG/LUT:** Wherever any duty free import is allowed or where otherwise specifically stated, the importer shall execute a Legal Undertaking (LUT)/Bank Guarantee (BG)/Bond with the Customs Authority before clearance of goods through the customs, in the manner as may be prescribed. In case of indigenous sourcing, the licence/certificate/permission holder shall furnish LUT/BG/Bond to the licensing authority before sourcing the material from the indigenous supplier/nominated agency.

- **Exemption from Bank Guarantee:** All the exporters who have an export turnover of at least ₹5 crore in the current or preceding licencing year and have a good track record of three years of exports will be exempted from furnishing a BG for any of the schemes under this policy and may furnish a LUT in lieu of BG.
- **Private/Public Bonded Warehouses for Imports:** It may be set up in the Domestic Tariff Area as per the terms and conditions of notification issued by Department of Revenue. Any person may import goods except prohibited items, arms and ammunition, hazardous waste and chemicals and warehouse them in such private/public bonded warehouses. Such goods may be cleared for home consumption in accordance with the provisions of this policy and against licence/certificate/permission, wherever required. Customs duty as applicable shall be paid at the time of clearance of such goods. If such goods are not cleared for home consumption within a period of one year or such extended period as the custom authorities may permit, the importer of such goods shall re-export the goods.

Q10. What are the basic elements of an export sales contract? How is it different from domestic sales contract?

Or

Distinguish between domestic sales contract and export sales contract.

Ans. The export sales contract covers important terms for the delivery of products in international trade. Export sales contract can be informal or formal, depending on the foreign buyer. Basic elements of an export sales contract are as follows:

- **Name and Addresses of the Parties:** The parties to the contract should be clearly stated.
- **Product, Standards and Specifications:** The export contract should explicitly state the product name, as well as technical names if there are any; sizes in which the product is to be supplied (if this is required); the applicable national or international standards and specifications; specific buyer requirements, and sample specifications.
- **Quantity:** The quantity should be clearly stated in both figures and words, units of measure should be specified.
- **Inspection:** Although a number of goods are now subjected to pre-shipment inspection by designated agencies, foreign buyers may stipulate their own inspection agencies and conditions for inspection. Therefore, the parties should clearly state the nature, manner and focus of the inspection envisaged, as well as the inspection agency.
- **Total Value of the Contract:** The total value of the contract should be put in both words and figures, and the currency should be specified.

- **Terms of Delivery:** Terms of delivery (one of the Incoterms 2000) should be stated in the contract.
- **Taxes, Duties and Charges:** The prices quoted by the seller may be inclusive of taxes, duties and charges. Levies, if any, in the country of importation may be the buyer's responsibility. Responsibility for payment of all such taxes should be clearly specified in the contract.
- **Period of Delivery, Shipment, etc:** The place of dispatch and delivery should be clearly specified, also whether the period of delivery will run from the date of the contract, from the date of notification of the issue of an irrevocable letter of credit, or from the date of receipt of the notice of issuance of the import licence by the seller.
- **Part-shipment, Trans-shipment, Consolidation of Cargo:** The contract should explicitly state whether the parties to it have agreed on part-shipment or trans-shipment. The contract should also indicate the port of trans-shipment and the number, if any, of partial shipments agreed. If the goods are likely to be shipped under a consolidation of export cargoes scheme, this should be mentioned in the contract.
- **Packaging, Labelling and Marking:** Packaging, labelling and marking requirements should be clearly stated in the contract.
- **Terms of Payment, Amount, Mode and Currency:** When quoting different payment terms, the exporter should specify whether the prices are based on the current rate of exchange of the South African rand, or on the basis of another currency (e.g. the US dollar). Fluctuations in the rate of exchange should also be addressed.
- **Discounts and Commissions:** The contract should specify the amount of discount or commission to be paid and by whom (i.e. by exporter or by the importer). If required, the basis on which commission is calculated and the rate to be applied should also be clearly stipulated. Discount or commission rates may, or may not, be included in the export price agreed upon by the exporter and importer.
- **Licences and Permits:** Import licences may be difficult to obtain in the buyer's country. Parties to the contract should therefore clearly state whether the export transaction will require any export or import licences, whose responsibility it will be to obtain them, and at whose expense.
- **Insurance:** A contract should provide for the insurance of goods against loss, damage or destruction during transportation. The contract should specify the type of risk covered and the extent of coverage.
- **Documentary Requirements:** Documents required by the buyer/importer, and which the exporter agrees to provide, should be stated. Where the exporter is required to take out marine

insurance, it is important that he is asked to provide a certificate of insurance, rather than the policy, to enable him to ship consignments under an open policy.

- **Product Guarantee:** The length of the period of guarantee should be fixed.
- **Delay in Delivery:** The contract should define the damages due to the buyer from the seller in the event of late delivery owing to reasons other than force majeure.
- **Force Majeure or Excuse for Non-performance of Contract:** Parties should include certain provisions in the contract defining the unforeseeable circumstances that would relieve them of their liability for non-performance of the contract. Such provisions are intended to identify the relief which may be available to either party to the contract should supervening circumstances occur during the period of validity of the contract.
- **Remedial Action:** As defaults in contractual obligations by any of the parties can occur, it is always advisable to include in the sale or purchase contract certain specific remedial actions. These remedial actions should reflect the mandatory provisions of the law applicable to the contract.
- **Applicable Law:** The contract should state the law of the country that is to govern the contract.
- **Arbitration:** The contract should include an arbitration clause to facilitate the amicable and quick settlement of disputes or differences that may arise between the parties.
- **Signature of the Parties:** The signing of the contract indicates the agreement of both parties to the terms and conditions of the contract.

The passing of ownership is still a matter of uncertainty in international trade. It is not, as many believe, linked to the transfer of the bill of lading when shipment is by sea. In the case of road, rail or air transport, a bill of lading is not provided. It would therefore be prudent to have a reservation of ownership clause in the sales contract, to the effect that the exporter reserves ownership of the goods sold until he has received the purchase price.

Distinction between Domestic Sales Contract and Export Sales Contract

A major point of distinction between a domestic and export contract lies in identifying the proper law governing the export contract. This is not a problem for domestic sales contract because the proper law will always be the Indian law in India. It will be the respective national laws in each country so far as their domestic transactions are concerned. But in export transactions, there are two nations, that of the exporter and importer. Therefore, the question arises, which country's law will apply to an export contract. This is a very complex problem but the principle generally followed is that the parties to the contract may agree mutually about the applicability of particular country's law. The country chosen must be either that of the exporter or the importer. In special circumstances, a third country's law may be chosen, provided that the country has something to do with the contract. For example, that may be the country where the goods will be re-exported by the importer subsequently. Only when the parties fail to mention the applicable law and a dispute arises later on, the court will decide which law should apply.

Each country's law has developed a set of rules which the courts consider while deciding on this issue. This is commonly known as 'conflict of laws' situation. Some of the factors considered by the courts are: the place where the contract is signed, the language in which the contract is written, the place of business of the parties, etc. However, these days, the courts normally identify as 'proper law', i.e., the law applicable to the contract (as the one where the contract is to be carried out, i.e. the place where the delivery is to take place). Since in most export transactions, delivery is made in the exporter's country (normally when the goods are placed on the carrier in the exporter's country), the applicable law becomes the exporting countries law. Read GPH books and score excellent marks.

Q11. Explain briefly various contract terms under INCOTERMS.

Ans. International Commercial Terms (INCOTERMS) are universally recognised set of definitions of international trade terms, such as FOB, CFR and CIF, developed by the International Chamber of Commerce (ICC) in Paris, France. It defines the trade contract responsibilities and liabilities between buyer and seller. It is invaluable and a cost-saving tool. The exporter and the importer need not to undergo a lengthy negotiation about the conditions of each transaction. Once they have agreed on a commercial term like FOB, they can sell and buy at FOB without discussing who will be responsible for the freight, cargo insurance, and other costs and risks.

The INCOTERMS was first published in 1936 as "INCOTERMS 1936" and it is revised periodically to keep up with changes in the international trade needs. The complete definition of each term is available from the current publication INCOTERMS 2000. These terms are as follows:

(1) Ex-W (Ex-Works)

'Ex' means 'from' and 'Works' means 'factory, mill or warehouse which is the seller's premises'. Ex-W applies to goods available only at the seller's premises. Buyer is responsible for loading the goods on truck or container at the seller's premises, and for the subsequent costs and risks. In practice, it is common that the seller loads the goods on truck or container at the seller's premises without charging loading fee.

The term Ex-W is commonly used between the manufacturer (seller) and export-trader (buyer), and the export trader resells on other trade terms to the foreign buyers. Some manufacturers may use the term Ex Factory, which means the same as Ex-Works.

(2) FCA (Free Carrier)

The delivery of goods on truck, rail, car or container at the specified point (depot) of departure, which is usually the seller's premises, or a named railroad station or a named cargo terminal or into the custody of the carrier, at seller's expense. The point (depot) at origin may or may not be a customs clearance center. Buyer is responsible for the main carriage/freight, cargo insurance and other costs and risks. In the air shipment, technically speaking, goods placed in the custody of an air carrier is considered as delivery on board the plane. In practice, many importers and exporters still use the term FOB in the air shipment.

(3) FAS (Free Alongside Ship)

This term means that goods are placed in the dock shed or at the side of the ship, on the dock or lighter, within reach of its loading equipment so that they can be loaded aboard the ship, at seller's expense. Buyer is responsible for the loading fee, main carriage/freight, cargo insurance, and other costs and risks. The FAS term is popular in the break-bulk shipments and with the importing countries using their own vessels.

(4) FOB (Free On Board)

In Free On Board, the seller/exporter/manufacturer clears the goods for export and is responsible for the costs and risks of delivering the goods past the ship's rail at the named port of shipment. The Free On Board term is used only for ocean or inland waterway transport. The "named place" in Free On Board and all "F" terms is domestic to the seller. Normal payment terms for Free On Board transactions include cash in advance, open account, and letters of credit.

The Free On Board term is commonly used in the sale of bulk commodity cargo such as oil, grains, and ore where passing the ship's rail is important. However, it is also commonly used in shipping container loads of other goods.

The key document in FOB transactions is the 'On Board Bill of Lading'.

(5) CFR (Cost and Freight)

In cost and freight, the seller/exporter/manufacturer clears the goods for export and is responsible for delivering the goods past the ship's rail at the port of shipment (not destination).

The seller is also responsible for paying for the costs associated with transport of the goods to the named port of destination. However, once the goods pass the ship's rail at the port of shipment, the buyer assumes responsibility for risk of loss or damage as well as any additional transport costs.

(6) CIF (Cost, Insurance and Freight)

The cargo insurance and delivery of goods to the named port of destination (discharge) at the seller's expense. Buyer is responsible for the import customs clearance and other costs and risks. In the export quotation, indicate the port of destination (discharge) after the acronym CIF, for example CIF Pusan and CIF Singapore. Under the rules of the INCOTERMS 1990, the term CIF is used for ocean freight only. However, in practice, many importers and exporters still use the term CIF in the air freight.

(7) CPT (Carriage Paid To)

'Carriage Paid To' means that the seller pays the freight for the carriage of the goods to the named destination. The risk of loss of or damage to the goods, as well as any additional costs due to events occurring after the time the goods have been delivered to the carrier, is transferred from the seller to the buyer when the goods have been delivered into the custody of the carrier.

(8) CIP (Carriage and Insurance Paid To)

'Carriage and Insurance Paid To' means that the seller has the same obligations as under CPT but with the addition that the seller has to procure insurance against the buyer's risk of loss of or damage to the goods during the carriage. The seller contracts for insurance and pays the insurance premium. When only land transportation is involved, CIP should replace the incorrect use of CIF.

(9) DAF (Delivered At Frontier)

'Delivered At Frontier' (DAF) means that the seller fulfils his obligation to deliver when the goods have been made available, cleared for export at the named point and placed at the frontier, but before the customs border of the adjoining country.

The seller is expected to provide the buyer at the seller's expense with the usual document or other evidence of the delivery of goods at the named place at the frontier. The seller is also expected to provide the transport normally obtained in the country of dispatch covering on usual terms the transport of the goods from the point of dispatch in the country to the place of final destination in the country of importance named by the buyer.

(10) DES (Delivered Ex Ship)

Under this type of contract, the seller fulfils his obligation to deliver when the goods have been made available to the buyer on board the ship uncleared for import at the named port of destination. The seller also pays the costs of customs formalities necessary for exportation as well as all duties, taxes or other official charges payable upon exportation and where necessary, for their transit through another country prior to delivery at the named port of destination.

(11) DEQ (Delivered Ex Quay)

In 'Delivered Ex Quay', the seller/exporter/manufacturer clears the goods for export and is responsible for making them available to the buyer on the quay (wharf) at the named port of destination, not cleared for import.

The buyer, therefore, assumes all responsibilities for import clearance, duties, and other costs upon import as well as transport to the final destination. This term can be used in for sea or inland waterway transport.

(12) DDU (Delivered Duty Unpaid)

'Delivered Duty Unpaid' means that the seller's obligation to deliver is fulfilled when the goods have been made available at the named place in the country of import. The seller has to bear the costs and risks involved in bringing the goods there (excluding duties, taxes and other office charges payable upon import) as well as the costs and risks of carrying out customs formalities. The buyer has to pay any additional costs and to bear any risks caused by his failure to clear the goods for import in time.

(13) DDP (Delivered Duty Paid)

The seller is responsible for most of the expenses, which include the cargo insurance, import customs clearance, and payment of customs duties and taxes at the buyer's end, and the delivery of goods to the final point at destination, which is often the project site or buyer's premises. The seller may opt not to insure the goods at his/her own risks.

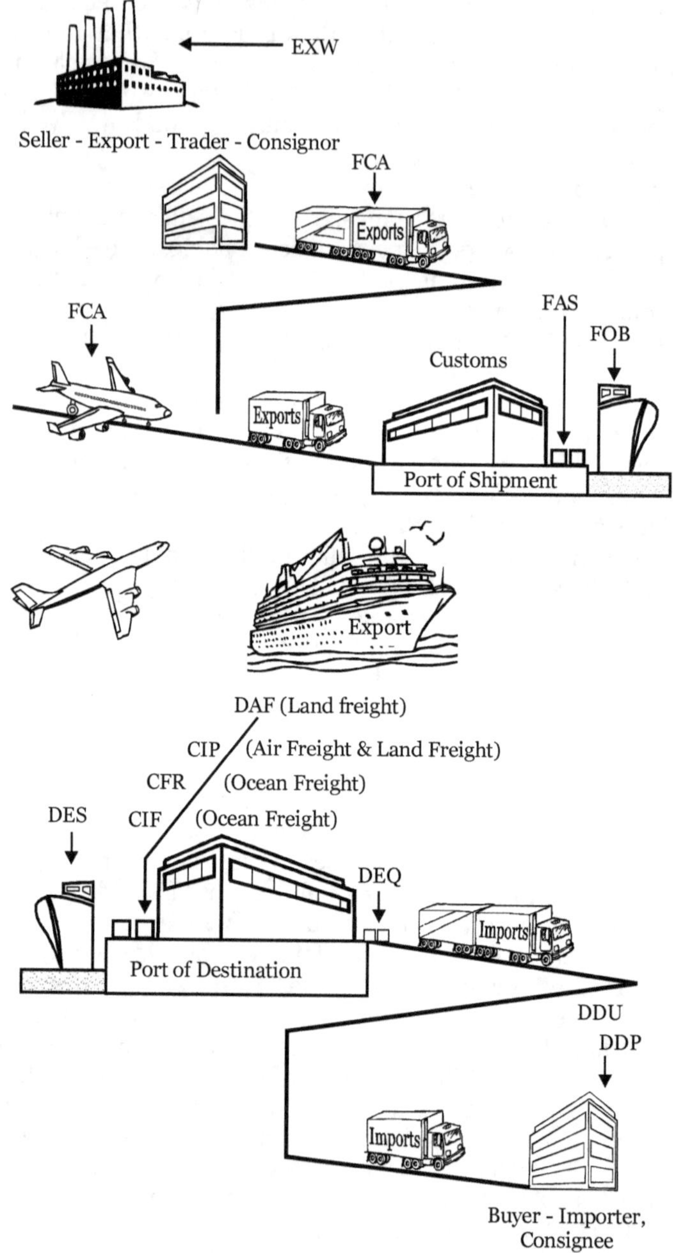

Fig. 1.3: International Commercial Terms

Q12. What are the duties of exporter and importer under FOB contract?

Ans. The duties of exporter and importer under FOB contract are as follows:

Exporter

- Supply the contracted goods in conformity with the contract of sale and deliver the goods on board the vessel named by the buyer at the named port of shipment.
- Bear all costs and risks of the goods until such time as they shall have effectively passed the ship's rail.
- at his own expense the customary clean documents in proof of the delivery of the goods.

Importer

- Reserve the necessary shipping space and give due notice of the same to the exporter and
- Bear all costs and risks of the goods from the time they have effectively passed the ship's rail and pay the price as provided for in the contract.

Q13. What are the duties of exporter and importer under CIF contracts?

Ans. Following are the duties of the exporter and importer under CIF contract:

Exporter

- Supply the goods in conformity with the contract of sale, arrange at his own expense for the shipping space by the usual route and pay freight charges for the carriage of goods.
- Obtain at his own risk and expense all documentation regarding governmental - authorisation necessary for the export of goods,
- Load the goods at his own expense on board the vessel at the port of shipment. He should procure at his own cost in a transferable form a policy of marine insurance for a value equivalent of CIF plus 10 per cent.
- Bear all risks until the goods have effectively crossed the ship's rail and furnish to the buyer a clean negotiable bill of lading.

Importer

- Accept the document when tendered by the exporter, if these are in conformity with the contract of sale and pay the price.
- Receive the goods at the port of destination and bear all costs except freight and marine insurance incurred in respect of the carriage of the goods.
- Bear all risks of the goods, from the time they have effectively passed the ship's rail at the port of shipment.

Q14. What are the general conditions in export contracts?

Or

What are the aspects under general conditions in export contracts?

Ans. An export contract can be simple but sometimes it could be complex, complexity of any contract depends upon what is being exported. If the product is standard, such as garments, handicraft or light engineering goods, a simple set of general conditions will suffice. On the other hand, a contract for the sale of petrochemicals plant may run into hundreds of pages. For a majority of products being exported from India, the following aspects should be covered under the general conditions:

 (1) The parties
 (2) The description of the products
 (3) Quality
 (4) Price per unit
 (5) Total value
 (6) Currency
 (7) Tax and Charges
 (8) Packing
 (9) Marking and Labelling
 (10) Mode of Transport
 (11) Delivery: Place and Schedule
 (12) Insurance
 (13) Inspection
 (14) Documentation
 (15) Mode of Payment
 (16) Credit period, if any
 (17) Warranties
 (18) Passing of Risk
 (19) Passing of property
 (20) Availability/non-availability of Export-Import Licences
 (21) Force Majeure
 (22) Settlement of Disputes
 (23) Proper Law of the Contract
 (24) Jurisdiction

Q15. What are the legal implications of FOB contract and CIF contract?

Ans. In export contracts, the applicable law can be the law of either party or that of a third party. It will be the Indian Contracts Act, if Indian law will apply. This act also provides that if the parties use special trade terms, the duties and the liabilities under the act can be changed by the expressed provisions in the contract. Similar provisions exist in acts of other countries as well. Further, over the centuries, courts in various countries have interpreted trade contracts. This has given rise to some accepted interpretations of contract terms, such as FOB and CIF. Principal features of these two types of contracts are as follows:

(1) FOB Contract

Under FOB contracts, the seller has the duty to place the goods onboard the carrier, which has been nominated by the buyer. However, sometimes due to reasons of convenience, the exporter himself may contract with the carrier.

In both cases, the freight has to be paid by the importer. The exporter's responsibility ends when he delivers the goods to the carrier.

The major legal implications of FOB contracts are:

(a) The delivery is completed by delivering the goods to the carrier. This means that delivery to the carrier operates as delivery to the buyer, unless the seller has reserved the right of disposal over the goods.

(b) The price in a FOB contract covers all expenses upto the loading of the goods on the carrier. All costs subsequent to that point will be on the buyer's account.

(c) Risks in the goods pass from the seller to the buyer at the same time when delivery is completed, i.e. when the goods are placed on the carrier.

(d) Normally, property in the goods should also be passed from the exporter to the importer along with risks. The passing of property may be postponed by a specific provision in the contract.

(e) Payments fall due when the delivery is completed. It is generally stipulated that property will pass only when the buyer fulfils his contractual obligations under the relevant terms. For example, acceptance of the Bill of Exchange submitted along with the Bill of Lading or the Airway Bill.

From a practical point of view, it is easier for an exporter to implement an FOB contract. This is because of the following two reasons:

(a) When the space is not available on ship, the exporter will be unable to export the goods. In FOB contract, reservation of ship is the duty of importer. Therefore, this is the fault of buyer.

(b) In FOB contract, risks associated with freight escalation has to be borne by the importer.

Though selling on FOB basis may be easier for an exporter, this is not good for the country as a whole. This is because since under an FOB contract, the importer will organise both shipping and insurance, he will give the business to local firms in his own country. As a result, the Indian shipping/Airlines and insurance companies stand to lose considerable amount of business.

(2) CIF Contracts

The exporter undertakes the responsibility of contracting the shipping space and also getting the insurance cover for the goods in a CIF contract. These responsibilities are in addition to what he does under an FOB contract.

The legal nature of a CIF contract is rather complicated as it necessarily involves three contracts, viz., contract of sale, contract of affreightment and contract of insurance.

Further, over the centuries, the nature of CIF contracts has evolved based upon court's interpretation all over the world. One of the objectives of CIF contract is to facilitate resale of goods while on transit on the basis of only shipping documents. The shipping documents represent title to the goods and, therefore, physical transfer of goods is not required for trading purposes. It is, therefore, said that legally speaking, a CIF contract is not a sale of goods themselves but a sale of documents relating to the goods. Under a CIF contract, the right of the buyer is to have the shipping documents and not the goods. The seller can claim payment only by tendering the relevant shipping documents.

The major legal implications of CIF Contracts are as follows:

(a)   The seller has to procure a contract of affreightment. This will enable him to ship the goods on the due date to the named port of destination.

(b)   He must deliver the goods on board the ship, collect the shipping documents and send to the importer.

(c)   He must also procure a contract of insurance covering the shipped goods and the risks, as desired by the importer.

(d)   He also has to send along with the shipping documents the payment document, such as the Bill of Exchange.

(e)   The importer has to make the payment on the basis of the documents tendered to him. He has a right to scrutinise the documents or reject them.

(f)   The property in the goods does not normally pass on shipment. It passes when the Bill of Lading is delivered to the buyer and thereby he acquires the right of disposal of the goods.

(g)   The property right that the buyer is acquiring is conditional.

(h)   The exporter's duty comes to an end when the goods have been placed on board the vessel. The goods will be at the importer's risks, though the freight and insurance premium have been paid by the exporter.

(i)   The CIF contract is so structured that even if the buyer knows that the goods have already been lost or damaged, he is under an obligation to pay. The importer has his remedy either under the contract of affreightment against a ship owner or under the policy of insurance against the insurance company.

Q16. What are the methods of dispute settlement?

Ans. There are two well-recognised methods for settlement of disputes, i.e. litigation and arbitration.

(1) Arbitration

If conciliation is not used or an agreement cannot be achieved, the next stop often used is arbitration. When all else fails, arbitration, rather than litigation, is the preferred method for resolving international commercial disputes. The usual arbitration procedure is for the parties involved to select a disinterested and informed party or parties as referee to determine the merits of the case and make a judgement that both parties agree to honour. Although informal arbitration is workable, most arbitration is conducted under the auspices of one of the more formal domestic or international arbitration groups organised specifically to facilitate the resolution of commercial disputes. These groups have formal rules for the process and experienced arbitrators to assist. In most countries, decisions reached in formal arbitration are enforceable under the law.

The popularity of arbitration has led to a proliferation of arbitral centers in countries, organisations, and institutions. All have adopted standardised rules and procedures to administer cases and each has its strengths and weaknesses. Some of the more active are the following:

- The Inter-American Commercial Arbitration Commission
- The Canadian-American Commercial Arbitration Commission (for disputes between Canadian and US businesses)
- The London Court of Arbitration (decisions are enforceable under English law and English courts)
- The American Arbitration Association
- The International Chamber of Commerce
- The Commercial Dispute Resolution Center of the Americas

The procedures used by formal arbitration organisation are similar. Arbitration under the rules of the International Chamber of Commerce (ICC) affords and excellent **example of how most organisations operates**. When an initial request for arbitration is received, the Chamber first attempts conciliation between the disputants. If this fails, the process of arbitration is started. The plaintiff and the defendant select one person each from among acceptable arbitrators to defend their case and the ICC Court of Arbitration appoints a third member, generally chosen from a list of distinguished lawyers, jurists, and professors.

The advantages of arbitrating an international contract dispute are many. The arbitrators may or may not be lawyers. For example, a construction contract dispute may have engineers as arbitrators. The arbitration process is likely to be faster than litigation. It may have a more streamlined process of getting to a hearing, especially when compared to the expensive and cumbersome discovery process in countries. A major factor in favour of arbitration is its lack of publicity. Unlike court proceedings, which are open to the public and often result in published decisions, arbitration is a private process. The ultimate decision is known only to the involved parties. A business concerned about the disclosure of confidential information will tend to try to resolve disputes through arbitration. Other advantages of arbitration include flexibility in rules on the admissibility of evidence, compellability to implement decisions, and limited rights of a party to appeal.

In order to arbitrate a dispute, the parties must agree to do so, usually in their initial contract. For example, a typical arbitration clause would have the parties agree to arbitrate any dispute 'arising from or related to' the contract before a specific group, such as the ICC; would designate a substantive law to govern the contract; would contain language allowing the enforcement of an arbitral award in court; could specify the number of arbitrators; and could choose a place and language for the arbitration proceedings.

Arbitration has become popular in both domestic and international business agreements. An arbitration clause may be inserted in an employment contract, credit card agreement, cruise ship ticket, or bank account application, as well as in big contracts.

However, arbitration can be expensive and even lengthy, despite its reputation as the quicker and cheaper alternative to litigation. A new trend is emerging-inclusion of a resolution mechanism for immediate problems in addition to arbitration, including a neutral advisor or special dispute passed.

(2) Litigation

Seeking justice in a court is generally avoided by parties to an agreement. The costs incurred, the frustrating delays involved, and extended aggravation make victories in law suits spurious. There are other grey areas also in litigation:

- Fear of creating a poor image and damaging public relations
- Fear of unfair treatment in a foreign court
- Difficulty in obtaining judgement that may otherwise have been possible in a mutually agreed settlement through arbitration
- The relatively high cost and time required to settle the dispute. The issue of paying compensation to victims of the Bhopal gas tragedy has been only recently decided though decades have gone by since the disaster occurred.
- Loss of confidentiality. Unlike arbitration and conciliation that are confidential, litigation is public.

Q17. Discuss the concept of International Arbitration.

Ans. Arbitration can take place either in the exporter's or importer's country, in the case of international transactions. Therefore, there is a need to resolve these arbitrations. The best method for resolving disputes arising from international commercial agreements and other international relationships is international arbitration. As with arbitration generally, international arbitration is a creature of contract, i.e. the parties' decision to submit disputes to binding resolution by one or more arbitrators selected by or on behalf of the parties and applying adjudicatory procedures, usually by including a provision for the arbitration of future disputes in their contract. The practice of international arbitration has developed so as to allow parties from different legal and cultural backgrounds to resolve their disputes, generally without the formalities of their respective legal systems. The International "New York Convention" on Recognition and Enforcement of Foreign Arbitral Awards 1967 has been ratified by 40 countries, which recognise and enforce arbitral awards given in the countries, which are signatories to his convention.

- ***Law for Enforcement of Foreign Awards in India:*** Countries which are parties to any of the International Convention have to pass implementing legislation giving effect to the respective Conventions. India, which is a party to the 1927 Geneva and the 1958 New York convention, has enacted the Arbitration (Protocol and Convention) Act, 1937 and the Foreign Awards

(Recognition and Enforcement) Act, 1961, respectively, giving effect to the two Conventions. The provisions of the two acts are made applicable to foreign awards made in such countries as are notified by the Government from time to time in the Official Gazette under the respective Acts.

- ***Procedure for Enforcement in India:*** Any person interested in a foreign award may apply in writing to any court having jurisdiction over the subject-matter of the award praying that the award be filed in the court. The application shall be numbered and registered in the court as a suit between applicant as plaintiff and the other parties as defendants. The court shall direct notice to be given to the parties requiring them to show cause why the award should not be filed. Thereupon, the court on being satisfied that the foreign award is enforceable under the act shall pronounce judgement according to the award. Upon the judgement so pronounced, a decree shall follow and no appeal shall lie from such decree expect in so far as the decree is in excess of or not in accordance with the award.

- ***Enforcement of Indian Awards in Foreign Countries:*** It is understood that awards made in India will be similarly enforceable in foreign countries, which are parties to any of the international conventions relating to the enforcement of foreign awards (according to the provisions of the respective conventions). However, enforcement of awards in countries, which do not adhere to either the 1937 or the 1961 convention or other similar international regulations is some what more difficult. The enforcement of awards in such other countries would largely depend on principles of private international law and might meet with considerable difficulties.

Q18. **What do you mean by export document? Discuss its perspectives.**

Or

Write a short note on Export Documents.

[Dec-2012, Q.No.-7(b)]

Or

Discuss the need for documents in international trade. Substantiate your answer with suitable illustrations.

[Dec-2013, Q.No.-2]

Ans. Export documents can be defined as the range of documents that an exporter must prepare to enable goods to leave the country, be accepted into the country of the importer and, frequently, to enable payment to be made through the international banking system.

Export documentation can be considered as the most complex but common part of overseas marketing. Persons may have come across such comments which tend to discourage them from entering into export business. It is therefore, necessary to emphasise that documentation is as much of an important activity as the conclusion of an export order and its fulfilment.

Documentation formalities are necessary to enable the importer to get the contracted goods and the exporter to get sale value as well as to secure export incentives. In other words, export documents are needed to comply with commercial, legal and incentive requirements. The perspective of export documentation with following terms are as follows:

(1) Commercial Perspective

The beginning of trade between two business firms located in different countries occurs with the conclusion of an export contract. Under the contract, the duty of the exporter is to ship the contracted goods in the agreed form (e.g., packing) and by agreed mode of transport as well as according to agreed time schedule. On the other hand, it is the duty of the importer to remit sale value to the exporter according to agreed terms of payment. In this process of physical movement of goods from the exporter to the importer and remittance of sales value in the reverse order, neither the exporter nor the importer is personally and physically involved.

Instead, the goods are handed over to a shipping company or an airline, which issues a receipt for these goods. Further, since goods in transit may be damaged or lost due to some accident, the exporter may be required to get an insurance policy. While these two documents will protect the interests of the importer, the exporter will ensure that these documents are not in the possession of the importer unless he has either paid for the goods or he has made a promise to make payment later. For this purpose, physical possession of the good will be linked with the acceptance of a payment document by the importer. In actual practice, a set of documents given proof of shipment and cargo insurance coverage along with a bill for payment is sent by the exporter to the importer through the banking channel.

This set of documents symbolises ownership in goods. This will be handed over to the importer by the bank in his country, which he has received it from the bank in the exporting country only when he has honoured the bill. In other words, the importer will get delivery of the goods from the carrier on the basis of the transport document, which is obtained through the bank, after he has complied with the agreed terms of payment.

(2) Legal Perspective

For the validity of terms and conditions, there is a need of legal force for any documents or documentation. Besides commercial necessity, documents for exports have a legal perspective. All over the world, laws regulating export-import trade as well as movement of foreign exchange have been enacted. In some countries, the regulations are few which can be enforced through simple procedural and documentation formalities. In other countries, the regulations are many and the enforcement procedures are complex.

There is perhaps no country in the world where movement of goods and money is absolutely free. The minimum regulations that one can think of are the one to record the movement of goods from and into a country. For this purpose, the exporter has to declare on a document the details of goods being exported by him. Other than these basic minimum requirements, the governments all over the world regulate movement of goods to protect political, economic, cultural and other interests and for implementing trade agreements with other countries.

Some countries do not have political relations with the others. As a result, goods originating from such a country are not allowed to be imported. Thus, a country, which does not permit flow of goods from certain countries, has laid down the requirement of Certificate of Origin, which states that the goods are of the country, which is exporting them. For example, some of the countries in West Asia do not allow imports from countries or companies having any relation with Israel.

Documents are needed for protecting the economic and social interests of the trading countries. For example, under the Indian Export policy, the government has listed out products, which either cannot be exported or can be exported after obtaining permission from the designated agencies. Some of the products are subject to restrictions because of their short supply in the country. Consequently, these products can be exported only after obtaining a quota, for which a documentary proof is to be submitted to the customs, authority for shipment purposes. Similarly, there are a number of government regulations governing quality, standards, foreign exchange flows, valuation of goods for calculating customs duties, etc. Compliance with these regulations necessitates documentation. Documents are also needed for fulfilling requirements under bilateral and multilateral trade agreements. For example, an Indian exporter will need to obtain GSP, Certificate of Origin for exporting certain specified products to those countries, which operate the Generalised System of preferences. Under this system, the developed country accord preferential duty treatment to specified goods originating from developing countries. The GSP certificate will enable the importer to pay concessional duty.

(3) Incentive Perspective

Incentive can be effective or sometimes necessary for export documentation. Therefore, export assistance and incentive measures have become an integral part of policy in larger number of countries. Since these incentives are to be given only to the export activity, documentary proof to this effect is required to be given by the claimant to the disbursing authorities. Such a documentary proof should state that the claimant is eligible to receive the incentive, that the goods will be or have been exported according to the export contract and that the claim has been filed in the manner specified in the policy. In other words, bonafides of the claim have to be established for receiving incentives and assistance. It is notable that for making a claim, the exporter has to file an application on the specified form that summarises the shipment and other details. This application is to be accompanied by a number of supporting documents to enable the incentive disbursing authority to check the authenticity of details given in the application.

Q19. What do you understand by Certificate of Origin? Explain briefly.

Ans. The Certificate of Origin is an instrument to establish evidence on the origin of goods imported into any country. The certificates are issued under the ambit of the Rules of Origin of any importing country that grants such concessions to tariffs or merely stipulates a non-preferential certificate without granting any tariff concession.

It is on this basis that various countries have formulated their Rules of Origin which grant greater access to goods from the developing and the least developed countries under the preferential mode. There are two categories of Certificate of Origin, viz.

(1)   Preferential and

(2)   Non-preferential.

India is signatory to World Trade Organisation because of which Indian exports are accorded preferential treatment available to all WTO members.

Secondly, India has also entered into bilateral and multilateral trade pacts with its trade partners because of which Indian exports get into these countries at concessional import duty regime. In order to avail the preferential treatment, the Indian exporters are required to furnish the proof that the goods manufactured are, indeed, of Indian origin. Hence, the need for Certificate of Origin arises.

Certificate of Origin

Exporter Name and Address:	Blanket Period : (DD/MM/YYYY)
	FROM:
Tax Identification Number	TO:
Producer Name and Address:	Importer Name and Address:
Tax Identification Number:	Tax Identification Number:

Description of Good(s)	TARRIF CLASSIFICATION NUMBER	PREFERENCE CRITERION	PRODUCER	NET COST	COUNTRY OF ORIGIN

I CERTIFY THAT

- Information provided in this certificate is based on facts and is accurate and I assume the responsibility for proving such representations. I understand that I am liable for any false statement or material omission made on or in concern with this document.
- I agree to maintain and present upon request documentation necessary to support this certificate and to inform, in writing, all persons to whom this certificate was given of any changes that would affect accuracy or validity of this certificate.
- This certificate consists of ___________________ pages including all attachments.

Authorised Signature:	COMPANY:	
Name: (Print or Type)	TITLE:	
Date: DD/MM/YYYY	Ph: xxxxxxxxxxxxxxx	Fax: xxxxxxxxxxxxxxxxx	Customs Form:

Fig. 1.4: Format of Certificate of Origin

Q20. What is commercial invoice? Write its functions.

Or

Write a short note on commercial invoice.

[Dec-2013, Q.No.-7(d)]

Ans. Commercial invoice is a type of commercial document, which is required for export or import. It is required, after the pro-forma invoice is accepted by the importer, the exporter must prepare a commercial invoice. The commercial invoice is required by both the exporter (to obtain the necessary export documents to enable the consignment to be exported, to prove ownership and to enable payment) and importer (who require the commercial invoice to facilitate the import of the goods into the country in question). In exporting, the commercial invoice is considered a very important document as it serves as the starting or initiating document that underpins the rest of the export transaction. *This is the first basic and the only complete document among commercial documents for the shipment.* Besides fulfilling the obligation under the export contract, the exporter needs this document for a number of other purposes including:

- obtaining export inspection certificate;
- getting excise clearance;
- getting customs clearance; and
- securing incentives.

Thus, this document is prepared at both the pre-shipment and post-shipment stages.

In the first place, Commercial Invoice is a document of contents that describes details of goods sent by exporter. It is the statement of account, which must contain identification, marks and numbers, description of goods and quantity of goods.

Every shipment has identification marks, which identify the cargo with various documents. These are private marks, which are made on the packages. These marks could be either in the form of symbols (say, a star, triangle, rectangle, etc.) or numericals. Similarly, every package under a shipment is numbered, usually written serially. The commercial invoice must specify the serial numbers given in a particular consignment.

Commercial invoice must describe the goods shipped by the exporter. The description of goods must correspond exactly with the description given in the contract or the letter of credit. It means that there should not be any difference (including spelling) between these descriptions. Thus, if a contract describes the goods as "Ten Thousand Pairs of Blouses and Skirts", the exporter should not describe them as "Ten Thousand Blouses and Ten Thousand Skirts", though logically both the descriptions mean the same.

Sometimes description of the goods includes the number of packages and the type of packing material. Thus, if the contract specifies shipment to be made in "ten new gunny bags", the exporter should send the contracted goods and describe them as needed. If the commercial invoice wrongly describes the shipment as "ten gunny bags" instead of "ten new gunny bags", the bank may refuse to honour shipping documents and not pay for them.

The quantity described on the commercial invoice should neither be less or more than the contracted quantity. In other words, the exporter should not ship less than contracted quantity, unless the contract permits part shipment. However, if the goods are being shipped under a letter of credit, part shipment is permitted, unless it is specifically prohibited. On the other hand, quantity shipped should not be more than contracted quantity. This is so even if the exporter may not be charging for the additional quantity.

Second function of the commercial invoice is that it is the seller's bill given to the buyer. As a bill, it must contain the name and address of the buyer, unit price, amount and authorised signatures with designation. Unless required by the buyer, the total invoiced value should be net of any commission or discount; in other words, it should be the realisable amount of goods as per the trade terms. Sometimes a contract requires a detailed breakup of the amount to be recorded on the invoice for enabling the customs authority in the importing country to calculate import duty. The following details should appear in the commercial invoice:

- The document title should clearly state "Commercial Invoice";
- The name of the exporter (referred to as the shipper) and their contact details (tel, fax, cell, e-mail), including physical (not postal) address;
- The name of the importer (referred to as the consignee, meaning the person or firm to whom the goods are to be sent) and their contact details (tel, fax, cell, e-mail) including physical (not postal) address (In the case of transshipment, there may be an intermediate consignee and their contact details and address should then also be included on the invoice);
- If the person or firm buying the goods (the importer) is not the same as the person or firm to whom the goods are being sent, then you should include both their contact details and addresses in the commercial invoice;
- The name of the person and company to notify once shipment has taken place and their contact details and physical address (here the contact details such as telephone, fax and cell number and e-mail address are more important than the physical address);
- A commercial invoice reference number;
- A purchase order number or similar reference to correspondence between the supplier and importer;
- The date of issue of the commercial invoice;
- A complete, detailed and clear description of the goods in question, incorporating the appropriate HS codes and brandmarks, if applicable (here the importer may ask you to remove these codes as they may not be the same in the importing country and may thus incur additional or higher duties to the importer's detriment because of their inadvertent misuse);
- The quantity of goods in question, including the number of units/items;
- The packing details unless provided in a separate packing list, including their external dimensions, cubic capacity, weight, numbers and contents of each package shipped, and kinds of packaging involved (pallets, boxes, bags, etc.) - if a separate packing list is used, reference should be made in the commercial invoice to the packing list;
- The grand total price of the goods for the whole consignment;

- Where applicable, the unit prices should be indicated - the unit price multiplied by the number of units/items should be reflected in the line total. The various line totals (in the case where different items are included in the same commercial invoice, or where additional services are itemised in the invoice), should add up to the total price for the whole consignment (also referred to as the 'Grand Total');
- The currency in which the goods will be sold (e.g. US dollars or rands);
- The type and amount of any discount given, where applicable;
- The likely delivery schedule and delivery terms;
- The payment methods (for example, cash in advance, documentary collection, L/C, etc.);
- The payment terms (for example 30 days on sight);
- The Incoterm to be used (Incoterms 2000- FAS, CIF, CFR, DDP, etc.);
- Who is responsible for the banking fees and other related costs (insurance and freight costs are covered by the incoterm in question);
- What the freight and insurance charges are;
- The exporter's banking details;
- A declaration of the country of origin of the goods;
- The expected country of final destination;
- Any freight details such as the port of loading and discharge;
- Any additional exporter-provided services that should be added to the invoice to come to the grand total;
- Any trans-shipment requirements;
- The validity of the commercial invoice, that is, when does the offer expire (leaving it open-ended could be very risky);
- Any other information relevant to the order;
- Make sure the commercial invoice is signed, together with the signature's name written underneath, with initials, title and position. Best help books for IGNOU students—GPH books.

Q21. What are the differences between pro forma invoice and commercial invoice?

Ans. The pro forma invoice is oftenly used as a form of quotation. Goods, merchandise and documents that are imported or exported between countries must typically include appropriate documentation, which may include either a commercial invoice or a pro forma invoice. Both types of invoices have certain differences. On the basis of format, responsible party, purpose and considerations, differences between them are as follows:

(1) **Format:** There is no specified format for either a commercial invoice or a pro forma invoice, according to the US Customs and Border Protection website. However, a commercial invoice must disclose certain required information, including a description and quantity of each item being shipped, the value of the

shipment in both US dollars and in the foreign currency, the country of origin, location of purchase, and the names and address of both the seller and the purchaser. US Customs and Border Protection does not require the same information on a pro forma invoice. A pro forma invoice only needs to include sufficient information to allow for a determination of duties and examination. Since there is no required format for either type of invoice, a commercial invoice and a pro forma invoice may appear virtually identical or they may appear radically different.

(2) **Responsible Party:** The exporting business is always responsible for providing a commercial invoice to customs officials when shipping goods, merchandise or documents that involve monetary value such as stock certificates, across international borders. In some instances, when no monetary transaction has occurred, such as when goods are shipped as gifts or as samples for an anticipated future transaction, the exporting business may not provide a commercial invoice. Documents that have no monetary value, such as a legal contract or a last will and testament, typically don't require a commercial invoice either. However, customs officials still require documentation of the shipment. In these instances, the importing business may provide a pro forma invoice to the customs officials. The exporting business provides the commercial invoice; the importing business provides a pro forma invoice.

(3) **Purpose:** A commercial invoice is designed to provide customs officials with enough information to determine appropriate import duties and to determine the eligibility of the merchandise to be shipped into the country. A commercial invoice is a true invoice. A pro forma invoice is not a true invoice; nothing has been billed by the exporting business and the importing business has no financial obligation. The pro forma invoice is typically only used when a financial transaction has not yet taken place. It may include a description of merchandise and list its value to indicate a commitment of a future transaction between the importer and the exporter. The importing business may provide an additional copy of the pro forma invoice to the exporting business because it contains valuable information regarding requirements for entry purposes, according to the US Customs and Border Protection website.

(4) **Considerations:** In most cases, a commercial invoice is required at the time of entry. The exporter prepares two copies of the commercial invoice - one to accompany the bill of lading and another to accompany the merchandise from its point of departure to the customs department at the point of entry at the international border. An importer who provides a pro forma invoice to US Customs and Border Protection must produce any related commercial invoice within 120 days.

Q22. **What do you mean by Bill of lading? Explain various types of Bill of lading.**

Or

Distinguish between 'Received for shipment B/L' and 'On board ship B/L' as also between 'Clean B/L' and 'Claused B/L'. **[June-2013, Q.No.-3]**

Ans. A bill of lading is a type of commercial document that is used to acknowledge the receipt of a shipment of goods. A transportation company or carrier issues this document to a shipper. In addition to acknowledging the receipt of goods, a bill of lading indicates the particular vessel on which the goods have been placed, their intended destination and the terms for transporting the shipment to its final destination.

This bill is issued by the shipping company or its agents stating that goods are either being shipped or have been shipped. A bill of lading can be used as a traded object. The standard short form bill of lading is evidence of the contract of carriage of goods and it serves a number of purposes:

- It is evidence that a valid contract of carriage, or a chartering contract, exists and it may incorporate the full terms of the contract between the consignor and the carrier by reference (i.e. the short form simply refers to the main contract as an existing document, whereas the long form of a bill of lading issued by the carrier sets out all the terms of the contract of carriage);

- It is a receipt signed by the carrier confirming whether goods matching the contract description have been received in good condition (a bill will be described as clean if the goods have been received on board in apparent good condition and stowed ready for transport); and

- It is also a document of transfer, being freely transferable but not a negotiable instrument in the legal sense, i.e. it governs all the legal aspects of physical carriage, and, like a cheque or other negotiable instrument, it may be endorsed affecting ownership of the goods actually being carried. This matches everyday experience in that the contract a person might make with a commercial carrier like FedEx for mostly airway parcels is separate from any contract for the sale of the goods to be carried. However, it binds the carrier to its terms, irrespectively of which the actual holder of the B/L, and owner of the goods, may be at a specific moment.

As a receipt, the bill of lading can be of various types, which are as follows:

  (1) **Received for Shipped B/L:** This bill is issued by the shipping company when goods have been given into the custody of the shipping company but have not yet been placed on board the ship. Such B/Ls are required in case of FOB shipments.

  (2) **On Board Shipped B/L:** This bill certifies that the goods have been received on board for shipment, goods are waiting for shipment and are under the custody of the shipping line. Such B/Ls will work in case of FAS (Free Alongside Ship) shipments.

(3) **Clean B/L:** The clean bill of lading bears an indication that the goods were received without damages, irregularities or short shipment, usually the words "apparent good order and condition", "clean on board" or the like are indicated on the B/L. Thus, a B/L reflects the carrier received the goods in good condition. The opposite term is soiled bill of lading, which reflects that the goods are received by the carrier in anything but in good condition.

(4) **Claused or Dirty B/L:** This bill, with many terms, is known as foul bill of lading, unclean bill of lading, dirty bill of lading or claused bill of lading. It is the opposite of the clean bill of lading. It bears an indication that the goods were received with damages, irregularities or short shipment, usually the words "unclean on board" or the like are indicated on the B/L, for example, "insufficient packing", "missing safety seal" and "one carton short".

This bill bears a superimposed clause an annotation, which expressly declares a defective condition of the goods. The clause may state "package number 20 broken" or "bale number 20 hook-damaged". By superimposing such clauses on the B/L, the shipping company limits its responsibility at the time of delivery of goods at the destination. It is very important to note that only a clean B/L is acceptable for negotiation of documents with the bank.

(5) **Through B/L:** It covers goods being transshipped enroute but where the first carrier has the responsibility as the principal carrier for all stages of the journey. For example, goods may be shipped from Bombay to Dubai and trans-shipped from Dubai to a port in Latin America.

A through bill of lading is a contract that covers the specific terms agreed to by a shipper and carrier. This document covers the domestic and international transportation of export merchandise. It provides the details of the agreed upon transportation between specific locations for a set monetary amount. An airway bill is a bill of lading that establishes terms of flights for the transportation of goods both domestically and internationally. This document also serves as a receipt for the shipper, proving the carrier's acceptance of the shipper's goods and agreement to carry those goods to a specific airport.

(6) **Combined B/L:** It covers several modes of transport for performing the complete journey from the exporting country to the importer's warehouse. For example, part of the journey may be completed by ship while subsequent parts may be undertaken by road; rail and air.

(7) **Transshipment B/L:** It has similar characteristic as the Through **B/L** except that, in this case, the first carrier acts only as an agent for effecting trans-shipment of cargo.

(8)   Charter Party B/L: It covers shipment on a chartered ship. The contract or the letter of credit will specify the nature of bill of lading that the exporter has to procure for the importer. Generally, the importers insist on the "clean on-board shipped" bill of lading, with the prohibition of the trans-shipment of goods.

Bill of lading is a document of title that will enable the lawful holder of any of the original B/L to take delivery of the goods at the stipulated port of destination. Thus, a claimant of title to goods is required to surrender an original B/L (also popularly known as negotiable copy of B/L) for claiming goods from the shipping company or its agents. It is not a negotiable instrument, though it is transferable by endorsement and Policies delivery. Transferability enables the banks to pay money to the exporter against surrender of shipping documents, including B/L, even before the goods reach the destination. Similarly, it enables the goods to be resold by the importer before goods reach the destination. For creating transferability, the bill of lading has to be made in such a way that the goods are consigned to the 'order of a party'.

The party could be either the exporter himself, or a negotiating or paying bank or any other party as provided in the contract or letter of credit. For example, if B/L is prepared in the following way, it can be transferred through endorsement in the same manner as in a cheque. Notifying is the party to whom the shipping company is to send "notice of arrival". There are three main columns in B/L. By filling these columns, transferability can be created in the following manner:

Consignor: ABC Company, New Delhi
Consignee: (Or Order of) Bank of XYZ, New Delhi
Notifying Party: KNM, London

By not striking-off the words "Or Order Of" and, writing the name of the negotiating bank, the bank becomes the first endorsee. Title to goods will be transferred from the negotiating bank to the paying bank to importer on endorsements by the negotiating and the paying banks in succession.

In contrast to the "Order B/L" is the consignee-named B/L. The consignee-named B/L is made out in the name of a specific party. Hence, title to goods cannot be transferred to a third party. The exporter should not ship goods under this kind of B/L as goods can be released by the shipping company at the destination without the presentation of the 'original' B/L. Thus, if payment from the importer has not been secured, the exporter may lose hold over goods and may not get paid. However, if payment in advance has been received or if goods are being shipped under irrevocable letter of credit, the consignee named B/L is a valid document.

Q23. What do you mean by Airway Bill? What are its functions?

Ans. An airway bill is a type of through bill of lading because it may cover both international and domestic transportation of goods. By contrast, ocean shipments require both inland and ocean bills of lading. Inland bills of lading are necessary for the domestic transportation of goods and ocean bills of lading are necessary for the international carriage of goods. Therefore, through bills of lading may not be used for ocean shipments. This document constitutes prima facie evidence of the conclusion of the contract of affreightment of receipt of goods and of conditions of carriage. This document, therefore, performs the triple functions as a forwarding note for the goods, receipt for the goods tendered and authority to obtain delivery of goods.

By itself, AWB is not a document of title, nor this is document transferable. However, AWB can be made into a transferable document by which it can be transferred to a third party by endorsement like the B/L. But, by and large, the business and commercial practice does not treat AWB as a document of title.

The functions of AWB are similar to B/L in regard to its characteristics as an evidence of contract and as cargo receipt. The AWB may be given as a receipt either for cargo given to the carrier pending shipment or for cargo loaded on board the aircraft. It may either be a clean receipt or a claused receipt. As regards the document of title characteristics, AWB is not a document of title, but this feature can be incorporated in it by making an order AWB. General practices in the trade are to get the consignee-named AWB. Consequently, goods are delivered to the consignee named in the AWB. The consignee will have to identify himself as the party named in AWB and goods may be delivered to him without any hindrance. But if the interests of the exporter have not been protected, the consignee may get hold of the goods and may also not pay for them. Hence, exporters provide for a clause in the contract, which requires AWE to be made in the name of the paying bank, which will ensure exchange of goods for payment by the importer. On the other hand, the importer can protect him against the seller's re-routing of the goods by obtaining the consignor's copy of the AWB (marked "Original 3 for Shipper"), which is sent to him through the banking channel by the exporter alongwith other shipping documents.

The airway bill or air consignment note or airway bill of lading, serves as a receipt for goods and an evidence of the contract of carriage, but it is not a document of title to the goods. Hence, the AWB is non-negotiable.

The goods in the air consignment are consigned directly to the party (the consignee) named in the letter of credit (L/C). Unless the goods are consigned to a third party like the issuing bank, the importer can obtain the goods from the carrier at destination without paying the issuing bank or the consignor. Therefore, unless a cash payment has been received by the exporter or the buyer's integrity is unquestionable; consigning goods directly to the importer is risky.

The AWB must indicate that the goods have been accepted for carriage, and it must be signed or authenticated by the carrier or the named agent for or on behalf of the carrier. The signature or authentication of the carrier must be identified as carrier, and in the case of agent signing or authenticating, the name and the capacity of the carrier on whose behalf the agent signs or authenticates must be indicated.

Q24. Write short notes on the following:
(i) Post parcel receipt

Ans. Post parcel receipt (PPR) evidences merely the receipt of the goods exported through postal channels to the buyer. The original copy of the receipt is signed by the banker, which is submitted to the post office for booking of the post parcel. The postmaster shall forward the original copy to the office of the RBI. The duplicate copy will be retained by the dealer bank that will be given the original documents for collections of remittances of foreign exchange from abroad, within the prescribed time limit of 21 days.

Post parcel receipt is both a receipt and evidence of dispatch. It does not evidence the title to goods. The parcel is consigned to the consignee named in the contract between exporter and importer. The consignee can identify himself with the postal authorities at the destination and obtain delivery of the goods.

(ii) Insurance certificate or policy

Ans. Cargo Insurance Policy (also called marine insurance policy) provides protection to cargo owners in the event of loss or damage to cargo in transit. This loss or damage is caused by accidents, which cannot be known in advance and against which no protection is possible. These may be caused by natural calamities as well as by manmade accidents. It is therefore, necessary that the risk of loss or damage to the cargo be minimised by obtaining a suitable insurance cover from an insurance company.

It must be pointed out that insurance cover is given irrespective of the mode of transport used including sea, air, road and rail carriers. Further, insurance cover can be secured for cargo going from the warehouse of the consignor to the warehouse of the consignee.

Generally, the export contract determines the party (exporter or importer) that will procure insurance cover. In the FOB and C&F contracts, importer obtains insurance cover after the goods have been laid on board on carrier. On the other hand, in a CIF contract, it is the obligation of the exporter to insure goods.

Sometimes, the export contract specifies the submission of 'insurance certificate' instead of the policy to bank for negotiation of documents. Insurance certificate, which is one stage prior to insurance policy, comes into being when a large and regular exporter obtains an open cover or concludes an open policy. Under these two arrangements, insurance certificates are issued on declaring shipments by the exporter as and when these are affected. Insurance certificate has an advantage as it cuts downtime in getting the insurance document from the insurance company.

Q25. What do you mean by bill of exchange? State some differences between demand bill and usance bill.

Ans. Section 5 of Negotiable Instrument Act defines a Bill of Exchange as an instrument in writing containing an unconditional order, signed by the maker, directing a certain person to pay a certain sum of money to a certain person or to the order of that certain person or to the bearer of the instrument.

Bill of exchange (B/E) is an important commercial document, which bridges the time gap between shipment of goods and receipt of sale amount. This document is prepared by the exporter and given to the bank alongwith other shipping documents for securing the sale amount. In this sense, B/E is attached to other documents, which will be given to the make payment at a future date.

Simply stated, the maker of B/E is the exporter (drawer) and the person who is directed to pay is the importer (drawee), while the person who is entitled to receive payment is the exporter (payee) or anyone directed by him. The sum of money to be paid by the drawee is the amount billed in the commercial invoice and recorded in B/E. B/E is to be honoured either on demand or on presentation to the drawee make payment at a future date.

A bill of exchange is a useful means of settlement in that it:

- provides written evidence of a debt which can be used in a court of law;
- enables the exporter to obtain immediate payment, by presentation if it is a sight bill, or by negotiation if it is a usance bill;
- enables the importer to delay payment until the maturity of the bill.

If a bill of exchange is a documentary bill, it will be accompanied by the documents relating to the goods for which payment is sought. The exporter presents the documents called for in the contract between the importer and himself to his bank and instructs the bank to deliver them to the importer against either acceptance or payment of the bill. If the documents are to be released against the importer's acceptance of the bill, the bill is called a D/A bill (documents against acceptance) and if upon payment then the bill is a D/P bill (documents against payment). If a bill is a sight or demand bill, the documents will be handed over only against payment of the bill. If the bill is a usance bill, the documents are usually handed over against acceptance.

The distinction between Demand Bill and Usance Bill can be stated as under:

- A demand bill is due for payment immediately after presentation, whereas, a usance bill is due for payment after a certain specified fixed period of time.
- A demand bill does not attract stamp duty, whereas, the usance bill attracts stamp duty.
- Bank normally purchases demand bill whereas usance bill is discounted. Remuneration from the former is exchange, whereas, in the latter case, it is discount.
- A demand bill does not require acceptance, whereas a usance bill has to be accepted.
- The collecting bank against acceptance delivers documents of usance bill by the drawee or his authorised agent. In case of demand bill, documents are delivered against full payment.

Q26. What are the legal documents required for exports from India and importing countries?

Or

Write a short note on Shipping Bill. [Dec-2014, Q.No.-7(c)]

Ans. Legal Documents for Exports from India

There are two types of regulatory export documents. Documents needed for different kinds of registrations of the firm and documents which are specific to a shipment.

(1) **Documents needed for different Kinds of Registrations of the Firm:** The first category documents included applications and supporting document for obtaining:

(a) Code Number from the Reserve Bank of India which once allotted is valid for the firm's life time,

(b) Importer-Exporter Code Number valid for the firm's life time, and

(c) Registration-Cum-Membership Certificate (RCMC) from the relevant export promotion council, commodity board, development authority, etc. valid for a specified time period. RCMC is strictly not a legal requirement for exporting from India, but is needed for claiming some of the important export incentives.

RBI Code Number is required for the purpose of monitoring the flow of foreign exchange against export of goods by a firm. For obtaining the RBI Code Number, the application in duplicate in the prescribed form, called CNX form is to be made to the Exchange Control Department of the Reserve Bank in whose jurisdiction to the Head Principal office of the exporter falls. This form is routed through the bankers of the applicant.

The application of the Importer-Exporter Code Number (IEC) is to be made in the prescribed form. Supporting documents to be submitted with the application are: (i) photocopy of RBI Code allotment letter; (ii) photocopy of the registration Certificate of either DGTD or Directorate of Industries, as the case may be; (iii) photocopy of industrial licence, if any; (iv) photocopy of Registration-cum-Membership Certificate or RCMC; and (v) photocopy of Permanent Income Tax Account Number.

RCMC is obtained from the concerned registering authority, which may be either an export promotion council or commodity board, or a development authority. Application is to be made on the prescribed form available from the registering authority.

Each STP unit will have to maintain a separate account; this should not be mixed up with any other accounts of the company. The Jurisdictional Director of STP issues necessary certificate for filling the application with the RBI.

(2) **Shipment Specific Documents:** The second category documents included those documents, which an exporter or his agent has to prepare for shipment of goods. These documents are:

(a) Foreign Exchange Regulation requires that all exports other than exports to Nepal and Bhutan shall be declared on the following forms:

 (i) GR Form: It is required to be filled in duplicate for all exports in physical form other than by post.

 (ii) PP Form: It is required to be filled in duplicate for all exports to all countries made by post parcel, except when made on "value payable" or "cash on delivery" basis.

 (iii) VP/COD Form: It is required to be filled in one copy for exports to all countries by post parcel under arrangements to realise proceeds through postal channels on "value payable" or "cash on delivery" basis.

 (iv) SOFTEX Form: It is required to be prepared in triplicate for export of computer software in non-physical form.

 All these documents serve the purpose of monitoring the realisation of sale amount by the exporter in the stipulated manner.

(b) For goods that are subject to the Export Trade Control policy of the Government of India, documents in the form of application have been specified. On the basis of that the concerned authorities will grant documents either an export Licence or an export permit will be granted by the concerned authorities. Licence or permission is generally given on the customs document known as shipping bill. For obtaining export Licence from the licensing authorities, the application is either the A-X Form or B-X Form, which is submitted alongwith the shipping bill and other documents, if any. In many cases, specific permission may have to be obtained from particular government ministries departments, in which case exporter has to apply on his letter head.

(c) For a number of products under the Export (Quality Control and Inspection) Act, 1962 and various other regulations, it is obligatory for an exporter to obtain Inspection Certificate from the notified agencies. For obtaining this certificate, the exporter has to apply in a document called intimation for inspection alongwith supporting documents (commercial invoice, technical specifications, etc.) to an Export Inspection Agency. Thereafter, a certificate of inspection will be issued, which along with other documents will be submitted to the customs authorities before permission to ship goods is given.

> (d) Under the Indian Customs Act, goods cannot be loaded on board the carriers unless permission from the customs authorities has been obtained. This permission is accorded on a document prescribed by the customs authorities. When goods are sent by sea or by air, this document is known as Shipping Bill. When goods are exported by land or by rail, it is called Application for Export. Post parcel consignment requires custom declaration form to be filled in.

There are four types of shipping bills. These are:

(a) Free Shipping Bill: Usually printed on white paper, it is used for export of goods which neither attract any export duty or cess nor are entitled to the duty drawback (an export incentive).

(b) Dutiable Shipping Bill: Printed on yellow paper, it is used in case of goods which are subject to export duty fees.

(c) Drawback Shipping Bill: It is usually printed on green paper and is used for export of goods entitled to duty drawback.

(d) Shipping Bill for Shipment ex-bond: It is printed on yellow paper for use in case of imported goods for re-export which are kept in the customs bounded warehouses.

Legal Documents in Importing Countries

There are various documents, which are needed in importing countries because of the legal necessity. These documents are, however, obtained by the exporter to be sent to the importer.

(1) Consular Invoice: Issued on the specified form, it is signed and stamped by the local consulate of the country to which goods are exported.

(2) Customs Invoice: It is also made out on a specified form prescribed by the customs authority of the importing country. The details given in the document will enable the customs authority of the importing country to levy and charge import duty.

(3) Legalised invoices: These invoices constitute a sworn affidavit by the exporter about the genuineness and correctness of the sale. These could be sworn before the appropriate consulate or the chamber of commerce, as the case may be, which will put their stamp on them.

(4) Certified Invoice: This is the self-certified invoice by the exporter about the origin of the goods.

(5) Certificate of Origin: This certificate is issued by independent bodies like the Chamber of Commerce on a prescribed form.

(6) GSP Certificate of Origin: Goods which get the benefit of preferential import duty treatment in countries which implement the Generalised System of Preferences should be accompanied by the GSP Certificate of Origin. This certificate is given on the forms prescribed by the importing countries.

(7) Health Veterinary Sanitary Certificates: Many importing countries require such certificates particularly in case of imports of foodstuff, livestock, hides, marine products, etc. to safeguard against the dangers of diseases and health hazards. The exporter has to get the required certification from the respective health, veterinary or sanitary authorities, before he is able to dispatch his goods.

Q27. What do you mean by the Bill of Entry? Describe the use of Bill of Entry.

Or

Discuss the concept of Bill of Entry.

Or

What are the types of Bill of Entry?

Ans. Bill of Entry is a document certifying that the goods of specified description and value are entering into the country from abroad. If the goods are cleared through the (Electronic Data Interchange) EDI system no formal Bill of Entry is filed as it is generated in the computer system, but the importer is required to file a cargo declaration having prescribed particulars required for processing of the entry for customs clearance. The Bill of entry, where filed, is to be submitted in a set, different copies meant for different purposes and also given different colour scheme. There are three types of Bill of Entry:

- Bill of Entry for home consumption: It is to be submitted when the imported goods are to be cleared on payment of full duty for consumption of the goods in India. It is white coloured.
- Bill of Entry for Warehouses: It is to be submitted when the imported goods are not required immediately by the importer but here they are to be stored in a warehouse without payment of duty
- Bill of Entry for Ex-Bond Clearance: It is used for clearing goods from the warehouse on payment of duty. The goods are classified and valued at the time of clearance from the Customs Port. Value and classification are not determined on such Bill of Entry.

In the non-EDI system along with the bill of entry filed by the importer or his representative, the following documents are also generally required:

- Signed invoice
- Packing list
- Bill of Lading or Delivery Order/Airway Bill
- GATT declaration form duly filled in
- Importers declaration
- Licence wherever necessary

- Letter of Credit/Bank Draft/wherever necessary
- Insurance document
- Import Licence
- Industrial Licence, if required
- Test report in case of chemicals
- Adhoc exemption order
- DEEC Book/DEPB in original
- Catalogue, technical write up, literature in case of machineries, spares or chemicals as may be applicable
- Separately split up value of spares, components machineries
- Certificate of Origin, if preferential rate of duty is claimed
- No Commission declaration

Bill of Entry is not required in the following cases:

- passengers baggage,
- favour parcels,
- mail box and post parcels,
- boxes, kennels of cargos containing live animals or birds,
- unserviceable stores, e.g. dunnage wood, empty bottles, drums, etc. of reasonable value,
- ship's stores in small quantities for personal use,
- cargo by sailing vessels from customs ports when landed at open bundles only for imports through the medium of post there is no bill of entry. Instead, it is prepared by the foreign post office for assessment of duty.

It is obligatory on the part of importers to submit Exchange Control copy of Bills of Entry for Home Consumption/Postal/Wrappers to the authorised dealer through whom relative remittance was made as evidence that the goods for which the payment was made have actually been imported into India. Authorised dealer should ensure that in all cases these are submitted by their importer customers and are verified. In respect of imports made on D/A basis, since goods would normally be cleared before the due date of payment, authorised dealers should insist on production of documentary evidence of import, i.e. Exchange Control copy of Bill of Entry for Home Consumption/Postal/Wrappers at the time of effecting remittance of the import bill. Authorised dealers should also advise this requirement to their importer customers in writing while delivering the documents against acceptance.

In case an importer does not furnish the Exchange Control copy of Bill of Entry within three months from the date of remittance, the authorised dealer should issue a reminder to the importer asking him to reduce it forthwith. If there is still no response, a reminder by registered post with acknowledgement due should be issued not later than one month from the date of the first reminder.

Q28. What are the standardised pre-shipment export documents?

Ans. Forms of documents prescribed by different agencies/bodies differ in size and layout even though much of the information is common.

Consequently, these documents are required to be prepared individually and separately. This method of preparation of documents caused delays in processing of documents by the concerned agencies/bodies besides resulting in errors and discrepancies. Considering the problems caused by the non-standardised documentation, a number of countries have been following a system of documentation known as the "Aligned Documentation System". This system is based on the "UN Layout Key" and is in use in a number of countries where exporters have benefited because of economy, speed, accuracy and convenience in documentation work.

By adopting the similar system, Government of India has developed Standardised Pre-shipment Export Document. With the help of this system, as many as 17 of the 25 documents can be prepared from only 2 Master Documents. In this method, the information is created on a set of standardised form printed on paper of the same size. This is done in such a way that items of identical information occupy the same position on each of them. The effort has been made to standardise both the Commercial and Regulatory documents. These documents can be discussed as follows:

(1) Commercial Documents

These documents are required for effecting physical transfer of goods and their title from the exporter to the importer and the realisation of export sale proceeds. These documents can be divided into:

    (a)   Principal Export Document, and

    (b)   Auxiliary Export Document.

Principal Export Documents are:

- Commercial invoice
- Packing list
- Bill of lading/Combined transport document
- Certificate of inspection/quality control
- Insurance certificate of policy
- Certificate of origin
- Bill of exchange
- Shipment advice

Auxiliary Export Documents are:

- Pro forma invoice
- Intimation for inspection
- Shipping instructions
- Insurance declaration
- Shipping order
- Mate receipt
- Application for certificate of origin
- Letters to the bank for collection/negotiation of documents

Out of above mentioned 16 documents, 14 documents have been standardised. Two documents, i.e. shipping order and bill of exchange have not been standardised. The standardised system involves the use of standardised trade documents which are also aligned in relation to one another. The documents are prepared on the same size of paper which have the requisite information in a standard format. Commercial documents are to be prepared as under:

Standard size of Paper

Paper	:	A4		
Size	:	Length	-	297 mm
		Width	-	210 mm
Margins	:	Top	-	10 mm
		Left	-	20 mm
		Right	-	6 mm
		Bottom	-	7 mm

Inside Measurements

Length	-	280 mm
Width	-	184 mm

Tolerance limits

±1 mm

Since these documents are aligned to one another, a Master Document is first prepared containing the information common to all documents. Thereafter, individual documents are prepared from the master documents with the help of a suitable marking and reproduction technique.

(2) Regulatory Documents

These documents are required by different government departments or organisations like central excise, customs, RBI, Export Inspection Council, etc. Documents required at pre-shipment stage are as follows:

Central Excise

Invoice

AR4/AR5 Forms

Customs

Shipping bill/Bill of export

Port Authorities (Port Trust)

Export Applications/Dock challan/Port Trust copy of Shipping Bill

Receipt for payment of port charges

vehicle/cart ticket/chit

RBI

GR/PP Form

Others

Freight Payment Certificate

Insurance premium

Out of these 9 pre-shipment regulatory documents, only 3 documents have been standardised. These three documents are as follows:

- Shipping Bill/Bill of Export
- GR Form
- Export Application/Dock Challan/Port Trust copy of Shipping Bill including receipt for payment of port charges.

Regulatory documents are to be prepared as under:

Standard size of Paper

Paper: Full scape size

Length	-	34.5 cms
Width	-	21.5 cms

Margins:

Top	-	1.5 cms
Left	-	1.8 cms
Right	-	0.5 cms
Bottom	-	1.5 cms

Inside Measurements

Inside Management

Length	-	31.5 cms
Width	-	19.2 cms

Tolerance limits

±1mm

Q29. Describe the steps involved in the receipt, examination and confirmation of an export order.

Ans. Processing of an export order starts with the receipt of an export order. An export order may be either in the form of export sales contract, which is concluded and incorporated in the form of a document or in the form of evidence or an instrument evidencing the conclusion of a contract.

Simply stated, it means that there should be an agreement, which is mostly reduced in a documentary form, between the exporter and the importer before the exporter can start arrangements for production or procurement of goods and their shipment. Generally, an export order may take the following forms:

- Pro forma Invoice accepted and signed by the importer;
- Purchase Order accepted and signed by the exporter;
- Letter of Credit opened by the importer in favour of the exporter.

A pro forma invoice is prepared and sent by the exporter to the importer. After accepting the terms and conditions given in it as given in a documented contract, if any, the importer returns a copy of this invoice to the exporter. Such a process helps in accepting the offer of the exporter by the importer, and thus, the conclusion of an export contract. In the case of long-term contract, the exporter may be required to send pro forma invoice for any intended shipment. Alternatively, the export contract may require a purchase order to be sent by the importer to the exporter. If the purchase order is in accordance with the terms and conditions of the contract, the exporter will duly accept it. Opening of a letter of credit is also a common method of receiving the export order. Although an instrument of payment, the letter of credit states major terms and conditions of shipment and enables the exporter to start processing the export order.

In order to avoid disputes, it is necessary to enter into an export contract with the overseas buyer. For this purpose, export contract should be carefully drafted incorporating comprehensive but in precise terms, all relevant and important conditions of the trade deal.

There should not be any ambiguity regarding the exact specifications of goods and terms of sale including export price, mode of payment, storage and distribution methods, type of packaging, port of shipment, delivery schedule, etc. The different aspects of an export contract are enumerated as under:

- Product, Standards and Specifications
- Quantity
- Inspection
- Total Value of Contract
- Terms of Delivery
- Taxes, Duties and Charges
- Period of Delivery/Shipment
- Packing, Labeling and Marking
- Terms of Payment— Amount/Mode & Currency
- Discounts and Commissions
- Licences and Permits
- Insurance
- Documentary Requirements
- Guarantee
- Force Majeure of Excuse for Non-performance of contract
- Remedies
- Arbitration

Court proceedings do not offer a satisfactory method for settlement of commercial disputes, as they involve inevitable delays, costs and technicalities. On the other hand, arbitration provides an economic, expeditious and informal remedy for settlement of commercial disputes.

A new exporter who is very keen to get into the business may tend to ignore certain aspects of the export order. It is not uncommon that s/he encounters difficulties while complying with the contracted obligations. In the process, he may suffer a loss. For example, the importer may specify inspection to be undertaken by an agency, which does not operate from India. Such a problem will be discovered only after the goods have been manufactured. At this stage, it may be difficult to persuade the importer to change this condition. Consequently, the exporter may suffer a loss.

Q30. Discuss the procedures of central excise clearance and pre-shipment inspection.

Ans. Central Excise Clearance

As soon as goods have been manufactured/procured, the process for obtaining clearance from central excise duty starts. The Central Excise and Sale Act of India and the related rules provide the refund of excise duty paid. This also provides exemption from the payment of excise duty both on the final export production and inputs used in the manufacture of export products, popularly known as rebate in excise duty. The documents used are Invoice and AR4/AR5 forms.

When goods are ready for despatch to the port for shipment, the production department of export firm is to apply to the central excise authority for excise clearance of the goods.

The exporters prepare six copies of AR4/AR5 forms (now ARE-1 forms). The exporters are now allowed to remove the goods for export on their own without getting the goods examined or after the examination by the Central Excise Officers. In case of without examination, exporter submits 4 copies of AR4/AR5 form to the superintendent of Central Excise having Jurisdiction over the premise of the exporter within twenty four hours of the removal of the consignment. The Superintendent examines the AR4/AR5 form and having being satisfied, signs the form and returns it to the concerned persons.

Pre-shipment Inspection

In order to ensure the exporters from India strictly adhere to the quality expectations and standards of international trade, the government of India had introduced the Export Quality Control and Inspection Act in the Year 1963. As per this act, certain items means for exports have been put on compulsory pre-inspection list and these items can not be exported unless certificate of pre-inspection have been obtained from the Export Inspection Council of India based in New Delhi or from any of their regional offices situated Mumbai, Kolkata, Chennai, Kochi or Ahmedabad.

Inspection of export goods may be conducted under:

(1)   Consignment-wise Inspection

(2)   In-process Quality Control and

(3)   Self-Certification

For getting an inspection certificate, the application is to be made on a prescribed form known as Notice of Inspection and submitted to the Agency with the following documents:

(1)   A copy of the commercial invoice;

(2)   Crossed cheque of demand draft as inspection fee;

(3)   A copy of export contract; and

(4)   Importer's technical specifications and/or approved sample.

After the inspector has completed inspection, the Export Inspection Agency will issue the inspection certificate in triplicate. The original certificate is for the customs verification. It is submitted to the customs authorities, along with other documents before permission to ship goods is granted. The second copy may be sent to the buyer, if needed. The third copy is for the exporter record.

Q31. Discuss the documentary formalities required for the appointment of clearing and forwarding agents.

Ans. Clearing and forwarding agents, also known as freight forwarders, perform a number of functions on behalf of the exporter. They provide specialised help in the exporter's warehouse to the importer's warehouse by undertaking the procedural and documentary formalities. It helps in packing, marking and labelling of consignment, arrangement for transport to the port, arrangement for shipment overseas, and customs clearance of cargo, procurement of transport and other documents. However, the main function of the agent is to obtain customs clearance of goods, ship them and procure the relevant transport document (Bill of Lading or Airway Bill). For performing the desired functions, the exporter is required to give detailed instructions to his agent, who in turn will charge fee for these activities. On completion of the process of clearance by the excise authorities as well as obtaining the Inspection Certificate, the production department dispatches the consignment to the port of shipment by either road or rail. Information to this effect is sent to the export department by signing the delivery note or by preparing a dispatch advice alongwith the following documents:

- Railway Receipt or Lorry Way Bill;
- Invoice;
- AR4/AR5 forms (Original and Duplicate); and
- Inspection Certificate (Original).

On receipt of these documents, the export department will appoint a clearing and forwarding agent by signing and sending a document, generally known as Shipping Instruction Sheet or simply the Shipping Instructions. This document contains full details of instructions of the exporter as well as details or the consignment to be shipped. Alongwith this document, following documents will be sent to the agent:

- Commercial Invoice (Generally 8-10 copies with at least one completed);
- Customs Declaration Form in Triplicate (This is a legal requirement whereby the exporter states that the declarations made to the customs authorities by the agent on his behalf are true);
- Packing list, if needed;
- Original Letter of Credit/Contract;
- Inspection Certificate (Original);
- GR Form- Original and Duplicate (It is a foreign exchange declaration form.);
- AR4/AR5 forms (Original and Duplicate) Invoice; and
- Railway Receipt/Lorry Way Bill.

Clearing and forwarding agents are authorised by the Government of India to not only help the importers and the exporters but also to bring it to the notice of the custom officials any irregularities in the customs rules and regulations updated by the customs, importer and exporter. The clearing agent should be converse with customs act rules and regulations.

Q32.Briefly explain formalities for claiming major export incentives.

Or

Describe the formalities for claiming duty drawback and excise rebate.

Ans. Formalities for claiming major export incentives are claiming export rebate and duty drawback.

Formalities of Getting Excise Rebate

After completion of the post-shipment formalities, the clearing and forwarding agent will file the following documents with the Maritime

Central Excise Collector or Jurisdictional Assistant Collector of Central Excise for claiming the refund of excise duty or for obtaining release from bond, as the case may be:

(1) AR4/AR5 forms (Duplicate copy) which has been certified by the Customs Preventive Officer, and

(2) Non-negotiable copy of the Bill of Lading and/or Shipping Bill certified by the Customs Preventive Officer.

Additional documents to be submitted for claiming refund of excised duty are: (a) Application for Refund in Form C; and (b) Pre-receipt.

Formalities of Duty Drawback

Duty drawback means the rebate of duty chargeable on imported material or excisable material used in the manufacturing of goods in and is exported. If the exporter intends to claim duty drawback on his exports, he has to follow prescribed procedures and submit necessary papers. For claiming duty drawback, the exporter's agent will file the customs attested copy of the Drawback Shipping Bill, alongwith the following documents, with the Drawback Department of the Customs House.

- Drawback Claim Pro forma (prescribed application form in five copies)
- Bank or Customs Certified copy of Commercial Invoice
- Non-negotiable copy of Bill of Lading
- Any other specifically prescribed document as E-BRC, EP copy of shipping bill, etc.

After finding the claim to be correct, the Drawback Department will dispatch the cheque of the claim amount to the exporter. Alternatively, if the exporter so desires, this amount will be sent to the exporter's bank for being credited to his account with intimation to the exporter.

▲ ▲ ▲

Feedback is the breakfast of Champions.

Ken Blanchard

You can Help other students.
"Inform any error or mistake in this book."

We and Universe
will reward you for Your Kind act.

Email at : feedback@gullybaba.com
or
WhatsApp on 9350849407

Terms of Payment and Export Finance

2

AN OVERVIEW

Terms of payment are often decisive in obtaining an export order. Therefore, an understanding of alternative payment terms is important for marketing goods abroad. Advance Payment, Documentary Credit, Documents Against Payment, Documents Against Acceptance, Open Account and Shipment on Consignment are six methods of receiving payments. Exchange control applies to all the rules and regulations designed to regulate transactions involving foreign exchange.

In India, the export credit facilities are provided largely by commercial banks. RBI and EXIM banks offer refinance. Export business has become very competitive and risky. Credit risk is greater in export transactions because reliable information about foreign buyers is difficult to obtain, and hence, it is difficult to evaluate their credit worthiness.

Foreign exchange transactions involve exchange of one country's currency for that of another country. The bank provides forward exchange cover for the risks arising out of fluctuations in exchange rates to both the importer and exporter. For this purpose, the parties enter into the forward contract for selling or buying of foreign currency in future.

Q1. What do you know by terms of payment? Briefly discuss the various methods of payment available for exporter.

Ans. Payment term in any business is a major part of sales contract. Terms of payment in exports and imports plays an important role in international business. The terms of payment play a very important role in export business. The terms are instrumental in attracting foreign buyers, and thus, expanding the export business. Many exporters are able to clinch an order on the basis of attractive payment terms, even though they may not be competitive from the viewpoint of price or quality. Payments are determined by a host of factors, such as exchange control regulations, trade practices, financial position of buyers and above all bargaining strength of the trading partners, in India, exchange control regulations play an important role in this regard. According to these regulations, the amount representing the full export value of the goods exported to all countries, other than Bhutan and Nepal, must be realised within six months from the date of shipment. Any deviation from the rule will require the Reserve Bank's prior approval. There are four methods of receiving payments from the overseas buyers. These methods carry risks of varying nature. Hence, the choice depends largely on the bargaining strength of the trading partners.

The following methods of payment are available for export:

(1) **Advance Payment (Cash-in-Advance):** With cash-in-advance payment terms, the exporter can avoid credit risk because payment is received before the ownership of the goods is transferred. Wire transfers and credit cards are the most commonly used cash-in-advance options available to exporters. However, requiring payment in advance is the least attractive option for the buyer, because it creates cash flow problems. The buyer may favour this method when he is an overseas affiliate of the exporter, or urgently requires the goods and the exporter is in a position to dictate his terms. Foreign buyers are also concerned that the goods may not be sent if payment is made in advance. Thus, exporters who insist on this payment method as their sole manner of doing business may lose from competitors who offer more attractive payment terms.

(2) **Open Account:** An open account transaction is a sale where the goods are shipped and delivered before payment is due, which is usually in 30 to 90 days. Obviously, this option is the most advantageous option to the importer in terms of cash flow and cost, but it is consequently the highest risk option for an exporter. Because of intense competition in export markets, foreign buyers often press exporters for open account terms since the extension of credit by the seller to the buyer is more common abroad. Therefore, exporters who are reluctant to extend credit may lose a sale to their competitors. However, the exporter can offer competitive open account terms while substantially mitigating the risk of non-payment by using one or

more of the appropriate trade finance techniques, such as export credit insurance.

(3) **Consignment Sales:** Consignment in international trade is a variation of open account in which payment is sent to the exporter only after the goods have been sold by the foreign distributor to the end customer. An international consignment transaction is based on a contractual arrangement in which the foreign distributor receives, manages, and sells the goods for the exporter who retains title to the goods until they are sold. Clearly, exporting on consignment is very risky as the exporter is not guaranteed any payment and its goods are in a foreign country in the hands of an independent distributor or agent. Consignment helps exporters become more competitive on the basis of better availability and faster delivery of goods. Selling on consignment can also help exporters reduce the direct costs of storing and managing inventory. The key to success in exporting on consignment is to partner with a reputable and trustworthy foreign distributor or a third-party logistics provider. Appropriate insurance should be in place to cover consigned goods in transit or in possession of a foreign distributor as well as to mitigate the risk of non-payment.

(4) **Documents against Acceptance (D/A):** In the documents against payment (D/P)-documents on payment (DOP or D/P)- The documents attached to the draft (bill) drawn by the exporter and needed to obtain goods are deliverable to the importer only after s/he has accepted the draft for payment later. The documents against acceptance (D/A) apply to a term draft.

(5) **Documents against Payment (D/P):** Like in D/A arrangement, here too the documents are sent to the buyer's bank with a draft (bill of exchange). However, this draft is a sight draft and not a usance draft. This draft has to be paid immediately on sight and only after the receipt of payment the shipment title documents are released. It means that the importer gets possession of the ownership documents of the shipment only after making payment for the same. The exporter, on the other hand, releases possession of shipment title papers only against the receipt of payment. No credit is involved here.

(6) **Letters of Credit (L/C):** A letter of credit is a very popular form of documentary credit. It is one of the most secure instruments available to international traders. An L/C is a commitment by a bank on behalf of the buyer that payment will be made to the exporter, provided that the terms and conditions stated in the L/C have been met, as verified through the presentation of all required documents. The buyer pays his or her bank to render this service. An L/C is useful when reliable credit information about a foreign buyer is difficult to obtain, but the exporter is satisfied with the creditworthiness of the buyer's foreign bank. An L/C also protects the buyer because no payment obligation arises until the goods have been shipped or delivered as promised.

Q2. List the various parties involved in the documentary credit.

Or

Discuss some parties involved in the documentary credit arrangement.

Or

Write a short note on Parties in Documentary Credits.

[Dec-2014, Q.No.-7(a)]

Ans. There are several parties in the documentary credit arrangement, which are as follows:

- **Applicant:** The buyer is responsible for providing precise and clear instructions for the issuance of credit and amendments thereafter. As he applies to the bank for the L/C, he is referred to as the applicant.

- **Issuing Bank:** This is the bank that issues the L/C. Before issuing the L/C, it must satisfy itself about the standing of the applicant making a request for the issuance of a letter of credit. Once the documents are presented, it has to examine them to ascertain whether the documents presented are compliant and meet the requirements of the credit. If so, they have to provide the payment to the bank (negotiating bank) from whom the documents were received.

- **Advising Bank:** The issuing bank will route the L/C through their correspondent bank (advising bank) in the exporter's country. The advising bank's responsibility is to establish apparent authenticity of the credit before advising it to the beneficiary.

- **Beneficiary:** The exporter or seller is the beneficiary of an L/C arrangement. On receipt of a properly worded, properly advised L/C; the beneficiary has to ship the goods, prepare the documents as per terms of L/C and submit them to his bank for negotiation.

- **Confirming Bank:** If the exporter does not have confidence in the standing of the issuing bank, he can demand a confirmed letter to credit. In this case, the issuing bank will request their correspondent bank (confirming bank) to add confirmation to the L/C. This bank will satisfy itself about the standing of the issuing bank, (making a request for adding confirmation to the letter of credit), before agreeing to add confirmation. By adding confirmation, it steps into the shoes of the issuing bank and it becomes bound to pay, accept or negotiate the documents drawn under L/C, if they comply with the terms and condition of the L/C. For adding confirmation, this bank will recover commission.

- **Negotiating Bank:** Upon shipment of goods, the exporter prepares the documents as per the terms of the L/C and submits these to his bank for payment. This bank is the negotiating bank, which must examine the documents to satisfy that they are drawn in compliance with the terms and conditions of the L/C. If so, then this bank will make the payment to the beneficiary and will forward the documents to the issuing bank to get the payment. The payment made by the negotiating bank to the exporter is 'with recourse' (i.e. the bank reserves a right to recover the payment from exporter in case it fails to get the payment from the issuing bank for any reason). However, in case of a confirmed L/C, the payment made is 'without recourse'.

- **Reimbursing Bank:** In case, the currency of the transaction is other than the currencies of the export and import countries, there will be a delay in getting the payment (e.g. an exporter in India has received the L/C issued by a bank in Dubai, which is denominated in US$). In this case, the negotiating bank in India will send the documents to the issuing bank in Dubai and will instruct them to remit proceeds to a bank in US, with whom negotiating bank maintains a US$ account. To avoid this delay, the issuing bank, at the time of issuing the L/C, will nominate a bank (their correspondents) in US as a reimbursing bank. In such a case, the negotiating bank will send all documents to the issuing bank but will simultaneously lodge a reimbursement claim with nominated bank in US. This will avoid the delay in getting the proceeds and the beneficiary stands to benefit.

Q3. Write the details included in Letter of Credit (L/C).

Ans. The advice of a documentary credit addressed to the beneficiary gives the following particulars though the format order varies among banks:

(1)   Name of the issuing bank and type of credit with number and date

(2)   On whose behalf the credit is issued (the applicant/buyer)

(3)   The amount (including the currency)

(4)   The date upto which the credit valid (expiry date). The last date for shipment may also be specified

(5)   Since the beneficiary is usually required to draw a bill of exchange (normally referred to as 'draft' in documentary credits) (a) the terms of the draft (i.e., sight or usance) (b) whether the draft is to be drawn on a named bank or the buyer

(6)   Brief details of the goods

(7)   Documents required - usually the documents are: Commercial Invoice, Packing List, Insurance Policy/Certificate, Inspection Certificate, Transport document - Bill of Lading, Airway Bill or Combined Transport Document

(8)   Port(s) of shipment and destination of shipment (only country's name may be written)

(9)   Price and terms of shipment (whether FOB, C&F or CIF)

(10)   Whether the part shipment and/or trans-shipment permitted

(11) Any other conditions applicable to the credit

(12) Certificate as the issuing bank's responsibility in the credit. If the certificate is omitted, it may be implied from type of credit indicated in (a) above, e.g. irrevocable, etc.

(13) Statement that the credit is subject to the provisions of the Uniform Customs & Practices for Documentary Credits.

Q4. What is the general procedure in a Letter of Credit?

Or

Write a short note on practical mechanism of letter of credit.

Ans. The general procedure in a letter of credit usually follows the below discussed sequence:

(1) The buyer and seller agree terms of sale, including payment by letter of credit

(2) The buyer issues an instruction to the issuing bank to issue the credit

(3) The issuing bank instructs the advising or confirming bank, including specification of documents

(4) The advising bank informs the beneficiary

(5) The beneficiary, if he accepts the advice and is happy with it, arranges shipment

(6) The seller obtains the bill of lading and the other required documents. He delivers them to the issuing, paying, accepting or negotiating bank, whichever is the appropriate one for the settlement.

(7) The bank checks the documents. If they are in accordance with the instructions from the issuing bank (or the applicant) if the issuing bank is the paying bank, effects payment as appropriate.

(8) If the paying bank is not the issuing bank, it sends the documents to the issuing bank. The issuing bank checks them and, if they are correct, release them to the buyer upon payment of the amount of credit.

(9) The buyer uses the documents to get possession of the goods.

Q5. What are the different types of Letter of Credit?

Ans. Banks may issue several types of L/C. It is best for importers and exporters to meet with their banking officer to determine which type of credit best suits their needs. The most common types of L/C are as follows:

(1) Revocable Letter of Credit: It allows issuing bank for amendments, modifications and cancellation of the terms outlined in the letter of credit at any time and without the consent of the exporter or beneficiary. So, this places the exporter at risk, revocable L/C are not generally accepted.

(2) Irrevocable Letter of Credit: It requires the consent of the beneficiary and applicant before any amendment, modification or cancellation to the original terms by the issuing bank. This type of letter of credit is commonly used and preferred by the exporter or beneficiary because payment is always assured, provided the documents submitted comply with the terms of the letter of credit.

(3) **Confirmed Letter of Credit:** It implies when a second guarantee is added to the document by another bank. The advising bank, the branch or the correspondent through which the issuing bank routes the letter of credit, adds its undertaking and commitment to pay to the letter of credit. This confirmation means that the seller/beneficiary may also look to the credit worthiness of the confirming bank for payment assurance.

(4) **Unconfirmed Letter of Credit:** It is when the document bears the guarantee of the issuing bank alone. The advising bank merely informs the exporter of the terms and conditions of the letter of credit, without adding its obligation to pay. The exporter assumes the payment risk of the issuing bank, which is typically located in a foreign country.

(5) **Back-to-back Letter of Credit:** These types of L/C are two individual L/C that together offer an alternative to a transferable letter of credit. The back-to-back letter of credit allows exporters (sellers or middlemen) who do not qualify for unsecured bank credit to use a letter of credit as security for a second letter of credit in favour of a supplier. In other words, if a foreign buyer will issue a letter of credit to an exporter, certain banks and trade finance companies will issue independent L/C to the exporter's suppliers so that the required goods can be purchased. Even if the initial letter of credit is not successfully completed, the second remains valid, and the issuing bank is obligated to pay under its terms. Although back-to-back L/C provide small and medium exporters virtually unlimited working capital to finance their sales and complete more export transactions, many banks are reluctant to take on this type of arrangement. Because back-to-back L/C involve two separate transactions, it is likely that several participating banks will be involved and the risk of confusion and dispute is high. To protect itself, a bank generally will require that the exporter present all relevant documents that are part of the first letter of credit before issuing the second letter of credit. The second document is worded to conform precisely to the original and dated to expire at some date prior to the first, ensuring that the seller has sufficient time to present documents within the time limits of the first.

(6) **Standby Letter of Credit:** Unlike a commercial letter of credit, which is basically a payment mechanism, a standby letter of credit is a form of a bank guarantee. It may be used as necessary to cover non-payment of a financial obligation. A standby letter of credit normally is intended to be drawn on only in the event of non-payment. The standby letter of credit is issued by the bank and held by the seller, who in turn provides the customer open account terms. If payment is made according to the seller's terms, the letter of credit is never drawn on. However, if the customer is unable to pay, the seller presents a draft, and all other documents as required, to the bank for payment. The standby letter of credit typically expires within 12 months.

(7) Transferable Letter of Credit: Here the L/C can be transferred to a second beneficiary. The L/C is only transferable if this is specifically stated when it is issued. The benefit of a transferable credit is that if the beneficiary is only an intermediary between the opener and the manufacturer and is interested in the margin/spread then he can make this without employing his own funds. Transferable credit can only be transferred once. The second beneficiary cannot transfer it again. However, a part or fraction can be transferred provided it does not exceed the total quantity/value of the original L/C and provided that partial shipment is allowed.

(8) Revolving Letter of Credit: A revolving letter of credit is where the credit available to the beneficiary gets reinstated after being utilised once. The amount of the credit is renewed or reinstated from time to time without a specific amendment. This credit may be limited by the overall credit available or the time period in which such a credit may be utilised or both.

(9) Anticipatory Credit or 'red clause' Letter of Credit: Under a red clause letter of credit, some part payment is made to the beneficiary before the shipment of goods and submission of documents stipulated in the credit. It is method of financing gets its name from the clause authorising the advising bank, which is typed or printed in red. This enables the beneficiary to purchase required raw materials and goods, etc. for the exporter. This amount of advance is either to be repaid by the exporter/beneficiary or is adjusted from the negotiation amount of the bill. If the exporter/beneficiary fails to repay or fails to submit the documents for negotiation, the ultimate responsibility is of the L/C opener to repay the money of advance.

Green clause letter of credit is an extension of red clause letter of credit in as much as, in addition to advance payment, it takes into account the grant of storage facilities at the part of shipment and its cost, including insurance charges, is met by opener. These L/Cs are very uncommon.

(10) Deferred Payment Credit: This letter of credit allows payment under the L/C in installment to the beneficiary and each installment is covered by a separate draft. The issuing bank will accept the drafts when the documents are submitted in accordance with the terms and conditions of letter of credit. The exporter can also discount the drafts with his banker or the issuing bank if the drafts are drawn under the credit.

(11) Restricted Credit: This refers that negotiations under a credit may be restricted by the issuing bank to a named bank.

(12) Payment Credit: This is a sight credit which will be paid at sight basis against presentation of requisite documents to the designated paying bank. In a payment credit, beneficiary may or may not be called upon to draw a draft. In many countries, because of stamp duties even on sight drafts, it has become increasingly customary not to call for drafts under credit available by sight payment.

(13) Acceptance Credit: This is similar to Deferred Payment Credit except for the fact that in this credit, drawing of a usance draft is a must. Under this credit, drafts must be drawn on the specified bank/drawee for specified period; the designated bank will accept the drafts and honour the same by making payment on the due dates.

(14) Negotiation Credit: This can be sight credit or a usance credit. But drawing a draft is must in Negotiation Credit. Further, the draft can be drawn either on the beneficiary or any other drawee as per credit terms. In a Negotiation Credit, the nomination can be restricted to a specific bank or it may allow free negotiation in which case it is called as 'Freely Negotiable Credit'. Under a Negotiation Credit, if the bank nominated as a Negotiated Bank refuses to negotiate, then the responsibility of Issuing Bank would be to pay as terms of that credit.

(15) Sight and Usance Credit: When a L/C states that the payment will be made by the bank at sight, on demand or on presentation, such credit is called Sight Credit. However, drawing of a draft is not always needed; payment can be made on presentation of specified documents. Under Usance Credit, L/C calls for drawing at a stated usance period. This type of credit is also referred to as 'Term Credit'.

(16) Fixed and Revolving Credit: When a credit is available for fixed amount and period, it is called fixed credit. In this type of credit, the credit gets exhausted once it is utilised for the stipulated amount or after the stated validity date.

(17) Under Revolving Credit: Under this credit, the amount is revived or reinstated without requiring re-enhancement in credit.

(18) Transit Credit: Normally, when an L/C is opened, it will be advised to the beneficiary by a bank that is based in the beneficiary's country. However, in a transit credit, the services of a bank situated in a 3rd country will be used. In such credit, the advising bank will be situated in a country other than the beneficiary's. Such a requirement may be called for, in cases where the opening bank has no correspondent relations with any bank in the beneficiary's country. Transit credit may also be opened by countries whose credit may not be readily accepted in the beneficiary's country. In such a case, a bank in a 3rd country may be requested to open the L/C.

Q6. What are the documents required under Letter of Credit (L/C)?

Or

"All parties in documentary credit deal only in documents". Discuss. [June-2013, Q.No.-2]

Ans. According to Article 4 of the Uniform Customs and Practice for Documentary credit, in credit operations all parties concerned deal in documents, and not in goods, services and/or other performances to which the documents may relate. Hence, it is necessary that the beneficiary tender documents in conformity with the requirements of letter of credit. Usual documents required in letter of credit are as follows:

(1) **Bill of Exchange:** It is an instrument drawn by one person (the seller of the goods) on another (the buyer) directing him to pay or to the order of drawer (i.e. the seller). The person whom payment is to be called 'payee', who can be either the drawer himself or a third person. Most L/C require that the exporter will prepare the bill, called the draft and submit it to the banker along with other documents. It is a document through which payment is arranged.

(2) **Commercial Invoice:** It is a document of content. It contains details about the goods sold, the price and any other charges, which may be on account of the buyer. It also contains information about any discount, if given by the seller. A correctly completed commercial invoice should conform to the sale contract.

(3) **Packing List:** This gives details of the individual parcels/packets shipped to the buyer.

(4) **Transport Documents:** As shipment is the most crucial condition of payment, all L/C insist on lodgement of documentary evidence in support of exporter's contention of having shipped the goods. Bill of Lading is issued in case of air consignment, Railway Receipt/truck Challan in case the goods are sent by land route. Combined Transport Document is issued where the exporter chooses a multimodel transport system. These documents are accepted as proof of shipment.

(5) **Inspection Certificate:** As the goods must conform to agreed quality standards, all L/C require an Inspection Certificate. The Inspection Certificate has to be submitted as a proof of the goods having been inspected by a qualified government or private agency.

(6) **Insurance Policy Certificate:** Insurance Policy is a legal evidence of contract of insurance, showing full details of risks covered. Insurance certificate, applicable in case of 'Floating' or

'Open' cover, contains a declaration regarding value of each shipment and is signed by the exporter himself. Insurance certificate is not normally acceptable unless specifically provided in the letter of credit.

Besides, some L/C require documents such as Certificate of Origin, Analysis and Weight Certificate, Health and Sanitary Certificate to be submitted to the negotiating bank.

Q7. Write the common errors exporters commit while making Letters of Credit. Give some tips to avoid these errors.

Ans. An exporter gets payment under letter of credit only if he has tendered correct documents. These documents are carefully scrutinised first by the negotiating banker in the exporting country, before he makes payment to exporters. The issuing banker in the importer's country also scrutinises it before reimbursing the negotiating banker. Any discrepancy in document can lead delays in payment. Documents are rejected on first presentation oftenly because they are either incomplete or incorrect. These typical errors are as follows:

(1) The letter of credit had expired.

(2) The bill of lading was claused (unclean or dirty).

(3) A charter party bill of lading was presented when L/C called on on-board shipment.

(4) The goods were shipped on deck when it was not permitted.

(5) Shipment was made between the ports other than stated in the letter of credit.

(6) Insurance cover was inadequate and expressed in a currency other than that required by the letter of credit.

(7) The description (or spelling) of goods on invoice(s) differed from that in the letter of credit.

(8) The weights, marks and numbers differed between export documents.

(9) The amounts of value shown on the invoice(s) and bill of exchange (draft) differed.

(10) The drawing was for less than the letter of credit amount (when part shipment) were not permitted.

(11) The bill of lading did not evidence whether freight was paid or not.

(12) The shipment was short.

(13) The bill of exchange (draft) was drawn on wrong party.

(14) The bill of exchange was payable on indeterminable date.

(15) The bill of lading, insurance documents or bill of exchange (draft) were not endorsed correctly.

(16) The copy of the freight account was not attached (when called for by the letter of credit).

(17) There was an absence of signatures of witnesses, when required, on document presented.

(18) The facsimile signatures were used when not allowed.

In view of such common errors, it is necessary to read the letter of credit very carefully and check the terms against the contract of sale. It is fundamental to check that the letter of credit:

(1) is of the type agreed, e.g. irrevocable and confirmed or just irrevocable;

(2) has an expiry date that is sufficiently far ahead for the goods to be shipped and the required documents obtained and presented in time;

(3) has terms and conditions that can be met and that the required documents can obtain exactly as called for; and

(4) has correct spelling, any misspelling should be taken up immediately with the buyer.

If any amendment or extension is necessary, the buyer should be asked immediately to instruct the issuing bank accordingly. A watch should be kept to see that advice of amendment of the credit is received without delay. It should be remembered that bank is not allowed to overlook or approve errors and inconsistencies; however, small in the documents presented and will not pay in such circumstances.

Q8. What is shipment on consignment basis? Discuss in brief.

Ans. Shipment on consignment basis implies that goods are sent to the importer on the understanding that the later will sell the goods and remit the sale proceed. Importer, in most cases, is either the exporter's own agent or certain marketing agencies who undertake to sell the goods on commission basis. A typical example of such sale is export of tea to UK. Tea is sent to London, where it is sold through periodic auctions, and the sale proceed is remitted back to exporters.

Under the exchange control regulations in India, Indian exporters are required to declare the minimum selling price of each consignment. In case the goods cannot be sold at the price declared at the time of shipment, reduction in price can be effected only with the permission from Reserve Bank of India.

Q9. What is foreign exchange? What do you understand by foreign exchange transaction?

Ans. Foreign Exchange Regulation Act, 1973 defines foreign exchange as foreign currency and it includes:

- all deposits, credit and balances payable in foreign currency
- any drafts, traveller's cheques, L/C and bills of exchange expressed or drawn in Indian currency but payable in any foreign currency and,
- any instrument payable at the option of the drawee or holder thereof or any other party thereto, either in Indian currency or foreign currency or partly in one and partly in the other.

Foreign Exchange Transactions

It is the ultimate of purchase or sale of one national currency against another arising out of import or export of goods and services, foreign remittances and foreign travel both inward and outward, etc. The goods refer to raw materials, intermediary or finished products capital goods, etc.

comprising the visible items of a country's foreign trade. Services refer to shipping, air travel, insurance, banking, supply of technical know-how, consultancy, transfer of capital by way of lending and or investment, interest on such capital and dividends on such investment, tourists income and expenses, cost of Indian students abroad and of foreign students in India, gifts and donations, remittances, etc. which taken together comprise the invisible items of a country's foreign trade. A foreign exchange transaction is thus transfer of purchasing power, i.e. acquisition or parting with the right to wealth in a foreign country. As we must be knowing that the foreign exchange is precious for a country. Hence, government regulates and controls the foreign exchange transactions.

Q10. What are the concerns and provisions of the Foreign Exchange Regulation Act (FERA), 1973 about exports?

Or

Discuss the provisions of foreign exchange regulations concerning exports under exchange control regulations.

[Dec-2012, Q.No.-6]

Ans. Exports are the reasons for earning huge amount of foreign exchange for any country. With earning foreign exchange, exports need to be checked and regulate for the regular earning. In India, the amended FERA, 1993 allows import and export of gold and silver under the provisions of exports - import policy of the Government of India. The bringing in or taking out of personal jewellery by travellers would be regulated by customs Act and Baggage rules. Import and export of any Indian currency or foreign exchange is prohibited except with the general or special permission of the Reserve Bank.

The important provisions include declaration of exports on prescribed forms, realisation of export proceeds in permitted methods, currencies prescribed period and prescribed manner. However, the provisions are discussed as follows:

Prohibition of Export

Export of all goods either directly or indirectly to any place outside India other than Nepal and Bhutan is prohibited unless the exporter furnishes to the authority a declaration in the prescribed form. It should be supported by such evidences as may be prescribed or so specified and true in all material particulars.

The prohibition shall not apply to the export of:

(1) Trade samples supplied free of payment.

(2) Personal effects of travellers, whether accompanied or unaccompanied.

(3) Ship's store, trans-shipment cargo and goods shipped under the orders of the Central Government in this behalf of or the military, naval or air force authorities in India for military, naval or air force requirements.

(4) Goods dispatched by air freight and accompanied by a declaration by the sender that they are more than ten thousand

rupees in value and that dispatch does not involve any transaction in foreign exchange.

(5) Goods dispatched by air freight and covered by a certificate issued by an authorised dealer that their export does not involve any transaction in foreign exchange.

(6) Goods export of which in the opinion of Reserve Bank does not involve any transaction in foreign exchange.

Export Declaration

Every exporter must make a true declaration in the prescribed form. The declaration is mandatory and includes:

(1) the full export value of the goods; or

(2) if the full export value of the goods is not ascertainable at the time of export, the value which the exporter, having regard to the prevailing market conditions, expects to receive on the sale of goods in the overseas market.

The declaration should be supported by an affirmation by the exporters to realise the required export proceeds. Exporter's affirmation has been mandatory made that the full export value declared is the same as contracted with the foreign importer. Any other invoicing or over-invoicing may attract penal provisions under the FERA act.

Permitted Methods

Export payment must be received in a currency appropriate to the country of final place of destination of the goods as declared on GR, etc. forms. Reserve Bank has granted permission for receiving payments for exports directly by exporters from their buyers in certain conditions.

Authorised dealers should receive remittances from foreign countries (other than Nepal and Bhutan) or obtain reimbursement from their branches and correspondents in these countries against payments due for exports from India. The other payments receivables should also conform these methods of payment indicated below:

(1) All countries other than member countries in the Asian Clearing Union (except Nepal), Bangladesh, Myanmar Islamic, Republic of Iran, Pakistan and Sri Lanka: Payment may be received in rupees from the account of a bank situated in any country in this group or payment may be received in any permitted currency.

(2) Member countries in the Asian Clearing Union (except Nepal), Bangladesh, Myanmar Islamic, Republic of Iran, Pakistan and Sri Lanka: Payment may be received for all eligible current transactions of debit to the ACU (Asian Clearing Union) dollar account in India of a bank of the participating country in which the other party to the transaction is resident, or by credit to the ACU dollar account of the authorised dealer maintained with the correspondent bank in the other participating country. In other cases, payment may be received in any permitted currency.

Permitted Currencies

The payment in foreign trade may be received or made in a foreign currency which is freely convertible. A freely convertible currency is permitted by the rules and regulations of the country concerned to be converted into major reserve currencies like US Dollar, Pound Sterling and for which a fairly active market exists for dealings against the major currencies. Authorised dealer may maintain balances and positions in any permitted currency and also in European Currency Unit (ECU) of the European Monetary System.

Prescribed Period

The amount representing the full export value of the goods exported shall be realised and be paid to the authorised dealer when it is due. The amount should be realised either on the due date for the payment or within six months from the date of shipment of the goods whichever is earlier. The period is extended to fifteen months where the goods are exported to a warehouse established outside India with the permission of the Reserve Bank. For exports to CIS countries and other East European countries Reserve Bank may permit realisation period upto 12 months. The Reserve Bank may extend the period of six months/twelve months or fifteen months if sufficient and reasonable causes are shown by the exporters.

Prescribed Manner

The manner in which the export proceeds are to be realised include:

    (1)   Payment should be received through an authorised dealer except in cases where general specific permission has been granted by Reserve Bank to receive the payment directly.

    (2)   Payment should be received in permitted currency.

    (3)   Payment should be received as per approved methods of payment.

Authorised dealers maintained with correspondent banks in the other participants case for imports into India from any of the ACU countries (except Nepal).

Some other provisions related to the export exchange regulations are as follows:

(1) Remittances connected with Exports

Exporters are permitted to retain upto 25 per cent (50 per cent in the case of EOUs located in EPZI Software Technology Parks/Electronics Hardware Technology Parks) of the receipts from export of goods in a foreign currency account with an authorised dealer in India. This account is known as Exchange Earners Foreign Currency (EEFC) account. According to the Monetary Policy (announced on 22 October 1997), Exporters are allowed to retain 50 per cent of their exchange earnings in the EEFC account as against the earlier 25 per cent. The account may be maintained in any permitted currency and in any form (current, savings without cheque facility or term deposit account). The balances in these accounts may be utilised for all bonafide payments of the account holder. Exporters maintain foreign Currency Accounts are not allowed to maintain EEFC accounts.

(2) Agency Commission on Exports

Authorised dealers may allow payment of commission, either by remittance or by deduction from invoice value, on application submitted by the exporter. The application, by letter, should give particulars such as Importer-Exporter code number, customs/shipping bill number and date, name of commodity, name and address of buyer/agent and export value and should be supported by an attested copy of invoice and documentary evidence in support of the amount to be remitted. The remittance may be allowed subject to the following conditions:

    (a)   Amount of commission has been declared on GR/PP/SOFTEX form and accepted by Custom authorities or Department of Electronics, Government of India as the case may be. In cases where the commission has not been declared on GR/PP/SOFTEX form, remittance thereof may be allowed after satisfying about the reasons adduced by the exporter for not declaring commission on Export Declaration Form provided a valid agreement/written understanding between the exporter and/or agent/beneficiary for payment of commission subsists.

    (b)   Rate of commission does not exceed 12.5 per cent of invoice value.

    (c)   Commission sought to be remitted is not on export of a canalised item, project exports or exports financed under lines of credit extended by Government of India or Exim Bank, or exports made by Indian partners towards equity participation in an overseas joint venture/wholly owned subsidiary.

    (d)   The relative shipment has already been made.

Export Claims

Authorised dealers are permitted to remit export claims by exporters on application by letter. The application contains particulars such as Reserve Bank Code Number, GR/PP form number, date of shipment, name of commodity, invoice value, name and address of claimant nature and amount of claim as also documentary evidence in support of the claim provided:

    (a)   the amount does not exceed 15 per cent of invoice value.

    (b)   the relative export proceeds have already been realised and repatriated to India. In case of exporters who have been in the export business for more than three years, remittances may be allowed without any percentage ceiling, provided:

        (i)   the exporter is not on the Exporter's caution list of Reserve Bank, and

        (ii) his track period is satisfactory.

In all such cases of remittances, the exporter should be advised to surrender proportionate incentives, if any, received by him.

Other Remittances: Authorised dealers may effect, on behalf of their exporter constituents, remittances connected with exporters like controlling charges, expenses incurred on dishonoured/unaccepted bills, legal expenses related to trade disputes, testing charges, etc. Exporters are expected to submit supporting documents for these remittances.

Dispatch of Goods not Involving Foreign Exchange

The dispatch of certain goods does not involve foreign exchange, for example, Gift parcels. In this case, GR/PP form is not applicable to exports by air freight and post parcel. Authorised dealers should certify that the exports do not involve any transaction in foreign exchange. This can be done in the following cases:

 (1) export is made by post parcel or air-freight;

 (2) authorised dealer is satisfied that the export does not involve any transaction in foreign exchange; and

 (3) the value of shipment does not exceed ₹25,000.

Export of Jewellery, Indian Currency, Foreign Exchange, Securities, etc.

Taking out of personal Jewellery from India by travellers is regulated under the Baggage Rules framed by the Ministry of Commerce under the Export-Import Policy.

 (1) **Export of Currency:** FERA Act prohibits taking or sending out Indian currency notes and coins from India without general or special permission of Reserve bank.

 (2) **Export of Foreign Exchange:** Export of foreign exchange in any form including currency notes or bank notes, other than foreign exchange obtained from an authorised dealer or authorised money-changer by the person exporting is prohibited unless it is covered by a general or special permission of Reserve Bank.

 (3) **Export of Securities:** Export of Securities to any place outside India requires permission of Reserve Bank.

Q11. Discuss about procedures for furnishing and declaration of the export declaration forms.

Ans. All exports to which the requirement of declaration applies must be declared on appropriate forms. These are as follows:

(1) Form GR/SDF

 (a) The declaration in form GR/SDF shall be submitted in duplicate to the Commissioner of Customs.

 (b) After duly verifying and authenticating the declaration form, the Commissioner of Customs shall forward the original declaration form/data to the nearest office of the Reserve Bank and hand over the duplicate form to the exporter for being submitted to the authorised dealer.

(2) Form PP

 (a) The declaration in form PP shall be submitted in duplicate to the authorised dealer named in the form.

 (b) The authorised dealer shall, after countersigning the declaration form, handover the original form to the exporter who shall submit it to the postal authorities through which the goods are being dispatched. The postal authorities after dispatch of the goods shall forward the declaration form to the nearest office of the Reserve Bank.

(3) Form SOFTEX

(a) The declaration in form SOFTEX in respect of export of computer software and audio/video/television software shall be submitted in triplicate to the designated official of Department of Electronics of Government of India at the Software Technology Parks of India (STPIs) or at the Free Trade Zones (FTZs) or Export Processing Zones (EPZs) in India.

(b) After certifying all three copies of the SOFTEX form, the said designated official shall forward the original directly to the nearest office of the Reserve Bank and return the duplicate to the exporter. The triplicate shall be retained by the designated official for record.

(4) Form VP/COD

This form is used to export to all countries by parcel post, under arrangements to realise proceeds through postal channels on value payable or cash on delivery basis.

Procedures for Furnishing the Forms

The declaration form GR (in duplicate) shall be submitted in duplicate to the commissioner of Customs. After duly verifying and authenticating the declaration form, the Commissioner of Customs will forward the original form to the nearest office of the Reserve Bank. The duplicate form is handedover to the exporter for being submitted to the authorised dealer with whom the export documents are negotiated.

The declaration form PP (in duplicate) shall be submitted to the authorised dealer in foreign exchange named in the form. The authorised dealer shall countersign on the form and handover the original form to the exporter. The exporter will submit the form to the postal authorities through which the goods are being dispatched. The postal authorities after dispatch of the goods, shall forward the declaration form to the nearest office of the Reserve Bank. On realisation of export proceeds the authorised dealer shall after due certification submit the duplicate form to the nearest office of the Reserve Bank.

The declaration form VP/COD (single copy) shall be submitted to the postal authority with the relative parcel at the time of dispatch. The postal authority shall send the form to the nearest office of the Reserve Bank.

On realisation of the export proceeds, the authorised dealer shall, after due certification, submit the duplicate of the GR/SDF, PP or as the case may be, SOFTEX form to the nearest office of the Reserve Bank.

Q12. What is the procedure and time period of export of computer software? Discuss in brief.

Ans. Export of Computer Software in physical form is done on GRPP forms. Export of computer software in non-physical form should be declared on SOFTEX form. The SOFTEX form is submitted in triplicate. Each exporter will have to designate a single branch of an authorised dealer to whom the export documents are submitted. Valuation of exports will be done by officials authorised by the Department of Electronics, Government of India. After verifying all the three copies of SOFTEX forms, the official will directly forward the original copy to the office of Reserve Bank under whose jurisdiction the exporter falls. The certified duplicate SOFTEX forms will be returned to the exporters together with all supporting documents and bills drawn on overseas buyers. The triplicate copy will be retained by the designated official for record to the Department of Electronics.

Period within which Export Value of Goods/Software to be Realised

The amount representing the full export value of goods or software exported shall be realised and repatriated to India within six months from the date of export:

- Provided that where the goods are exported to a warehouse established outside India with the permission of the Reserve Bank, the amount representing the full export value of goods exported shall be paid to the authorised dealer as soon as it is realised and in any case within fifteen months from the date of shipment of goods;

- Provided further that the Reserve Bank, or subject to the directions issued by that bank in this behalf, the authorised dealer may, for a sufficient and reasonable cause shown, extend the said period of six months or fifteen months, as the case may be.

Q13. What do you mean by pre-shipment finance? Enumerate the methods of pre-shipment finance.

Or

Write a short note on 'Packing Credit'.

[June-2013, Q.No.-7(e)]

Or

What is meant by Packing Credit? What are the conditions of eligibility for availing the facilities? What is the procedure adopted? Has the ECGC any role in such loans?

[June-2015, Q.No.-3]

Ans. A pre-requisite to pre-shipment financing is that the exporter should have a credit facility in place with a bank. Each bank has a credit process that determines the amount of funding the bank can give the company. Pre-shipment finance is provided to the exporters for the purchase of raw materials, processing them and converting them into finished goods for the purpose of export. Pre-shipment finance can be availed of only for the specific purpose of procuring raw materials, purchasing, manufacturing, processing, transporting, warehousing, packing and shipping the goods meant for export. Various pre-shipment advances available to the exporters are as follows:

(1) Packing Credit

Packing credit is meant for the purpose to enable the eligible exporters to procure, process, manufacture or store the goods needed for export. Packing credit refers to any loan to an exporter for financing the purchase, processing, manufacturing or packing of goods as defined by the Reserve

Bank of India. It is a short-term credit against exportable goods. Packing credit is normally granted on secured basis. Sometimes clear advance may also be granted. Many advances are clean at their initial stage when goods are not yet acquired. Once the goods are acquired and are in the custody of the exporter banks usually, convert the clean advance into hypothecation/pledge. The detail procedure of packing credit includes following:

Eligibility: All exporters can avail packing credit whether they are merchant exporters, Export/Trading/Star Trading/Super Star Trading Houses and manufacturer exporters. Manufacturers of goods supplying to Export/Trading/ST/SST Houses and merchant exporters are eligible for packing credit. The credit is given to eligible exporters for specified purposes against irrevocable letter of credit by the foreign buyer through the medium of a reputed bank. It is also available against a confirmed or firm export order/contract placed by the buyer for export of goods from India.

An exporter who holds an export order or Letter of Credit (L/C) in his own name to perform an export contract can avail of pre-shipment credit. Banks may also grant pre-shipment advances without insisting on prior lodgment of L/Cs or purchase orders. This is known as the "Running Account Facility".

Running Account Facility: The RBI has permitted banks to grant packing credit advances even without lodgement of L/C or firm order/contract under the scheme of Running Account Facility subject to the following conditions:

(a) The facility may be extended, provided the need for Running Account facility has been established by the exporters to the satisfaction of the bank.

(b) The banks may extend this facility only to those exporters whose track record has been good.

(c) L/C or firm order is produced within a reasonable period of time. For Commodities under selective credit control, banks should insist on production of L/Cs or firm orders within one month from the date of sanction.

(d) The concessive credit available in respect of individual pre-shipment credit should not go beyond 180 days.

Packing credit may also be given under the Red Clause letter of credit. In this method, credit is given at the instance and responsibility of the foreign bank establishing the L/C. Here, the packing credit advance is made against a simple receipt and is unsecured.

Amount: Banks will lend an amount to an exporter after factoring in a particular margin (this margin is calculated as a percentage of the value of the order). The margin differs from bank to bank. Margins are stipulated for the following reasons:

(a) to ensure that the exporter has some stake in the transaction

(b) to cover any erosion in the value of goods, and

  (c) to ensure that there is no lending against the exporter's profit margin.

The banking practice is that the exporter can obtain 90 per cent of the FOB value of the order or 75 per cent of the CIF value of the order.

Period: The RBI has allowed banks to grant this funding at a concession for a maximum period of 180 days. This period can be extended by the bank without referring to RBI for a further period of 90 days. Banks grant this extension in cases where the exporter faces genuine hardships in completing his order.

If an extension is required beyond 270 days (i.e. 180+90 days), the RBI has the discretion to grant another (maximum) extension of 90 days. However, if the exports do not take place at the end of this period, the bank will charge interest from day one, at a rate left to the bank's discretion.

Rate of Interest: The interest payable on pre-shipment finance is usually lower than the normal rate, provided the credit is extinguished by lodging the export bills on remittances from abroad. If the exporter fails to do so, they would not be able to avail concessional rate of interest. In order to avail the packing credit, exporters are expected to make a formal application to the bank giving details of credit requirements alongwith the required documents.

(2) Advance against Incentives

When the value of the materials to be procured for export is more than FOB value of the contract, the exporters may get packing credit advance more than the FOB value of the goods. The excess of cost of production over the FOB value of the contract represents incentives receivables. For example, when the domestic price of goods exceeds the value of export orders, the difference represents duty drawback entitlement.

Banks can grant advances against duty drawback at pre-shipment stage subject to the condition that the loan is covered by Export Production Finance Guarantee of Export Credit Guarantee Corporation (ECGC). This guarantee enables banks to sanction advances at the pre-shipment stage to the full extent of cost of production. The extent of cover and the premium are the same as for packing credit guarantee.

(3) Pre-shipment Credit in Foreign Currency

Oftenly, the pre-shipment borrowal is in the domestic currency, in the case of an exporter based in India, the Indian Rupee. The facility is available in any of the convertible currencies. The credit will be self-liquidating in nature and accordingly after the shipment of goods, the bills will be eligible for discounting/rediscounting or for post-shipment credit in foreign currency. The exporters can avail this finance under the following two options.

  (a) the exporters may avail pre-shipment credit in rupees and, then, the post-shipment credit either in rupees or in foreign currency denominated credit or discounting/rediscounting of export bills.

  (b) the exporters may avail pre-shipment credit in foreign currency discounting/rediscounting of the export bills in foreign currency.

PCFC credit will also be available both to the supplier units of EPZ/EOU and the receiver units of EPZ/EOU. The credit in foreign currency shall also be available on exports to Asian Clearing Union (ACU) Countries. This will be extended only on the basis of confirmed/firm export orders or confirmed LICs. The Running Account facility will not be available under the scheme. Read GPH books and score excellent marks.

Q14. What do you mean by Post-shipment Finance? What are the various methods through which post shipment finance can be granted?

Or

What are the various methods permitted under RBI regulations for realising export proceeds? Which in your opinion is safest from exporter view point and why?

[June-2014, Q.No.-4]

Or

Write a short note on post-shipment finance.

[June-2014, Q.No.-7(b)]

Or

Discuss various types of post-shipment finance.

Ans. Post-shipment finance means any loan or advance granted or any other credit provided by a bank to an exporter of goods/services from India from the date of extending credit after shipment of goods/rendering of services to the date of realisation of export proceeds. As per the period of realisation prescribed by FED, it includes any loan or advance granted to an exporter, in consideration of, or on the security of any duty drawback allowed by the Government from time to time. As per the current instructions of FED, the period prescribed for realisation of export proceeds is 12 months from the date of shipment.

While granting post-shipment finance, banks are governed by the guidelines issued by RBI, the rules of the Foreign Exchange Dealers Association of India (FEDAI), the Trade Control and Exchange Control Regulations and the International Conventions and Codes of the International Chambers of Commerce. The exporters are required to obtain credit limits suitable to their needs. The quantum of credit depends on export sales and receivables.

The exporter may choose the type of facility as per his requirements. The bank scrutinises the documents submitted for compliance of exchange control provisions like:

- the documents are drawn in permitted currencies and payment receivable as permitted method of payment;
- the relevant GR/PP form duly certified by the customs is submitted and particulars as stated in the GR/PP form are consistent with the documents tendered as well as the sale contract; firm order, etc.; and L/C;
- the documents are submitted within the time limit stipulated and in case of delay suitable explanation is made;

- the period of usance is in consonance with the time limit prescribed for realisation of export proceeds.

Post-shipment finance can be availed against export shipping documents and also against drawback claim. Post-shipment finance is granted generally in the following manner:

(1) Negotiation of Export Documents under L/C

The banks will negotiate the provided export bills where the exports are under L/C arrangements and it is drawn in conformity with it. When documents are presented to the bank for negotiation under L/C, they should be scrutinised carefully taking into account all the terms and conditions of the credit. All the documents tendered should be strictly in accordance with the L/C terms. It is to be noted that the L/C issuing bank undertakes to honour its commitment only if the beneficiary submits the stipulated documents. Even the slightest deviation from those specified in the L/C can give an excuse to the issuing bank of refusing the reimbursement of the payment that might have been already made by the negotiating bank.

Getting letter of credit is a safer method since there is a guarantee by the foreign bank to make payment on the strength of documentary evidences for having exported the goods. When an exporter, after having exported the goods, approaches a bank for post-shipment credit the bank sanctions a post-shipment credit limit based on the value of the goods exported.

(2) Purchase/Discount of Foreign Bills

Purchase or discount facilities in respect of export bills drawn under confirmed export orders are generally granted to the customers who are enjoying bill purchase/discounting limits from the bank. As in the case of purchase or discounting of documents drawn under export order, the security offered under L/C by way of substitution of credit worthiness of the buyer, i.e. importer by the issuing bank is not available, the bank financing is totally dependent upon the credit worthiness of the bank. The documents drawn on D/P basis are parted with through foreign correspondent only when payment is received. In case of D/A bills, documents are passed on to the overseas Importer against the acceptance of the draft to make payment on maturity. Banks generally opt for ECGC policies and guarantees to be issued in favour of the exporter/banks to protect their interest in case of non-payment or delayed payment. Under the policy, ECGC fixes limits and payment terms for individual buyers and the financing bank has to ensure that the limit is not exceeded so that the benefits of policy are available. Banks also secure a guarantee from ECGC on the post-shipment finance extended by them either on a selective or whole turnover basis. Banks sometimes do obtain credit reports on foreign buyers before they purchase the export bills drawn on the foreign buyer.

(3) Advances against Export Bills sent on Collection

In case the exporter wants to avail advance against export bills sent on collection, the bills are sent by the bank on collection basis as against their purchase/discounting by the bank. Post-shipment finance is granted against bills sent on collection basis in the following situations:

- when the accommodation available under the foreign bills purchase limit is exhausted;
- when some export bills drawn under L/C have discrepancies;
- where it is customary practice in the particular line of trade and in the case of exports to countries where there are problems of examination.

Advance against such bills is granted by way of a 'separate loan' usually termed as 'post shipment loan'. This type of facility is, however, not very popular and most advances against export bill are made by the bank by way of negotiation/purchase/discount.

(4) Advance against undrawn Balance

In certain lines of export, it is the trade practice that bills are not to be drawn for the full invoice value of the goods but to leave small part undrawn for payment after adjustment due to difference in rates, weight, quality, etc. to be ascertained after approval and inspection of the goods. Banks do finance against the undrawn balance if undrawn balance is in conformity with the normal level of balance left undrawn in the particular line of export, subject to a maximum of 10 per cent of the export value. The percentage of undrawn balance can be enhanced by the exporter against prior approval from the RBI. Accordingly, finance can be availed at higher rate.

(5) Advance against Retention Money

Banks also grant advances against retention money, which is payable within one year from the date of shipment, at a concessional rate of interest upto 90 days. In case the advances extend beyond one year, they are treated as deferred payment advance, which are also eligible for concessional rate of interest.

(6) Advance against Goods Sent on Consignment

Sometimes exports are affected on consignment basis. In such condition, payment is receivable subject to sale of goods. Goods are exported at the risk of exporter for sale. The banks may finance against such transaction subject to the exporter enjoying specific limit for such purposes. The overseas branch/correspondent of the bank is instructed to deliver the documents against Trust Receipt.

(7) Advance against Export Incentives

Advances against the export incentives are given at the pre-shipment stage as well as the post-shipment stage. However, the major part of the advance is given at the post-shipment stage. The advance is granted to an exporter in consideration of or on the security of any duty drawback incentives receivable from the Government. The banks follow their own procedure in granting the advance. The most common practice is to obtain a power of attorney from the exporter executed in their favour by the banks. It is sent to the concerned government department like the Director General of Foreign Trade, Commissioner of Customs, etc. These advances are not granted in isolation. It is granted only if all types of export finance are extended to the exporter by the same bank.

(8) Post-shipment Export Credit Guarantee and Export Finance Guarantee

Post-shipment finance given to exporters by banks through purchase, negotiation or discount of export bills or advances against such bills qualifies for this guarantee. Exporters are expected to hold appropriate shipments or contracts policy of ECGC to cover the overseas credit risks. Exporter Finance Guarantee covers post-shipment advances granted by banks to exporters against export incentives receivable in the form of duty drawback, etc.

(9) Post-shipment Credit in Foreign Currency

The exporters have the option of availing of export credit at the post-shipment stage either in rupee or in foreign currency. The credit is granted under the Rediscounting of Export Bills Abroad Scheme (EBR) at LIBOR interest rates. The scheme covers export bills with usance period upto 180 days from the date of shipment. Discounting of bills beyond 180 days requires prior approval from RBI. The exporters have the option to avail of pre-shipment as well as post-shipment credit either in rupee or in foreign currency. If pre-shipment credit has been availed of in foreign currency, the post-shipment credit necessarily to be under the EBR scheme. This is done because the foreign currency pre-shipment credit has to be liquidated in foreign currency.

Q15. **Write an explanatory note on financing of exports under deferred payment.**

Or

Describe how exports under deferred payments can be done.

Ans. Contracts for export of goods and services against payment to be secured partly of fully beyond 180 days are treated as deferred payment exports. The credit extended is termed as deferred payment term credit. For financing under deferred credit system, a single point approval mechanism within a three-tier system operates.

This system includes:

(1) Commercial banks who are authorised dealers in foreign exchange in India, can provide in principle clearance for contracts valued upto ₹25 crores. They can avail refinance from EXIM bank.

(2) EXIM bank is empowered to give clearances for contracts of value of above ₹25 crores and upto ₹100 crores.

(3) A working group considers proposals of contracts of value beyond ₹100 crores. The working group consists of representatives of all the above institutions to provide single window clearance.

Deferred credit facility is normally allowed only for export of engineering goods, turnkey projects involving rendering of services like designing, civil construction and erection and commissioning of plant or factory alongwith supply of machinery, equipment and materials. Project exports eligible of export finance are as follows:

    (1)   Turnkey Projects: These projects involve supply of equipment alongwith related services like design, detailed engineering, civil construction, erection and commissioning of plants, etc.

    (2)   Construction projects involve civil works, steel structural works as well as associated supply of construction materials and equipment.

    (3)   Technical and consultancy service contracts involve provision of personnel, furnishing of knowhow, skills, operation and maintenance services and management contracts.

These services include:

    (a)   Engineering services contracts involve supply of services such as design, erection, commissioning or supervision of erection and commissioning.

    (b)   Consultancy services contracts involve preparation of feasibility studies, project reports, preparation of designs and advice to the project authority on specifications for plant and equipments.

Deferred Credit Facilities

Export of goods on deferred payment terms can be financed under supplier's credit or Buyer's credit.

    (1)   **Supplier's Credit:** The exporter extends credit directly to the overseas buyer and seeks refinance from commercial banks/EXIM bank.

    (2)   **Buyer's Credit:** It is a loan extended by a financial institutions or a consortium of financial institutions to the overseas buyers for financing a particular contract.

Under *Buyer's Credit* scheme, credit is granted by EXIM Bank jointly with an authorised dealer to foreign buyers in connection with export of capital goods turnkey projects from India. The exporters are paid out of the buyer's credit on a non-recourse basis on their complying with the terms of the export contracts to be financed under the scheme. Before the exporter enters into any contract providing for credit terms to be financed under buyer's credit scheme, they should have detailed discussion with the bankers. While considering proposals under the scheme, the following factors are taken into account by EXIM Bank:

    (1)   competence and capability of Indian exporters in complying with the proposed commercial terms of the contract;

    (2)   justifiability of the contract on commercial considerations;

    (3)   economic viability of the overseas projects concerned of the importer and general economic conditions of his country;

    (4)   credit worthiness of foreign borrower.

Reserve Bank's permission is also required for the purpose of granting credit under the scheme since payment will have to be made to the exporter on behalf of non-resident buyer. Application to the Reserve Bank should be made by the authorised dealer in Form DPX 6 for the purpose.

Q16. **What are the various functions of Export Import Bank in financing exports from India? State various programmes offered by the EXIM Bank.**

Or

Discuss the role of Export Import Bank of India?

[Dec-2012, Q.No.-5(b)]

Or

Write a short note on Export Import Bank of India.

[June-2013, Q.No.-7(a)]

Or

What is the role of Export Import Bank in financing exports from India? Explain, and state its service programmes for commercial banks.　　　　**[Dec-2014, Q.No.-2]**

Ans. Export Import Bank of India (Exim Bank) is a specialised financial institution, wholly owned by Government of India, set up in 1982, for financing, facilitating and promoting foreign trade of India. It is the principal financial institution in the country for co-ordinating working of institutions engaged in financing exports and imports.

The major functions of Exim Bank are as follows:

(1) **Finance:** Exim bank finances export of India machinery, manufactured goods, consultancy and technology service on deferred payment terms. The finance is also made available at export production stages. It undertakes co-financing activities with global and regional development agencies and assists Indian exporters in their efforts to participate in overseas projects. The bank provides a variety of lending and service programmes to Indian entities, commercial banks and overseas entities. These financing activities facilitate the export-import business in the country.

(2) **Services:** International risks are the most challenging task before the Indian exporters. The bank provides information and advisory services to the exporters. These services include country studies, merchant banking services, advice on international marketing, data relating to projects funded by Multilateral Institutions, etc. These services help the exporters to evaluate the international risks, export opportunities and competitiveness.

The bank has wide network with financial institutions, trade promotion agencies and information providers across the globe. The bank helps Indian companies in their global operations through these networks. The bank assists in the identification of the technology suppliers and overseas partners and negotiating an alliance and consummating a joint venture.

(3) **Research and Analysis:** The bank undertakes research and analysis work on specific industry sub sectors with export potential and international trade related areas. These works are widely disseminated amongst exporters, academicians, industry

and trade organisations and Government. The bank is deeply involved in the creation of export capability, which helps in stimulating the economic growth of the country.

The following table, Table 2.1 gives us the details of various programmes offered by EXIM Bank.

Table 2.1: Lending and Service Programme of EXIM Bank

Programme	Use
For Indian Entities	
Export (Supplier's) Credit	Enables Indian Exporters to extend term credit to overseas Importer, of eligible Indian goods.
Financing of Rupee Expenditure for Project Export Contracts	Enables companies to meet cash flow deficits of projects being executed overseas on cash payment terms.
Finance for Consultancy and Technology Services	Enables Indian exporters of consultancy and technology services to extend term credit to overseas importers.
Pre-shipment Credit	Enables Indian exporters to buy raw material and other inputs for export contracts involving cycle time exceeding six months.
Finance for Deemed Exports	Enables Indian Companies to meet cash flow deficits of contracts secured in India and financed by multilateral funding agencies.
Foreign Currency Pre-shipment Credit	Enables eligible exporters to access finance for import of raw materials and other inputs needed for export production.
Finance for EOU's & Units in EPZs	Enables Indian companies to acquire indigenous and imported machinery and other assets for export production.
Foreign Currency Lines of Credit for Imports	Enables eligible export-oriented units to acquire imported machinery for export production.
Export Vendor Development Finance	Enables vendors of export-oriented units to acquire plant & machinery and other assets for increasing export capability.
Export product Development Finance	Enables Indian firms undertake product development, R & D for exports.
Overseas Investment Finance	Enables Indian promoters to finance equity contribution in joint ventures/WOS set up abroad.
Software Training Institutes	Enables setting up of institutes for software training.
Export Marketing Finances	Enables exporters to implement market development programmes and finances productive capabilities through loan financing.
Production Equipment Finance	Enables eligible export-oriented units to acquire equipment.
Services	
Underwriting	Enables Indian exporters to raise finance from capital markets through public/rights issues of equity shares/debentures with the backing of EXIM Bank's underwriting Commitment.

Contd...

Forfaiting	Enables Indian exported to convert credit sale to cash sale on without recourse basis.
Guarantee Facility	Enables Indian companies to provide requisite guarantees to facilitate execution of export contracts and import transactions.
L/C Confirmation	Confirmation of L/Cs covering import of capital goods.
Project Preparatory Services Overseas	Enables Indian consultancy firms undertake project preparatory studies in developing countries by grant/loan financing.
Business Advisory & Technical Assistance Services Overseas	Enables Indian consultancy firms undertake specific assignments in select countries through grant financing.
Cooperation Arrangement with African Management Services Co. (AMSCO) Amsterdam	Enables Indian consultants secure assignments in various projects that are managed by AMSCO in different parts of Sub-Saharan Africa, through grant financing.
Africa Enterprise Fund	Enables Indian Consultancy Firms to undertake specific assignments to assist small and medium entrepreneurs in Sub-Saharan Africa.
Africa Project Development Facility	Enables Indian consultancy firms undertake specific assignments in Sub-Saharan Africa through grant financing.
EC Investment Partners Facility	Enables Setting up of joint ventures in India between Indian companies and enterprise in the European Community.
For Commercial Banks	
Refinance of Export (Supplier's) Credit	Enables banks to offer credit to Indian exporters of eligible goods, who extend term credit over 180 days to importers overseas.
Small Scale Industry (SSI) Export Bills Rediscounting	Enables banks to rediscount export bills of their SSI customers with usance not exceeding 90 days.
Relending Facility	Enables banks overseas to make available term finance to their clients for import of eligible Indian goods.
Refinance of Term Loans to EOUs	Enables banks to offer credit to eligible export-oriented units to acquire indigenous and imported machinery and other assets for export production.
Bulk Import Finance	Enables banks to offer finance to importers for bulk import of consumable inputs.
Guarantee-cum Refinance Supplier's Credit	Enables banks to project their own cash flow as also its exporter client's cash flow an account of default by overseas buyer. Protects the Bank by not treating the Advance as a Non-performing Asset for provisioning Purposes.
For Overseas Entities	
Lines of Credit	Enables overseas financial institutions, foreign governments, their agencies to on lend term loans to finance import of eligible goods from India.
Buyer's Credit	Enables overseas buyer to import eligible goods from India on deferred credit terms.

Q17. What is the difference between Factoring and forfaiting?

Ans. There are following differences between factoring and forfaiting:

(1)   Factoring services are mainly meant for financing and collecting of receivables arising from short-term credit transactions say upto 180 days. As against this, forfaiting is meant for financing credit transactions of having deferred credit period of more than 1 year.

(2)   Factoring arrangement can be with recourse or without recourse depending on the terms of factoring contract between a client and a factor. As against this, forfaiting transaction is always without recourse where forfaiter absorbs credit risk also.

(3)   Factoring services can be considered either for domestic transaction or for export transaction. As against this, forfaiting transaction is always considered for export transactions only.

(4)   Factoring is done on the strength of sales invoices only. Whereas forfaiting involves use of avalised negotiable instruments like bill of exchange or promissory note.

(5)   In a factoring arrangement, a margin of 5 to 20 per cent is kept. In other words, finance is provided immediate on the purchase of invoice to the extent 80 to 95 per cent of invoice value. As against this, a forfaiter discounts the entire sale value of the export transaction without keeping any margin.

(6)   Factoring services include sales ledger, administration, collection of receivables and other advisory services. On the other hand, forfaiting is a pure financial arrangement.

(7)   Factoring is done on whole turnover basis, whereas, forfaiting can be done on transaction basis.

Q18. What do you mean by credit risk?

Ans. Credit risk is associated with any kind of credit-linked events, such as changes in the credit quality (including downgrades or upgrades in credit ratings), variations of credit spreads and the default event. In other words, credit risk is an estimate of the probability that a borrower will not repay all or a portion of a loan on time. The risk is that a loan will not be repaid.

Risks are inherent in all credit transactions but more so in export transactions. The fact that the buyer may not pay either due to insolvency or for any other reason exposes the exporter to the credit risk. Credit risk may arise even in cases where the buyer's credit standing has been thoroughly investigated. Too cautious an attitude in evaluating buyers may result in loss of hand to get business opportunities. Hence, credit risk is unavoidable specially in export business.

Credit risk has assumed large proportions today not only because the volume of export transactions has become larger but also because far-reaching political and economic changes that are sweeping the world. An outbreak of war, civil war, coup or an insurrection may block or delay the payment for goods exported. Balance of payment difficulties may lead to transfer delays. And all this is possible even where the buyer is fully in a position to pay. In addition, one has to contend with the possibilities of the insolvency or protected default of the buyers. In recent years, there has been a significant increase in insolvencies and business failures even in many developed countries. In such a high-risk situation, export credit insurance can be of immense help to (i) exporters and (ii) the banks who provide finance for the export transactions.

Q19. Explain about ECGC.

Or

What do you know about ECGC?

Ans. Export Credit Guarantee Corporation of India Limited was established in the year 1957 by the Government of India to strengthen the export promotion drive by covering the risk of exporting on credit. Being essentially an export promotion organisation, it functions under the administrative control of the Ministry of Commerce & Industry, Department of Commerce, Government of India. Board of Directors comprising representatives of the Government, Reserve Bank of India, banking, insurance and exporting community managed it.

ECGC is a government institute, which provides insurance policy to exporter against the risk of non-realisation of export proceeds due to occurrence of the commercial and political risk involved in exports and guarantees to commercial banks against losses that the banks may suffer in granting advances to exporter. It also finds the credit worthiness of the foreign buyer. It charges a small premium for its insurance and guarantees.

Q20. Describe various types of polices issued by ECGC.

Or

What are the types of insurance cover provided by ECGC?

Or

Describe the different kinds of policies and financial guarantees issued by ECGC. [Dec-2012, Q.No.-5(a)]

Or

What are the risks covered under the Standard Policy of ECGC?

Or

What are the risks not covered under the Standard Policy of ECGC?

Or

Write a short note on financial guarantees of ECGC. [Dec-2013, Q.No.-7(a)]

Ans. The covers issued by ECGC can be broadly divided into four groups, which are discussed as follows:

(1) Standard Policies
Standard policies issued to exporters to protect them against payment risks involved in exports on short- term credit. Under the Standard Policy, ECGC covers, from the date of shipment, the following risks:

    (a) Commercial Risks
        (i)   Insolvency of the buyer.
        (ii)   Failure of the buyer to make the payment due within a specified period, normally four months from the due date.

(iii) Buyer's failure to accept the goods, subject to certain conditions.

(b) Political Risks

(i) Imposition of restriction by the Government of the buyer's country or any Government action, which may block or delay the transfer of payment made by the buyer.

(ii) War, civil war, revolution or civil disturbances in the buyer's country.

(iii) New import restrictions or cancellation of a valid import Licence in the buyer's country.

(iv) Interruption or diversion of voyage outside India resulting in payment of additional freight or insurance charges which cannot be recovered from the buyer.

(v) Any other cause of loss occurring outside India not normally insured by general insurers, and beyond the control of both the exporter and the buyer.

Risks not covered under the Standard Policy of ECGC: The policy does not cover losses due to the following risks:

(a) Commercial disputes including quality disputes raised by the buyer, unless the exporter obtains a decree from a competent court of law in the buyer's country in his favour.

(b) Causes inherent in the nature of the goods.

(c) Buyer's failure to obtain necessary import or exchange authorisation from authorities in his country.

(d) Insolvency or default of any agent of the exporter or of the collecting bank. Loss or damage to goods which can be covered by general insurers.

(e) Exchange rate fluctuation.

(f) Failure of the exporter to fulfil the terms of export contract or negligence on his part.

(g) Loss or damage to goods, which can be covered by general insurers.

The ECGC also does not cover risks which can normally be insured with commercial insurers. An exporter may either take a comprehensive risk policy covering both political and commercial risks or secure himself against political risks only, depending upon his requirements. It must, however, be noted that ECGC does not issue policies to cover commercial risks only.

(2) Specific Policies

Specific Policies designed to protect Indian firm against payment risk involved in exports on deferred terms of payment; services rendered to foreign parties; and construction works and turnkey projects undertaken abroad.

Specific Policy for Supply Contracts: This policy may take any of the following four forms:

(a) Specific Shipments (Comprehensive Risks) Policy to cover both commercial and political risks at the post-shipment stage.

    (b)   Specific Shipments (Political Risks) Policy to cover only political risks at the post-shipment stage in cases where the buyer is an overseas Government or payments are guaranteed by a government or by banks, or are made to associates.

    (c)   Specific Contracts (Comprehensive Risks) Policy.

    (d)   Specific Contracts (Political Risks) Policy.

Contracts Policy provides cover from the date of contract. Losses that may be sustained by an exporter at the pre-shipment stage due to frustration of contract are covered under this policy in addition to cover risks provided by the Shipments Policy.

Insurance cover for buyers credit and links of credit: Buyers credit is a loan extended by a financial institution, or a consortium of financial institutions to the buyer for financing a particular export contract. In this credit system, a loan is extended to government or financial institutions in the importing country for financial import of specified items from the lending country. ECGC has evolved scheme to protect financial institutions in India which extend these types of credit for financing exports from India.

(3) Services Policy

When Indian firms render services to foreign parties, they would be exposed to payment risks similar to those involved in export of goods. This policy offers protection to Indian firms against such payment risks. The policy has been designed broadly on the lines of ECGC insurance policies covering export of goods, and is issued to cover specific transactions.

There are four types of policies available, as follows:

    (a)   Specific Services Contract (Comprehensive Risks) Policy to cover commercial as well as political risks;

    (b)   Specific Services Contract (Political Risks) Policy to cover political risks only;

    (c)   Whole turnover services (comprehensive policy); and

    (d)   Whole turnover services (Political Risks) policy.

(4) Construction Works Policy

Construction Works Policy has been designed to Indian Contractor who executes a civil construction job abroad. This policy protects the contractor from 85 per cent of the losses that may be sustained by him due to various risks.

Financial Guarantees

Financial guarantees are issued to banks to protect them from the risks of loss involved in their extending financial support to exporters at the pre-shipment as well as post-shipment stages. These financial guarantees protect the banks against any loss in their credit to exporters and thereby encourage banks to advance funds to exporters to fulfil their export commitments.

The ECGC provides different types of financial guarantees: (a) packing credit guarantee, (b) post-shipment export credit guarantee, (c) export finance guarantee, and (d) export production finance guarantee. The major non-financial guarantees extended by ECGC are: (a) export performance guarantee, (b) transfer guarantee, and (c) investment insurance guarantee. The last facility was introduced in September 1978 to protect Indian entrepreneurs willing to invest abroad against political risks arising out of war, expropriation, restrictions on remittances, etc.

The extent of guarantee cover provided by the ECGC has changed from time to time and is somewhat flexible.

Q21. What is the procedure for taking policy of ECGC?

Ans. For taking policy of ECGC, exporter should fill in a proposal form (no. 121) available with all ECGC offices and submit it to the nearest office. After examining the proposal, ECGC would send him an acceptance letter stating the terms of its cover and premium rates. The policy will be issued after the exporter conveys his consent to the premium rates and pays a non-refundable policy fee.

The premium rates are closely related to the risks involved and depend upon (i) length of the credit, (ii) terms of payment, (iii) credit worthiness of the buyer and his country and (iv) the past record of the exporter.

ECGC normally fixes a maximum limit of its liability for shipments in each of the policy years.

It is therefore, advisable for exporters to estimate the maximum outstanding payment due from overseas buyers at any time during the policy period and to obtain the policy with maximum liability for such value. The maximum liability fixed under the policy call is enhanced subsequently, if necessary.

There are following obligations of the policy holders:

(1) **Declaration of Shipments:** An exporter who has taken a shipment policy has to send, by the fifteenth of each month, a declaration of shipments made in the previous month, in the prescribed form (No. 203). An exporter who obtains a contract policy has to send a declaration of all outstanding contracts immediately after the policy is issued. Thereafter he shall send a monthly declaration of contracts concluded and shipments made by him during the previous month. Premium has to be paid along with the declaration at rates shown in the schedule attached to the policy.

(2) **Fixation of Credit Limit on each Buyer:** Commercial risks are covered by ECGC subject to approval of a credit limit on each buyer. Credit limit is the limit upto which claim can be paid under the policy for losses on account of commercial risks. As commercial risks are not covered in the absence of a credit limit, exporters would be well advised to apply to ECGC for approval of credit limit on buyer in the prescribed form (No. 144) before making shipment. If complete information regarding the buyer and his banker is given in the credit limit application, it will facilitate receipt of credit information expeditiously.

ECGC obtains credit information on overseas buyers through banks and credit information agencies. On the basis of credit information and its own experience, ECGC fixes suitable credit limits on overseas buyers. In case, an exporter has already obtained a credit report on the buyer or is in possession of other information that can help ECGC in fixing credit limit, the same may be furnished along with credit limit application to facilitate quick decision. If the exporter needs an enhancement in limit, he may apply in the prescribed form (No. 144A) giving the past experience with the buyer.

(3) **Reporting Defaults:** In the event of non-payment of any bill, policy holders are required to take prompt and effective steps to prevent or minimise loss. A monthly declaration of all bills that remain unpaid for more than 30 days should be submitted to ECGC in the prescribed form (No. 205) indicating action taken in each case. Granting extension of time for payment, converting bills from DP to DA terms or resale of unaccepted goods at a lower price require prior approval of ECGC.

Q22. What is the procedure for making a claim with ECGC?

Ans. An exporter can claim when any of the risks insured under the policy materialises. If an overseas buyer goes insolvent, the exporter becomes eligible for a claim one month after his loss is admitted to rank against the insolvent's estate or after four months for the due date, whichever is earlier. In case of protracted default, claim is payable after four months from the due. Claims in respect of additional handling; transport or insurance charges incurred by the exporter because of interruption or diversion of voyage outside India are payable after proof of loss is furnished. In all other cases, claim is payable after four months from the date of the event causing loss.

However, in case of exports to countries where long transfer delays are experienced, ECGC may extend the waiting period and claims for such shipments are payable after the expiry of such extended period. Sometimes the buyer does not accept goods or pay for them because of differences over fulfilment of the terms of contract by the exporter, counter claims or setoff. In such cases, ECGC considers claims after the dispute between the parties is resolved and the amount payable is established by obtaining a decree in a court of law in the country of buyer. This condition is waived in cases where the Corporation is satisfied that the exporter is not at fault and that no useful purpose would be served by proceeding against the buyer. Procedure for making a claim needed following preparation:

(1) Procedural Formalities

The ECGC has three types of claim forms: (a) Form No. 501 for claims arising due to non-payment for goods accepted by the buyer; (b) Form No. 502 for claims arising because of the non-acceptance of goods/documents by the buyer; and (c) Form No. 503 for claims on account of delay in transfer of funds to India. Claims due to the above cases should be filed in the respective prescribed form. Other types of claims can be filed by means of a letter, giving full particulars of the cause and extent of loss. The claims have to be submitted to the ECGC office that issued the policy. Again, the claim forms should be sent through the bank which handled the export bill concerned. No claim will be entertained by the ECGC if it is not filed within a period of 24 months from the due date of the concerned bills.

(2) Documents in Support of Claims

Every claim has to be supported by documentary evidence. Important documents that should accompany the claim forms are the following:

(a) Certified copy of the export order
(b) Certified copies of invoices
(c) Certified copies of bills of lading
(d) Copies of the correspondence with the buyer
(e) In case of insolvency of the buyer, copy of the letter from the official receiver/liquidator admitting the claim.
(f) In case of protracted default, (i) protest note, (ii) original of unpaid bills, (iii) advice of non-payment received from the bank, and (iv) copy of the plaintiff if a suit has been filed,
(g) In case of transfer delays, certified copy of payment advice received from the collecting banker indicating the date on which payment was made by the buyer in local currency. This should also certify that all exchange control formalities necessary for transfer of funds to India have been complied with by the buyer.

All claims are paid in Indian currency, i.e. rupees through the bank, which handled the bills concerned.

Q23.What is Foreign Exchange Rate? Write the factors, which determine the exchange rate of a currency.

Ans. Foreign Exchange Rate is the price of one currency in terms of another currency; it is the relative price of the two currencies. In other words, the rate at which one country's money or currency buys or exchanges for another country's money or currency is known as the rate of exchange. And foreign exchange is the mechanism by which the currency of one country gets converted into the currency of another country.

Factors determining the Exchange Rate of a currency

Following factors determine the exchange rate of a currency vis-à vis another currency:

- Balance of Payments
- Local Interest Rates
- Monetary Policy
- Exchange Control
- Regulations Inflation
- Central Bank Intervention
- Speculation Demand/Supply of a currency

Q24.Discuss the types of exchange rates.

Ans. Exchange rate can be maintained in spot rates or forward rates, which are as follows:

(1) Spot Rate

The spot rate is the current exchange rate. It is the rate at which most foreign exchange transactions are carried out. If the contract to buy or sell foreign currency is agreed upon and executed immediately, the transaction is known as a spot transaction and the rate quoted is the spot rate. By convention, the agreed payment date or "value date", as it is known is usually two business days after the transaction has originated. The two days period give ample time for the two parties to send the instructions necessary to debit and credit bank accounts here and abroad.

Exchange rate can be quoted by units in two ways:

(a) **Direct quote:** home currency price of a foreign currency

Example: ₹54.05/USD; ₹70.25/Euro

(b) **Indirect quote:** value of one unit of home currency in terms of a foreign currency

Example: Re= USD 0.0185; Re= Euro 0.0142

In the first method, the rate of exchange is expressed for a fixed unit of foreign currency. The difference in the rate is expressed by a variation in the home currency, viz the rupee. Such a method where the unit of foreign currency is kept constant and price variation is reflected in the units of home currency is known as 'direct' or 'home currency' quotation.

In the second method, the rate of exchange is expressed for a fixed unit of home currency. The difference in the rate is expressed by a variation in the foreign currency. Such a method, where the unit of home currency is kept constant and price variation is reflected in the units of foreign currency is known as 'indirect' or 'foreign currency' quotation.

In India, it was the practice to use the indirect method of quotation. The unit of India was ₹100. Thus, for example, an Authorised Dealer (AD) buying US dollars from an exporter would take $1.85 for ₹100. However, w.e.f. 2 August 1993 direct quotations are being used, i.e. an AD buying US$ from an exporter would give ₹54.05 for one USD in the above example.

Buying and Selling Rates

There are two rates of exchange quotation in foreign exchange transactions. The exchange quotation will have two rates. One at which the bank is willing to buy and the other at which the bank is willing to sell. The rate at which the bank is willing to buy is known as buying rate or bid rate and the rate at which it is willing to sell is known as selling rate or offer rate. There is always some difference between buying and selling rates. This happens because foreign exchange dealer would like to make profit from the exchange transactions. Let us take an example of direct quotation. The authorised dealer buys at US $1 = ₹35.3675 and sells at US $1 = ₹35.39. The dealer buys at lower rate and sells at a higher rate. It is notable the authorised dealer buys at a lower rate and sells at a higher rate.

(2) Forward Rate

It refers to the rate quoted for delivery of foreign exchange in future at some agreed date, i.e., when the value date is more than two business days in future, is called the forward rate. A forward bank enters into a contract to buy/sell a fixed amount of foreign currency at a specified future date at a pre-determined rate of exchange. The rate quoted for the transaction is the forward rate. The date of delivery of foreign exchange in future or the maturity of a forward foreign exchange contract can be a few days, months or years in some cases. The exchange rate is fixed at the time the transaction is agreed upon. But no money actually changes hands until the maturity date. There will be a specific exchange rate forward maturity and each of these rates almost always will differ from today's spot exchange rate.

Forward Quotations

It can be expressed in two ways. Commercial customers are usually quoted the actual price which is referred to the outright rate. On the other hand, in the interbank market, dealers quoted the forward rate only as a discount from, or a premium on the spot rate. This forward differential is known as the swap rate.

If the forward exchange rate for a currency is higher than the current spot rate, it is said to be trading at a premium for that forward maturity. If the forward rate is below the spot rate, then the currency is said to be trading at a discount. If the forward rate is the same as the spot rate, then it is said to be at par with the spot rate but it happens only rarely.

(3) TT (Telegraphic Transfer) Rate

Telegraphic Transfer rate may be either TT buying rate or TT selling rate. These can be discussed as follows:

TT Buying Rate

This rate is applied for purchase of foreign currency by banks where cover is already obtained by banks in India. This rate is applied for all clean remittances outside India. All foreign inward remittances which are made payable in India are converted by applying this rate. For example, suppose Nisha gets from Citi Bank in New York a demand draft for $10,000 drawn on Citi Bank, New Delhi. The New York bank will credit the New Delhi Citi Bank's account with itself immediately.

TT buying rate is calculated as:

TT Buying Rate = Base rate - Exchange Margin.

The base rate refers to the interbank rate. The Foreign Exchange Dealers Association of India (FEDAI) has prescribed exchange margin rate as between 0.025 per cent to 0.080 per cent. Banks have discretion to charge any rate of exchange margin this prescribed range. Let us take an example.

Suppose interbank rates for US$ are:

Spot US $1 = ₹35.2575 – 35.2625

This means that Base Rate	=	35.2575
Lass Exchange Margin @0.08%	=	0.0280

Round off Figure = 35.33

Suppose a customer wants to purchase a draft drawn on New York for $10,000. The customer will have to pay (35.23 × 10,000) = ₹3,52,300. The bank may charge commission.

TT Selling Rate

This rate is applied for all clean remittances outside India. It is applied for selling foreign currency to its customer by the bank such as for issuance of bank drafts, mail/telegraphic transfers, etc. The rate is computed as:

TT Selling Rate = Base Rate + Exchange Margin

Here, the base rate is the interbank selling rate. FEDAI has prescribed exchange margin rate for TT selling rate as between 0.125 per cent to 0.15 per cent.

Let us take an example.

Interbank exchange rate for US$ is:

Spot US $1	=	35.2625
Add Exchange margin say 0.15%	=	0.0528
		35.3153

Round off Figure = 35.32

Suppose a customer wants to purchase a draft drawn on New York for $10,000. The customer will have to pay (35.32 × 10,000) = ₹3,53,200. The bank may charge commission.

(4) Bill Rate

Bill rate may also be either bill buying rate or bill selling rate. It can be discussed as follows:

Bill Buying Rate

This rate is applied when a foreign bill is purchased. As we must be knowing that exporters draw bills of exchange on their foreign customers. They can sell these bills to an authorised dealer for immediate payment. The authorised dealer buys the bill and collects payment from importer. When the bill is purchased, the proceeds will be realised by the authorised dealer after the bill is presented to the drawee at the overseas centre. In case of sight bill, the payment is made on presentation of the bill. In the case of usance bill, the proceeds will be realised on the due date of the bill which includes the transit period and the usance period of the bill. The bank or the authorised dealer, therefore, makes an allowance for the loss of interest for the period of transit, the usance of the bill and the days of grace, if any. The authorised dealer loads the forward margin for an appropriate period. The period for which forward margin is to be loaded depends upon whether the foreign currency is at a forward premium or discount. The authorised dealers extract the rate which is most favourable for them. The rate is computed as:

Bill Buying Rate = The base rate - Forward discount for transit plus usance period rounded off to the higher month - Exchange Margin

Or

Bill Buying Rate = The base rate + forward premium for transit plus usance period rounded off to the lower month - Exchange Margin

FEDAI has prescribed exchange margin rate as between 0.125 per cent to 0.150 per cent.

Bill Selling Rate

This rate is applied for all foreign remittances outside India as proceeds of import bills payable in India. In this case, the importer requests the bank to make payment to a foreign supplier against a bill drawn on the importer. The bank handles documents related to the transaction. For this purpose, the bank loads margin over the TT selling rate. It is computed as:

Bill Selling Rate = TT Selling Rate + Exchange Margin

FEDAI has prescribed exchange margin rate as between 0.175 per cent to 0.200 per cent.

Q25. How forward rates are calculated?

Ans. Forward rates are calculated based on the following formula:

$$\text{Forward Rate} = \text{Spot Rate} \pm \text{Margin}$$

If forward rate is more than spot rate, then the local currency is quoting at a premium.

If forward rate is less than spot rate, then the local currency is quoting at a discount.

For example

(1) if today is 15 June and the spot rate of today is 54. You want a forward rate as of 15 July. The bank gives you 54.50. As the forward is more than the spot, rupee is quoting at a premium. The premium is 54.50 − 54.00 = 0.50. Thus, the premium is 50 paise.

(2) if today is 15 June and the spot rate of today is 54. You want a forward rate as of 15 July. The bank gives you 53.75. As the forward is less than the spot, rupee is quoting at a discount. The discount is 53.75 − 54.00 = −0.25. Thus, the discount is 25 paise.

Q26. How the exporters and importers are exposed to exchange risks. Discuss.

Ans. The exchange risk arises because there is a time gap between the shipment of goods and the receipt or payment of the price thereof. And the exchange rate of the currency involved may undergo a change in the time period involved. If we are an exporter, we receive less rupees than we had expected. If we are an importer, we might have to pay more than what we bargained for. Risk for both exporter and importer can be discussed as follows:

(1) Risk as an Exporter

An exporter may draw his export bills either in rupees or in foreign currencies. If he has drawn his export bills in Indian currency, i.e. rupees, we will not suffer any loss by any possible depreciation of foreign currencies or of Indian rupees. We are sure to receive the Indian rupees for which we have invoiced our goods. But it may always be possible for us to invoice our goods in rupees. Firstly, the foreign importer may insist that he is billed in his local currency. That will make the cost of goods imported by him certain in his own currency. Again, it is a matter of courtesy to the exporter to bill the importer in the currency of importer's choice. It is a good marketing strategy also. Moreover, the Government of India has now directed that exporters bill their importers in foreign currency only.

If we have billed our importer in a foreign currency, there is an equal possibility that the foreign currency may appreciate or depreciate by the time we are likely to receive payment. As a result, we may receive more or less in terms of rupees than we bargained for. Let us understand this by means of an example. Suppose we export goods worth US $100,000 on 1 January when the value of $1 is ₹35. We thus, expect a payment of ₹3.50,000. But the payment is due to be received by us on May 1. Suppose the value of the dollar decreases to ₹34 on the day. We will now receive only ₹3,40,000. The fact that Indian exporters operate on a very low margin, may mean that whatever profit he expected may be wiped out due to a decline in the value of the dollar. But if the value of the dollar increases to ₹36, the exporter will get ₹3,60,000 and may earn a profit that he never expected. Thus, while there is a possibility of the exporter making a windfall profit, there is a definite risk to which the exporter is exposed. The larger the depreciation of the foreign currency, the larger is the risk to which the exporter is exposed.

(2) Risk as an Importer

The position is entirely opposite of what it is for the exporter. If the importer is billed in rupees, he does not stand to loss at all whether the foreign currency appreciated or depreciates. But considering the position of the Indian rupees as it is, no exporter would like to bill the Indian importer in rupees. Hence, the importer is always exposed to an exchange risk. Let us suppose that an Indian importer contracts to purchase an equipment costing $10,000 on 1 January expecting to pay ₹3,50,000 in Indian currency. But if the value of dollar increases to ₹36 on May 1 when the payment is due, he will have to pay ₹3,60,000 and not ₹3,50,000. Of course, there is an equal possibility of the dollar going down to ₹34. In that case, the Indian importer will stand to gain. But the point is that he is exposed to a risk. The higher the appreciation of the dollar the higher is the risk to which he is exposed.

Q27. **What are the methods of dealing with foreign exchange risks?**

Or

Explain various methods to deal with the foreign exchange risks.

Or

Explain the various methods used for dealing with foreign risks.   **[Dec-2014, Q.No.-5]**

Ans. When we conduct business overseas, we will have to convert currencies involved at some prevailing exchange rate. The price of one country's currency in terms of another country is called the exchange rate. When the currency of one country depreciates (drops in value), there will be a corresponding appreciation of value in another country's currency. Depreciation occurs when it takes more currency to purchase the currency of another country. Appreciation is just the opposite; the currency is able to purchase more units of the other country's currency. Since most currencies are valued according to the marketplace, there are constant changes to exchange rates. This gives rise to exchange rate risk.

A firm can deal with foreign exchange risks in the following ways:

> **(1)** **Taking Risk:** The firm may decide to bear the risk if the foreign currency depreciates or appreciates and pocket the gain resulting therefrom. Bigger firms having both imports and exports can match the losses and gains on exports with gains or losses on imports. Matching will ultimately minimise the losses and gain if any. Matching is easier in a large diversified firm

than in a firm dealing in one product only. Large trading houses and export houses as also STC and MMTC can do it easily. An important point to be mentioned here is that losses and gains due to exchange fluctuations are taken into account for tax purposes. Thus, assuming that the rate of tax is 50 per cent, the impact of losses due to exchange fluctuations, if any, is reduced to 50 per cent only.

(2) Using a Hedging Clause: The exporter can use a hedging clause in the contract with the customer/supplier providing for a revision of price in the event of a significant change. This will tend to protect both parties as movement in exchange rates may both be the upwards and downwards. While we protect ourselves against a loss, we may lose the possibility of making a profit. However, the customer/supplier may not agree for such a clause in short-term agreement. But it is more easily possible in long-term contracts.

(3) Entering into Forward Contract: Forward contracts are deals between two parties who enter into the contract for buying or selling of the foreign currency at a future date. The firm can enter into a forward contract with his banker. If it is an importer, it can purchase foreign currency to be delivered in future (forward purchase). If it is an exporter, it can sell foreign currency to be delivered in future (forward sale). This will ensure that the firm receives or pays a certain amount of rupees irrespective of changes in the value of foreign currency involved.

Q28. Discuss forward contract as a method of dealing with foreign exchange risks.

Ans. Forward Contract is a hedging tool available to Indian corporate to safeguard against adverse movement in exchange rates. The rate at which a currency can be bought or sold at a future date can be fixed today thus effectively fixing the costs of imports or export receivables due at a future date. It, thus, renders debtors and creditors free from the risk arising out of exchange rate fluctuations. Authorised dealers have been delegated powers to book forward contracts subject to the following conditions:

- Forward facility can be extended to resident customers only.
- Forward cover can be for genuine transactions only and not for speculative transactions.
- AD should satisfy himself that the party for whom the forward cover is being booked is in fact exposed to exchange risk.
- While booking a forward contract, ADs should verify the necessary documents to ensure authenticity of the transaction.
- The underlying transaction should be firm and not anticipated or speculative in nature.
- A customer transaction can be covered in whole or in part. The period and extent to which cover can be obtained may be left to the customer though the cover should ordinarily match the maturity of the original transaction.

A forward exchange contract is a mechanism by which one can ensure the value of one currency against another by fixing the rate of exchange in advance for a transaction expected to take place at a future date. It is a tool to protect the exporters and importers against exchange risks. The uncertainty about the rate which would prevail on a future date is known as exchange risk. From the point of an exporter, the exchange risk is that the foreign currency in which the transaction takes place may depreciate in future and thus the expected realisation will be less in terms of local currency. The importer also faces exchange risks when the transaction is designated in a foreign currency. In this case, the foreign currency may appreciate and the importer may be compelled to pay an amount more than that was originally agreed upon in terms of domestic currency.

In the case of forward exchange contract, two parties – one being a banker from one country entering to a contract to buy or sell a fixed amount of foreign currency on a specified future date or future period at a predetermined rate. The forward exchange contracts are entered into between a banker and customer or between two parties. In a forward contract, the settlement of currencies is at a fixed date in future.

Q29. What do you mean by Cancellation and Extension of Forward Contracts?

Ans. A customer under forward contract knows in advance the time and amount of foreign exchange to be delivered and the customer is bound by this agreement. There should not be any variation and on the due date of the forward contract, the customer will either deliver or take delivery of the fixed sum of foreign exchange agreed upon. But, in practice, quite often the delivery under a forward contract may take place before or after the due date, or delivery of foreign exchange may not take place at all. The bank generally agrees to these variations provided the customer agrees to bear the loss, if any, that the bank may have to sustain on account of the variation.

Cancellation of Forward Contract

The customer is having the right to cancel a forward contract at any time during the currency of the contract. The cancellation is governed by Rule 8 of the FEDAI. The difference between the contracted rate and the rate at which the cancellation is done shall be recovered or paid to the customer, if the cancellation is at the request of the customer. Exchange difference not exceeding ₹50 shall be ignored. The spot rate is to be applied for cancellation of the forward contract on due date. The forward rate is to be applied for cancellation before due date. In the absence of any instruction from the customer, contracts which have matured shall on the 15th day from the date of maturity be automatically cancelled. If the 15th day falls on a holiday or Saturday, the cancellation will be done on the next succeeding working day. The customer is liable for recovery of cancellation charges and in no case, the gain is passed on to the customer since the cancellation is done on account of customer's default.

The customer may approach the bank for cancellation when the underlying transaction becomes infractions, or for any other reason he wishes not to execute the forward contract. If the underlying transaction is likely to take place on a day subsequent to the maturity of the forward contract already booked, he may seek extension in the due date of the contract. Such requests for cancellations or extension can be made by the customer on or before the maturity of the forward contract.

Cancellation of Forward Contract on Due date

When a forward purchase contract is cancelled on the due date, it is taken that the bank purchases at the rate originally agreed and sells the same back to the customer at the ready TT rate. The difference between these two rates is recovered from/paid to the customer. If the purchase rate under the original forward contract is higher than the ready TT selling rate the difference is payable to the customer. If it is lower, the difference is recoverable from the customer. The amounts involved in purchase and sale of foreign currency are not passed through the customer's account. Only the difference is recovered/paid by way of debit/credit to the customer's account.

In the same way when a forward sale contract is cancelled, it is treated as if the bank sells at the rate originally agreed and buys back at the ready TT buying rate. The difference between these two rates is recovered from/paid to the customer.

Extension of Forward Contract

An exporter may find that he is not able to export on the due date but expects to do so in about two months. So also, an importer may be unable to pay on the due date but is confident of making payment a month later. In both these cases, they may approach their bank with whom they have entered into forward contracts to postpone the due date of the contract. Such postponement of the date of delivery under a forward contract is known as the extension of forward contract.

For extension of sales contract, the exchange control regulations provide that the contract may be extended if the relative letter of credit or firm contract is extended for shipment and the import licence is valid for the extended period.

When the bank enters into a forward purchase contract with a customer, it covers its own position by selling in the inter-bank market the same amount for the same delivery period. On the due date when the contract is extended, irrespective of the fact that the customer has not delivered foreign exchange, the bank has to meet its commitment. For this purpose, the bank buys spot from the market and delivers under the original contract. Supposing the customer requires extension of two months, after two months the bank would be in receipt of foreign exchange under the extended contract. To cover its position, the bank enters into a forward contract for two months.

The bank will charge from the customer the loss suffered by it as also interest on the outlay of funds for the extended period. It will also make a flat charge.

Extension on Due date

An exporter finds that he is not able to export on the due date but expects to do so in about two months. An importer is unable to pay on the due date but is confident of making payment a month later. In both these cases, they may approach their bank with whom they have entered into forward contracts to postpone the due date of the contract. Such postponement of the date of delivery under a forward contract is known as the extension of forward contract.

The earlier practice was to extend the contract at the original rate quoted to the customer and recover from him charges for extension. The reserve bank has directed that, with effect from 16 January 1995 when a forward contract is sought to be extended, it shall be cancelled and rebooked for the new delivery period at the prevailing exchange rates.

Q30.Discuss currency option in the context of dealing with foreign exchange risks.

Ans. A currency option provides the buyer with the right, but not the obligations, to buy or sell an agreed amount of currency at an agreed exchange rate. This agreed exchange rate is known as the strike price. An option that provides the right to buy is known as a call option and an option that gives the right to sell is known as a put option. A call option on one currency is simultaneously a put option on another. For, if a person has the right to buy DM with US$ at a given dollar rate, then he also has the right to sell US$ at a particular DM rate. The person who buys an option is called the buyer or purchaser or holder of the option and the person who sells it is called the seller or the writer or the grantor of the option.

The date on which an option contract matures or expires is known as the expiration date. It is the last day on which the option may be exercised. The time period between the contract date and the expiration date is the lifetime of an option.

Q31. Discuss the meaning and objectives of exchange control.

Ans. Exchange control means regulating the demand for and supply of foreign exchange with the objective of making rational use of available foreign exchange for various purposes according to a scheme of priorities laid down by the policy. It was introduced during the Second World War on a systematic and long-term basis. It became essential in view of the substantial requirements of foreign exchange for the planned developmental effort undertaken by them.

Exchange control is usually imposed on both, i.e. on payments as well as on receipts. The purpose of introducing the exchange control on receipts is to pool the country's foreign exchange reserves to facilitate. Their judicious use, while the purpose of imposing exchange control on payments is to restrain the demand and contain it within the permissible limits.

Objectives of Exchange Control: The objectives of the exchange control are as follows:

- to prevent flight of capital
- to ensure the availability of sufficient foreign exchange for specific purposes such as meeting the international commitments
- to stabilise the external value of the domestic currency, and
- to insulate the economy from external economic pressures.

Q32. Discuss administration and scope of Foreign Exchange Regulation Act (FERA), 1973.

Or

What is the scope of Foreign Exchange Regulation Act (FERA), 1973?

Ans. Foreign Exchange Regulation Act (FERA) was enacted in September 1973 and it came in force from 1 January 1974. It was amended by the Foreign Exchange Regulation (Amendment) Act 1993 and later in 2000. Until 31st May 2002, all foreign exchange management in India was governed by Foreign Exchange Regulation Act 1973 (FERA). On 1 June 2002, FERA was replaced by Foreign Exchange Management Act 1999 (FEMA).

In India, the Ministry of Finance, Government of India determines the exchange control policy. The Act is administered by the Reserve Bank in accordance with the general policy laid down by the Central Government in consultation with the Bank. The Central Government is empowered to give to the Reserve Bank such general or special directions as it thinks fit. The Bank is obliged to comply with these directions in the discharge of its functions under the act.

It is also related to and supplemented by the trade control. India's foreign trade (exports and imports) is regulated under the provisions of the Foreign Trade (Development and Regulation) Act, 1992 and Foreign Trade (Regulation) Rules, 1993. Trade control is concerned with the physical transfer of goods whereas exchange control involves related financial transactions. Exchange control is more comprehensive and covers not only exports and imports but invisibles and capital transactions as well. Thus, a close co-ordination is maintained in the administration of the two controls. The customs authorities have also an important role to play in the administration of certain aspects of exchange control for example valuation of exports. Hence, a close is maintained with them.

For enforcing the provision of Foreign Exchange Regulation Act, and dealing with prosecutions and adjudication for evasion or contravention of the regulation, there is a separate machinery. This is known as Directors of Enforcement having its headquarter in New Delhi and branches in all important places in the country. The central Government may appoint such persons as it thinks fit to be officers of Enforcement.

Purchase and sale of foreign exchange can be effected only by authorised dealers duly Licenced by the Reserve Bank. These licences are generally granted only to commercial banks. However, in the recent years licences have been given to some State Corporative Banks as well. Restricted licences have been granted to Industrial Development Bank of India and Export Import Bank. Licences have also been granted to certain established firms, hotels and other organisations for dealing in foreign currency notes, coins and travellers cheques. They are called Money Changers.

Scope of the Act

The Foreign Exchange Regulation Act covers the types of transaction having international financial implications. Broadly, the Exchange Control regulates the following transactions have been discussed below:

    (1)   Purchase and sale of and other dealings in foreign exchange and maintenance of balances at foreign centres.

    (2)   Procedures for realisation of proceeds of exports.

    (3)   Payments to non-residents or to their accounts in India.

    (4)   Transfer of securities between residents and non-residents; and acquisition and holdings of foreign securities.

    (5)   Foreign travel with exchange.

    (6)   Export and Import of currency, cheques, drafts, travellers cheques and other financial instruments, securities, etc.

    (7)   Activities in India of branches of foreign firms and companies and foreign nations.

    (8)   Foreign direct investment in India including investment by non-resident Indian nationals/persons of Indian origin and corporate bodies predominantly owned by such persons.

    (9)   Appointment of non-residents and foreign nationals and foreign companies as agents in India.

    (10)   Setting up to Joint ventures/subsidiaries outside India by Indian companies.

    (11)   Acquisition, holding and disposal of immovable property in India by foreign nationals and foreign companies.

    (12)   Acquisition, holding and disposal of immovable property outside India by Indian nationals resident in India.

The main aim of GPH book is to provide knowledge as well as good marks in exam.

3 | Shipment of Export Cargo

AN OVERVIEW

The Government of India has set up several institutions for export promotion. In international trade, goods are properly packed to protect them, to keep a consignment together, to protect the goods from damaging the environment and be affected by it. Now-a-days, containerisation has become a predominant form of unitised transport.

With the rapid technological development and the establishment at the International Air Transport Association (IATA), the movement of cargo traffic by air has been increasing.

Cargo or marine insurance is the practice of providing risk cover to the cargo-owners against loss or damage that the cargo may suffer in transit due to accidents and mishaps. A cargo insurance contract is between the insured and the insurance company, which is in the nature of a financial indemnity. The insured has certain responsibilities to fulfil, if he is to recover the loss from the insurance company without a hitch.

Exporters have to comply with procedural formalities of the customs and port authorities before the shipment of the goods. Export goods are either exempted from indirect taxes or these taxes are refunded.

Q1. What is packing of goods or export packing? What should we keep in mind while packing goods for export?

Ans. Export packaging is also sometimes referred to as transport packaging. It is one of the three main types of packaging that may be needed for exported goods:

- Export packaging is the outermost layer of packaging and is designed to protect your goods in transit.
- Outer packaging is an intermediate layer of packaging that protects the final product packaging.
- Sales packaging is the immediate layer of packaging around our goods, which remains in place when the goods reach their end user.

While the 'outer layer' export packaging, we should consider all of our packaging requirements together since they are interrelated. When packing goods for export we should take the following into consideration:

- We should choose the most appropriate packing materials for the mode of transport that we are using.
- We should find out whether the country of destination has any specific regulations with regard to the packaging of goods that we need to comply with.
- Where possible, consolidate smaller packages into one larger consignment to provide better protection and reduce shipping costs.
- We should bear in mind that during shipment other consignments may be stacked on top of ours. We should make sure our method of packaging will provide protection if this should happen.
- We should secure and protect our goods within the packaging. Heavy goods may need to be bolted to the support. We should also consider using a filling material between the goods and the outer packaging.
- We should make sure that we have adequate insurance in place while our goods are being packed. (This is particularly important if we are using an outside company to carry out our export packaging.)

Q2. Write short notes on the following:

(a) Bulk cargo

Ans. By nature, bulk cargo is commodity cargo that transported unpackaged in large quantities. These cargos are usually dropped or poured, with a spout or shovel bucket, as a liquid or as a mass of relatively small solids (e.g. grain, coal), into a bulk carrier ship's hold, railroad car, or tanker truck/trailer/semi-trailer body. They are used in large quantity because their market demand does not frequently change since they are free from attacks of product development, changes in design, obsolescence, deterioration and depreciation. These cargoes have low unit-value, and hence, they can be transported and warehoused at low per unit cost only when transported and warehoused in large quantity. The cargoes which have these characteristics are the primary commodities and industrial raw materials such as iron ore, foodgrains, coal, fertilisers, oils, petroleum products, chemicals and liquefied gas. Bulk cargo has been divided into two categories, viz., Dry Bulk (e.g. foodgrains) and Liquid Bulk (e.g. oil and petroleum products).

(b) General Cargo

Ans. General cargo vessels vary in length between 80 and 160 m, the latter having a deadweight of about 20,000 tons. The cargo holds of these multipurpose vessels are able to handle both containers and all sorts of cargo. Dependent of the specific trade, the ships vary from medium speed, slender project cargo vessels to slow speed extremely high block vessels with a large load capacity.

General Cargo comprises manufactured, semi-manufactured, processed and semi-processed goods and materials moving in small quantities in cases, packages, parcels, bales, etc. Examples of such cargo are engineering goods, leather products, textiles, drugs and pharmaceuticals, tobacco, spices and marine products. In contrast to Bulk Cargo, General Cargo cannot be carried and stored in large quantities, mainly because of their susceptibility to fast changes in their demand due to changes in fashion, design, season, technology, etc. On the other hand, they need not to be carried and stored in large quantities because of their higher unit-value, and thus, their ability to bear a higher per unit transportation and warehousing cost.

Q3. Explain the salient features of liner and tramp shipping services.

Or

What are the features of liner and tramp shipping services?

Or

Distinguish between Liner and Tramp shipping services.

[Dec-2014, Q.No.-3(a)]

Ans. Linear Shipping

Liner shipping service is a service that operates within a schedule and has a fixed port rotation with published dates of calls at the advertised ports. A liner service generally fulfils the schedule unless in cases where a call at one of the ports has been unduly delayed due to natural or man-made causes.

For example: The UK/NWC continent service of MSC which has a fixed weekly schedule calling the South African ports of Durban, Cape Town and Port Elizabeth and carrying cargo to the UK/NWC ports of Felixstowe, Antwerp, Hamburg, Le Havre and Rotterdam.

Features of Liner Shipping: Liner shipping has the following features:

(1)   It is designed to carry a variety of cargo, with spaces for bales, bundles, boxes, barrels, drums, etc. as well as for refer (refrigerated) cargo. The designs of the holds and number of decks will be different from those of a tramp. With the increased share of containerised cargo, specially designed container ships for carrying different categories of containers operate.

(2) The cargo handling equipment on a liner will be varied and sophisticated for quick loading and unloading of cargo to ensure quick turn-round, which means that the ship spends the least possible time in the port and most of its time in transit.

(3) It operates regularly between fixed ports and normally loads in several ports. It serves a number of discharging ports along a predetermined route.

(4) In order to ensure speedier carriage, it is fitted with sophisticated and expensive propelling machinery.

(5) It provides pre-announced scheduled services on given terms and conditions of carriage.

These terms and conditions mostly relate to the responsibilities and liabilities of the ship owners in receipt, carriage and delivery of cargo. Liners, thus, provide services on terms and conditions which are not negotiable.

(6) It generally offers carriage on fixed and stable freight rates.

Tramp Service

A Tramp Service or tramper on the other hand is a ship that has no fixed routing or itinerary or schedule and is available at short notice (or fixture) to load any cargo from any port to any port.

For example: A ship that arrives at Durban from Korea to discharge cargo might carry some other cargo from Durban to the Oakland in the West Coast of USA which in an entirely different direction. From Oakland say, for example, it could carry some cargo and go to Bremerhaven.

Features of Tramp shipping: A tramp carrier has the following characteristic features:

(1) It is primarily designed to carry the more simple and homogeneous cargo in large quantity. It is, therefore, designed to fully utilise its carrying capacity for carriage of one type of cargo. For example, a grain-carrying ship will be designed in such a way that a full cargo of grains in bulk can be accommodated in the lower holds, feeders and bins.

(2) Since one kind of homogeneous cargo is to be handled, a tramp will have comparatively simple equipment. Bulk cargoes are normally loaded and discharged by mechanical equipment, elevators, pumps, etc.

(3) Because of the comparatively low unit value of commodities carried, a tramp will be operated at the lowest possible cost. This objective can be achieved by operating ships having relatively less speed by fitting less expensive propelling machinery.

(4) A tramp generally carries cargoes of one or two ship users. Hence, loading and discharging are confined to a few ports.

(5) It does not have a fixed route and predetermined schedule of departure as it is to be engaged by one/two users as and when their need arises.

(6)   It offers services at terms and conditions, including freight/hire charges, which are not fixed and given but are negotiable.

Difference between liner shipping and tramp shipping is tabulated as follows:

Table 3.1

S. No.	Liner Shipping Service	Tramp Shipping Service
(1)	It is designed to carry a variety of cargo, with spaces for bales, bundles, boxes, barrels, drums, etc, as well as for reefer (refrigerated) cargo.	It is primarily designed to carry the more simple and homogeneous cargo in large quantity. It is, therefore, designed to fully utilise its carrying capacity for carriage of one type of cargo.
(2)	It operates regularly between fixed ports and normally loads in several ports. It serves a number of discharging ports along a predetermined route.	It does not have a fixed route and predetermined schedule of departure as it is to be engaged by one/two users as and when their need arises.
(3)	It generally offers carriage on fixed and stable freight rates	It offers services at terms and conditions, including freight/hire charges, which are not fixed and given but are negotiable.
(4)	In order to ensure speedier carriage, it is fitted with sophisticated and expensive propelling machinery.	Because of the comparatively low unit value of commodities carried, a tramp will be operated at the lowest possible cost. These ships have relatively less speed and it is fitted with less expensive propelling machinery.

Q4.   What is shipping conference practice? Discuss.

Ans. A shipping conference is an association of independent shipowners which is organised to restrict/eliminate competition in the trade, regulating and rationalising sailing schedules and ports of call. The conferences operate on the basis of written agreements, providing for a permanent secretariat and describing rights and obligations of members. The members are expected to follow the rules set by the conference under the agreement. In the event of violation of the agreed rules of discipline by a member, the agreement provides for imposing a penalty, which is generally the forfeiture of an agreed bond amount deposited with the conference.

The first conference was formed in 1875, known as the UK-Calcutta Conference. Since then, almost all trade routes have been covered by the shipping conference system. The basic aim of a shipping conference is to minimise losses or to maximise profits by combating competition among shipowners. At the same time, conference binds shippers (shipping services users) and obtains continuous cargo support from them through a number of freight concessional arrangements and agreements. Major methods which have been evolved to achieve this aim are designed to eliminate competition from within and fight competition from outside.

Competition among the conference members is regulated by (i) Rate Agreements; (ii) Control of Sailing Schedules; (iii) Pooling Arrangements; and (iv) Good Faith or Performance Bonds. The conferences fight competition from outsiders including shipping lines and shippers in a number of ways. The competition from other shipping lines is encountered through: (i) extending conference membership to the growing outside lines; (ii) agreements with other conferences operating on alternative routes in such a way that one conference operates on one route.

Competition from the skippers is blunted through three main devices for securing cargo support from the shippers. These devices are as follows:

- Deferred rebate on commissions arrangements;
- Immediate cash rebate agreements;
- Dual rate agreements.

Q5. What are the various forms of chartering of the shipping services? Explain.

Or

Briefly explain the various forms of chartering the shipping services.   **[Dec-2014, Q.No.-3(b)]**

Ans. When a tramp carrier is engaged, it is said to be under charter, as one-charterer hires either the whole or the bulk of its space. A tramp may be chartered in a number of ways. Three most important forms of engagement are as follows:

(1) The Voyage Charter

The charterer hires the vessel for a single voyage. The owner and his crew manage the vessel. According to Black's Law Dictionary, a voyage charter is a charter under which the ship-owner provides a ship and crew, and places them at the disposal of the charterer for the carriage of cargo to a designated port. The voyage charterer may lease the entire vessel for a voyage or a series of voyage or may lease only a part of the vessel (by space charter party). Under a voyage charter, the vessel is let out to the charterer for a specific voyage. The ship-owner will be paid 'freight' which will cover its costs, including fuel and crew, as well as its profit. Legally, freight is a special type of payment, as the usual rule of set off will not apply to it. A set time, 'lay time', will also be provided for the loading and discharging operations. If these operations exceed the permitted lay time, the ship-owner will be compensated by 'demurrage' at the rate set down in the charter. For its part, the ship-owner owes the charter the duty of proceeding with reasonable dispatch on the charter party voyage, or voyages, in the case of a consecutive voyage charter. In voyage charter, the ship-owners are not only to meet all expenses of running the ship such as officers and crew wages, stores and provisions, insurance of ship, depreciation, etc. but also the operating expenses like fuel cost, port charges, light dues, etc. The ship-owners recoup their expenses and earn profits from the freight paid by the charterers.

A voyage charter differs from time charter in many respects, but primarily in that it is a contract to carry specific goods on a defined voyage or voyages, the remuneration of the ship-owner being a freight calculated on the basis of the quantity of cargo loaded or carried or sometimes a lump sum freight.

A voyage charter party usually carries a cancellation clause that gives the charterer the right to cancel the charter if the ship is not as his disposal at the port of loading at the specified time. The charterer would have to fix a cancellation date before exercising this right.

(2) The Time Charter

Here the vessel is hired for a specific amount of time. The owner still manages the vessel but the charterer selects the ports of destination and controls the operation of the ship. It is a more permanent arrangement than the voyage charter and more representations are made about the ship to the charterer.

According to Black's Law Dictionary, "charter for a specified period, rather than for a specific task or voyage; a charter under which the ship-owner continues to manage and control the vessel but the charter designates the ports of call and the cargo carried. Each party bears the expenses related to its functions and for any damage it causes."

A charter by demise operates as a lease of the ship itself, to which the services of the master and the crew may or may not be superadded. The charterer becomes for the time being the owner of the vessel; the master and crew become his servants and through them, the possession of the ship is in him.

Under a charter not by demise, the ship-owner agrees with the charterer to render services by his master and crew to carry the goods that are put on board his ship by or on behalf of the charterer. In this case, it was held that the ownership and also the possession of the ship remained with the original owner through the master and crew though the charterer has the temporary right to have his goods loaded and conveyed in the vessel.

In a time charter engagement, the responsibility of scheduling the ship's employment and meeting port expenses, canal dues, fuels cost, cargo expenses, etc. remain with the charterers.

However, running expenses of the vessel like officers and crew wages, stores, provisions, insurance, etc. have to be met with the ship-owners. Another feature of the time charter engagement is that the charterers can either operate themselves or sublet the vessel on voyage charter depending upon their requirements (provided the latter action is not specifically prohibited in the agreement between the ship-owners and the charterers). If the market improves after the vessel is taken on time charter and the charterers sublet it, the charterers may earn more money than what is payable to the ship-owners by way of charter hire. Sometimes ships are time chartered on a long-term basis to fulfil the contractual obligations like the Contract of Affreightment. Such long-term charters are entered into so as to protect the charterers from the vagaries of fluctuation in the freight market.

(3) Demise or Bareboat Charters

This arrangement is completely different from the previous two. The charterer takes full control of the vessel along with the legal and financial responsibility for it. The demise shifts the control and possession of the vessel.

The ship-owners have the minimum responsibility and act as if they are 'dead'; and have no concern about the ways the ship will be used. Also known as "Demise Charter", the charterers in this case become the disponent owners and are responsible for staffing as well as operating the ship like the owners of the ship.

Since the ship is at the disposal of charterers, they have the right to appoint the Master and the Chief Engineer, however, subject to the approval of the owners. They bear all costs and expenses for the operation of the ship. For the time period, the ship-owners are paid a fixed sum calculated at a certain rate per ton dead weight on summer free board per calendar month payable in advance. 'The ship is put at the disposal of the charterers in the seaworthy condition and after the expiry of the time period, it is redelivered to the ship-owners in the same good order and condition as and when delivered, minus the ordinary wear and tear.

Q6. What are the factors which change the real fundamental of air freighting? Also, discuss air freight rates, documentation and clearing house in the context of air freighting.

Or

What are the roles of International Air Transport Association (IATA) in air freighting? Discuss.

Or

Write a short note on procedure for export by air.

[June-2014, Q.No.-7(c)]

Ans. The bulk of international cargo traffic moves by sea, but nowadays, the movement of cargo traffic by air has been increasing. As a result, a variety of cargo, which hitherto was exclusively moving by sea, is now also being moved by air.

The real fundamental change in favour of air freighting can be traced to four factors. These are:

    (1)   Technological developments in the area of civil aviation;

    (2)   Technological developments in the field of cargo handling and communications;

    (3)   Change in the composition of world trade; and

    (4)   Establishment of the International Air Transport Association (IATA).

Over the years, there has been a marked change in the composition of world trade. We find that high unit-valued products including fashion items and sophisticated machinery, which require fast delivery, extra handling and care, are able to bear a high incidence of freight cost. Therefore, air carriage has become more suited to carry variety of cargo. The establishment of IATA in 1945 has considerably helped in the development of air freighting. IATA is an organisation of airlines of the world. It was set up to ensure smooth and fast development of air services. For its role, particular mention should be made of:

(1)   Standardisation in the rate-making;

(2)   Standardisation in Documentation; and

(3)   Clearing House and Other facilities.

Air Freight Rates

Air freight rates are chargeable either on gross weight or gross volume or volumetric basis (i.e., weight or volume whichever is higher). The rates quoted by the airlines are from one specified airport to another airport in one direction and include two elements, viz., basic rates and trans-shipment charges. An important aspect of the air rates is that there is a minimum rate for a minimum acceptable weight. In other words, if the cargo offered for carriage is less than the minimum acceptable weight, it will be charged at the stipulated minimum rate. Further, air rates generally provide for concessions at certain weights such that higher tonnage will be carried at the concessional rates. The weight at which these concessions become applicable are known as "break points". For example, there could be a concession of 10 per cent on the rate in a schedule if the cargo offered is 100 kg or more.

Under the IATA agreements, airlines offer specific commodity rates from and to agreed ports to the stipulated products or product groups. These are the concessional rates offered to those products which are available for carriage in large quantities over a period of time. Thus, the airlines agree to provide concessional services in return of regular tonnage. Products which are not included in this group are charged, with some exception, either the 'normal rate' or 'quantity rate'. Normal rate is a non-specific commodity rate between two defined airports in one direction of product less than 45 kgs. If the weight of these become 45 kgs and above, a concessional 'quantity rate' is charged, which is 25 per cent less than the 'normal rate'. Aircrafts can also be chartered, in which case the freight rate is negotiable which periodically fluctuates depending on the conditions of demand and supply.

Documentation

Airlines all over the world use a standardised transport document, known as Airway Bill (or Consignment Note). Besides functioning a carrier receipt and evidence of contract of affreightment (transport) between airline and shipper, this document also operates as an instruction sheet for the onward carriers. It is not a document of title but can be made one by getting an "order" bill.

Clearing House

IATA provides an important facility to the carriers and the users in the form of the Clearing House. This facility is useful in the inter-line claim settlements, when the cargo is moving through more than one carrier, as in the case of trans-shipment. Therefore, the shipper may book the cargo through one carrier and pay total freight, a part of which will be paid to the onward carriers.

Q7. Discuss the system of quality control and pre-shipment inspection.

Or

What are the important methods of quality control and pre-shipment inspection? Explain briefly.

Or

Write a short note on consignment wise pre-shipment inspection. **[Dec-2012, Q.No.-7(d)]**

Or

Write a short note on 'Self-certification system of quality control and inspection of export cargo'.

[June-2013, Q.No.-7(b)]

Or

What are the various systems of quality control in our export trade? Discuss. **[Dec-2013, Q.No.-4]**

Or

Discuss the significance of quality control and preshipment inspection in exports. What are the different system of preshipment inspection and give a detailed account of procedure involved in any one of them.

[June-2014, Q.No.-3]

Or

Write a short note on Self-Certification Scheme.

[Dec-2014, Q.No.-7(b)]

Ans. An important aspect about the goods to be exported is compulsory quality control and pre-shipment inspection. In other word, according to the prevailing law in India, a fairly large number of export goods are subjected to compulsory quality control and/or inspection by the agencies authorised by the Government of India before being allowed to be exported from the country. In 1965, the Export Inspection Council was set up to formulate and supervise the inspection schemes with the help of Export Inspection Agencies, which have a network of offices spread all over the country. These agencies have trained manpower and are equipped with laboratory facilities to carry out inspection tests and issue Inspection Certificates. There are three systems/methods for quality control and inspection. These are as follows:

(1) Consignment wise Inspection

Under this system, each and every export consignment is subjected to a detailed inspection by the Export Inspection Agencies based on a statistical sampling plan. If the samples are found to conform to the recognised specifications/standards, an inspection certificate for export is issued to the exporter. The Inspection Certificates carry a specific validity period within which the export consignment must be shipped.

This system is applicable to all the notified products by the Export Inspection Council other than those for which the Inprocess Quality Control system is applicable. Procedurally, for obtaining the Inspection Certificate, the exporter has to apply to the Export Inspection Agency well in advance to avoid shipment delays. The application is to be made on prescribed form known as Notice of Intimation alongwith.

(a)　Crossed Cheque or Demand Draft for the inspection fee

(b)　Copy of Commercial Invoice

(c)　Copy of Export Contract

(d)　Importer's Technical Specifications

This application will be registered in the Office of Agency, which will appoint an Inspector for carrying out physical examination of the goods.

The inspector will examine the goods in the exporter's premises with reference to the agreed specifications, which should not be inferior to the notified specifications. Samples may be drawn and sent to the laboratory, if required. Thereafter, the inspector prepares the Field Inspection Report, which becomes the basis for the issuance of the Inspection Certificate. The original of the Certificate is to be submitted to the customs authorities for clearance of goods for export.

(2) Inprocess Quality Control

Under this system, export-oriented manufacturing/processing units are approved as "export-worthy" units because they possess the requisite infrastructure for manufacturing/processing products of standard quality. Such a unit is allowed to inspect and clear goods for export without an inspection by the Export Inspection Agency. The Agency will issue certificate of inspection on the declaration by the unit.

For the approval of a unit, it is to apply to the Export Inspection Agency on the prescribed pro forma. After a preliminary visit by the officer of the agency, a panel of experts will be appointed. This panel thoroughly investigates the quality control facilities of the unit right from the raw material stage to packing. It submits its report to the agency with its recommendations. On the basis of these recommendations, the unit is accorded the status of an export-worthy unit.

For obtaining the inspection certificate under this system, the exporter submits the following documents to the Export Inspection Agency:

(a)　Application (Notice of Intimation)

(b)　Crossed Cheque/Demand Draft for fee

(c)　A Copy of Commercial Invoice

(d)　Importer's Technical Specifications.

On receipt of these documents, the agency will issue inspection certificate in triplicate. The original certificate is for the customs authorities.

(3) Self-Certification

With the experience gained over the years in operating the Compulsory Quality Control and Pre-shipment Inspection Scheme in India, there has been a qualitative change in the inspection system also. Recently, self-certification system has been introduced which is based on the concept that manufacturing unit having established reputation for its products with sufficient in-built responsibility for quality assurance could be permitted to certify its own products for export. For the purpose of operating this system, a manufacturing unit found qualifying against the prescribed norms, which amongst other include the following:

- (a)   Product Quality;
- (b)   Design and Development;
- (c)   Raw Materials/Bought out Components;
- (d)   Organisation and Personnel for Quality Control;
- (e)   Process Control;
- (f)   Laboratory;
- (g)   Quality Audit;
- (h)   Packaging;
- (i)   After-Sales-Service; and
- (j)   House-keeping and Maintenance.

The unit approved under this system is recognised by notification under Section 7 of the Act as the agency for quality control and inspection of specific products manufactured in the unit. The system removed the need for the manufacturing unit to seek certificate of inspection from an outside agency, which provides an added advantage in the mechanism of exportation.

Q8. Write a short note on marking and labelling of goods.

Ans. Every export package must be properly marked and labelled. Marking, including handling instructions, help quick and safe transportation of goods. There are two types of marking—marking of origin and shipping marks. In addition to making, handling instructions on export packs must be clearly states. Where these are given in the form of written language, these must be in the language of exporting and importing countries. In case of goods requiring careful handling and storage, the international practice is to give these instructions in the form of symbols.

Q9. What do you mean by ISO 9000? What are the benefits of these standards?

Ans. ISO 9000 is a *family* of standards for quality management systems. ISO 9000 is maintained by ISO, the International Organisation for Standardisation and is administered by accreditation and certification bodies. The rules are updated, as the requirements motivate changes over time. Some of the requirements in ISO 9001:2008 (which is one of the standards in the ISO 9000 family) include:

- a set of procedures that cover all key processes in the business;
- monitoring processes to ensure they are effective;
- keeping adequate records;
- checking output for defects, with appropriate and corrective action where necessary;
- regularly reviewing individual processes and the quality system itself for effectiveness; and
- facilitating continual improvement.

Following are the major benefits of ISO 9000 Quality Systems:

- Better product design;
- Improved product quality;

- Reduction in scrap rework and customer complaints;
- Efficient utilisation of men, machines and materials, resulting in higher productivity;
- Elimination of bottlenecks in production and tension-free work environments leading to good human relations;
- Creation of quality awareness and greater job satisfaction among employees, improving the company's quality culture;
- Improvement of confidence among customers; and
- Improvement of a company's image and credibility in international markets which is essential for success in the export business.

The ISO standards have been accepted worldwide as the norm assuring high quality of goods. The standards have been taken without change into the national standard systems of about 91 countries worldwide. The customers all over the world have started demanding their suppliers to adhere to ISO 9000 or equivalent standards. The British equivalent system is BS-5750. The European community has developed the EN 29000 series of standards which is technically equivalent to ISO-9000. European Community (EC) is today the largest trading partner of India. Hence, there is a dire need to adopt ISO 9000 for Indian exporters to cater to the vast requirements of European countries.

Export Inspection Council and its agencies are actively engaged in disseminating information on ISO 9000. In order to win the market, Indian Industry should certainly gear itself for adopting ISO 9000. The manufacturers who have acquired the ISO 9000 or any other internationally recognised equivalent certification of quality will be eligible for grant of special import Licences. The Licences shall be granted for such value or bearing such proportion to the value of their exports for the import of non-prohibitive items included in the Negative List of imports as may be specified by the Government.

Q10. What are the roles of clearing and forwarding agents in export trade? Discuss.

Ans. For smooth and timely shipment of cargo, the exporter should appoint a suitable Clearing and Forwarding (C&F) Agent. Nevertheless, he should prepare the shipping documents himself as there are many intricacies and technicalities which he alone would know properly. He should not depend too much on the Clearing and Forwarding Agent, who should be entrusted with getting the documents processed and shipment only.

Clearing and forwarding agents are a link between the owners of goods and owners of means of transport. They help the cargo owners in efficient movement of goods to the buyers by completing a number of procedural and documentary formalities. They are experts and knowledgeable in laws and regulations governing shipment of goods through the customs authorities as well as in commercial practices, especially the ones concerning transport. Since they are in constant touch with various government authorities, they keep themselves abreast with the developments in the field of their activity. In addition to these functions, the agents can undertake a number of activities including marking, labeling and packing of goods, arranging internal transport, advising exporters of trade laws and price quotations as we'll as on developments in the transport field, file duty-drawback claims on behalf of the exporters, etc. In fact, the agents can perform all activities except perhaps selling the goods. Above all, the agents act as trouble- shooters for the exporters in case of movement problems. We may categorise various activities in the following groups:

    (1)   Advising exporters on trade laws;

    (2)   Providing transport and handling cost information;

    (3)   Packing, marking and labeling;

    (4)   Arranging transport;

    (5)   Completing customs and port formalities;

    (6)   Preparing and procuring documents; and

    (7)   Educating exporters on development in transport.

Q11. Explain different types of policies covered under the contract of cargo insurance in international trade transactions.

Ans. A contract for cargo insurance to cover all shipments from time to time as declared, a policy being issued in respect of each, having three forms. These are as follows:

(1) Specific Voyage Policy

A voyage policy covers the risks that may arise during a journey from specific place to another. The terms and conditions of the insurance are set out in the appropriate Institute of London Underwriters (ILU) and other clauses. The clauses cover mainly the perils and risk covered under the policy as well as conditions related to the insurable value and claims. According to the Indian Stamp Act, each policy must be stamped. The stamp duty is recoverable from the insured. For creating transferability, the policy is required to be assigned by black endorsement by writing "for and on behalf of" followed by the name of the insured (e.g., exporting firm) and the signature of the director or partner.

The insurance policy comprises "MAR" Policy form, which contains no insurance conditions and the Institute Clauses (A, B, C and War and Strike Clauses) which contain insurance conditions. It must be noted that Duration Clauses, which provide warehouse-to-warehouse cover, are part of the Institute Cargo Clauses. Hence, unless specifically deleted, the warehouse-to-warehouse cover is deemed to be effective. In this way, Voyage Policy also becomes a Time Policy.

(2) Open Cover

Open cover is an insurance arrangement designed specifically to the need of those firms, which have substantial import export turnover and frequent transactions. Such firms are spared the inconvenience of negotiating insurance contracts every time the transaction is to be made. Main features of an open cover arrangement are as follows:

    (a)   Unlike an insurance policy, open cover is not an enforceable contract, instead, it is an agreement under which the insurance company would honour and accept declarations of shipment of cargos and issue stamped specific certificate of insurance against each declaration.

(b) Under all open cover arrangement, agreement between the insured and the insurer is reached about the subject matter (e.g. goods) insured, packing conditions, voyages, risks covered, rates and other conditions of the cover. The insured can obtain insurance cover within these agreed conditions.

(c) No premium is charged when an open cover is issued, but the insurance companies usually require the insured to furnish either a bank guarantee or cash deposits towards payment of premium against each declaration, as declarations are made.

(d) The validity period of an open cover is twelve months.

(e) It is customary to make an open cover agreement subject to two limitation clauses, i.e. Par Bottom and Par Place clauses. The effect of these clauses is to limit the liability of the insurance company to an agreed amount. Thus, if the loss in an accident is more than this amount, the loss will be partly recoverable upto the agreed amount, For example, in an open cover, if the limitation clause was for ₹10 lakh and the loss were ₹20 lakh, the insurance company will pay only ₹10 lakh.

(f) An open cover may be cancelled by either party by giving 30 days notice in writing. This stipulation does not cover war and strikes risks for ocean voyage. For ocean voyages other than from/to USA, the notice period for cancellation of war and strikes risk is 7 days and for shipments from/to USA is 48 hours.

(3) Open Policy

Marine cargo insurance that provides blanket cover against loss or damage to all goods transported by a specific carrier, or by a specific shipper, during a stated period. Under its terms, the insured is required to periodically provide the insurer with the description, quantity and value of goods shipped during that period. It is also known as open cover.

This policy benefits clients with substantial turnover and a large number of dispatches. Thus, it covers a series of consignments with all stipulations of the open cover, except that:

(a) Open policy is an enforceable contract of insurance, and is hence, duly stamped.

(b) Open policy is for an agreed amount against which a series of consignments may be dispatched and declared as a result of which the sum insured will gradually diminish by the amount of each declaration until it is finally exhausted.

(c) Even though the open policy ceases on expiry of one year from the date of its issue, the sum insured is of paramount importance. Therefore, the sum insured may exhaust prior to the expiry of the policy.

(d) Open policy is subject to cancellation by either party after giving 15 days notice of cancellation in writing.

Q12. Describe various types of perils in cargo insurance policy against which insurance cover can be obtained.

Ans. The events which lead to loss or damage to the cargo are the perils against which insurance cover can be obtained. These perils can be discussed as follows:

(1) Maritime Perils

These caused by either an Act of God (i.e., a natural calamity) or an Act of Man (manmade event, either through negligence or through connivance) and it exposed to cargo in transit. The perils may occur while the cargo is in transit either on land, inland water and sea or in air. An Act of God may also be described as "extraordinary and violent action of waves and winds". Common examples of Acts of God are earthquake, volcanic eruption and lightening, entry of seawater into the vessel, washing overboard of cargo and rainwater damage. Common examples of manmade perils are: fire, explosion, smoke and water used to extinguish fire, piracy, barratry and deliberate (i.e. vandalism, sabotage, arson or scuttling).

(2) Extraneous Perils

These types of perils are the incidental perils to which the cargo is exposed. These are caused mainly on, account of the faults in loading, keeping, carrying and unloading of cargo. Examples of such perils are: improper stowage, rough handling, breakage and leakage, hook and sling damage, contract with mud oils and acids and theft, pilferage and non-delivery.

The maritime and extraneous perils are incorporated in the Institute Cargo Clauses standardised by the Institute of London Underwriters. These clauses constitute the terms and conditions of the insurance and are appended to the policy form known as MAR policy form.

(3) War Perils

These types of perils covered by the Institute War Clauses refer to following events:

(a) War, civil war, revolution, rebellion, insurrection or civil strike or any hostile act by or against a belligerent power;

(b) Capture, seizure, arrest, restraint or detainment of carrier or craft arising from event mentioned in (i) above. Thus, confiscation by the customs authorities of goods being smuggled cannot be insured; and

(c) Derelict (abandoned) mines, torpedoes, bombs or other derelict weapons of war. It is clear from the above that war risk insurance is not only against hostile or warlike acts but also for perils, which continue to exist after war is over.

War risk cover is provided with certain restrictions about the duration of the cover. Some of the major restrictions are:

(a) The cover is restricted to the period while the goods are water-borne in the ship or are in the craft;

(b) The cover attaches as the goods are loaded into the vessel aircraft or craft used to carry the goods to the vessel;

(c) The cover terminates either as the goods are discharged from the vessel/aircraft at the final port of discharge or on the expiry of 15 days from the midnight of the day of the arrival whichever is earlier. The limit of 15 days also applies to cases where vessel/aircraft carrying cargo cannot go to the final port and the cargo is discharged at some other port; and

(d) In the case of shipments 15 day limit does not apply where cargo after being discharged from the overseas vessel into a craft for delivering the cargo to the shore. The time limit for goods in crafts is 60 days after discharge from the overseas vessel.

(4) Strike Perils

In marine insurance, strike perils mean events, which lead to loss or damage to cargo caused by:

(a) strikes, lock-out workmen or persons taking part in labour disturbances, riots or civil commotions; and

(b) a terrorist or any person acting from a political activities.

It is clear from the above that strike perils are not only the ones which are caused by the striking workmen. These also include perils caused by the political activities, which participate or lead the strike. In fact, strike perils, as opposed to war perils are the handiwork of citizens of the same country. The perils covered under the Institute's Strike Clauses supplement of the perils covered under the Institute War Clauses. It is, therefore, customary for war and strike risks to be covered jointly on payment of a single premium. However, strike clauses have been so designed that they can be used separately from the war risk cover.

Regarding the duration of the cover, the strike risks cover is from warehouse of the exporter to warehouse of the importer. It exists throughout the whole period of transit. This stipulation is in contrast to the 15 day time limit for war cover at either the final port of discharge or at an intermediate port. However, even when cover is from the warehouse of the seller to that of the buyer, there is an implied time limit for transport of cargo from the final port of discharge to the warehouse of the buyer. This time limit is 60 days in the case of marine (sea) transit and 30 days for air transit, after the final discharge at the port.

Q13. Discuss the nature and need of cargo insurance policy.

Or

Discuss the nature of cargo insurance policy.

Or

Why do we need cargo insurance? Discuss.

Or

Describe the need of cargo insurance in international business.

Ans. A cargo insurance policy has an international character and, therefore, a policy taken in one country is acceptable in other country. This is because of the adoption of universally acceptable uniform rules governing insurance in different countries. Marine insurance, also known as cargo insurance, in India is subject to the following legislations:

(1) The Insurance Act, 1938; Insurance Rules, 1939; and

(2) Marine Insurance Act, 1963.

In India, the cargo insurance cover is provided only by the Nationalised Insurance Companies. These companies operate within the standard rules and regulations including those, which are provided in the "All India Marine Cargo Tariff".

Marine Insurance Contract: Article 3 of the Indian Marine Insurance Act, 1963 define marine insurance contract as, "It is an agreement whereby the insurer undertakes to indemnify the assured in the manner and to extent thereby agreed, against marine losses, that is to say, the losses incidental to marine adventure". Before we explain different aspects of the marine insurance contract, it should be clearly understood that the word "marine" used in the definition does not have any specific connotation. Despite the usage of this word, cargo insurance principles as stated in the definition are equally applicable to all modes of transport used in the carriage of goods.

Indemnity and Insurable Value: The insurance contract is in the nature of indemnity. The literal meaning of indemnity is protection against loss or making good the loss. The object of an insurance contract is to place the insured, after a loss, in the same relative position in which he would have stood had no loss occurred. In other words, an insured can claim only that much that he has suffered (or lost). If cargo has been damaged by 10 per cent of the insured value, the insured will be paid only that much amount, even though he has paid premium on the total insured value. But it must also be understood that the indemnity undertaking of the insurance company is only a "commercial" indemnity. The insurance company will place the assured in the same "financial" position as he was before the loss. Since the insurance companies cannot undertake to reinstate or replace cargo in the event of a loss, they pay a sum of money, agreed in advance, between the insured and the insurer, called "insurable value". Insurable value is calculated with reference to the "market value" of the insured goods to which is added an agreed percentage to cover general overheads as well as to provide a margin of profit on the transaction. From this range, an indemnity in insurance does not cover either a gambling loss or a sentimental loss (if tangible loss). Consequently, over-insurance, i.e. insurance more than the market value plus a certain percentage is not the principle of cargo insurance.

In practice, the amount of loss payable is based on the c.i.f. value of goods to which is added an agreed percentage. According to prevailing practice in India, maximum insurable value for export cargo is equal to c.i.f. plus 15 per cent. Generally, the percentage added to c.i.f. value is ten. It is customary in the insurance business to issue "duty" policies to cover duty payable on the imported goods. In such cases, claims are payable either on the basis of actual duty paid or on the basis of the sum insured, whichever is less. Thus, the sum payable cannot exceed the actual loss of the duty amount paid by the insured. It is also implied that the sum insured in the policy would not include any percentage to cover general overheads and the margin of profit.

Need of Cargo Insurance Policy

The term cargo insurance is popularly known as marine insurance applies to all modes of transportation. The need for export (or import) cargo insurance often differs from exporter to exporter (or importer to importer) and from consignment to consignment. Unless the insurance is mandatory in a trade term, the exporter or the importer may opt not to insure the goods at his/her own risks.

Depending on the international commercial terms, either the seller (the exporter) or the buyer (the importer) is responsible for insuring the cargo. The seller is obligated to insure the cargo in the CIF and CIP terms. The seller may opt not to insure the cargo at his/her own risks in the DDU and DDP terms. The trade terms DDU and DDP are often used in the turnkey projects where the amount at stake is large. In practice, the seller usually insures the cargo in the DDU and DDP terms.

There are two reasons for securing the insurance cover. The first reason concerns the legal dimension of limited liability of the carriers and other intermediaries. However, the second reason concerns commercial considerations. These are explained as follows:

- **Legal Dimension:** When the goods are ill transit from the exporter to the importer, they are at different stages in the custody of different agencies and authorities including the clearing and forwarding agents, carriers, port and customs authorities, etc. If there is any loss or damage to the goods, while in their custody, the concerned intermediary may be held liable to pay damages to the cargo owners. The nature and extent of liabilities of various intermediaries have been defined in the respective laws enacted by the government all over the world.

  According to these laws, the intermediaries cannot be held liable for loss to the cargo, if it was caused by reasons or events beyond their control. For example, if the loss is due to natural disasters or war or strike, the intermediaries will not be liable to pay for the loss. Further, if the loss has occurred even after the concerned intermediary has exercised reasonable care in keeping the goods, it is legally exempted from the liability. In such situation, the cargo owners who suffer the loss cannot recover it from the intermediaries and they have no other option but to obtain appropriate insurance cover. The laws also state that where the carriers or other intermediaries are liable for loss or damage, the maximum amount of recovery is limited to the sum stipulated in the respective laws.

- **Commercial Dimension:** From the point of view of an exporter, a transaction is complete as soon as the importer either pays for the Bill of Exchange on its presentation or he undertakes to make payment at a future date by accepting the Bill. Sometimes even before the Bill of Exchange is presented to the importer, he comes to know about the loss of goods in transit and does not accept the bill when presented. In such a situation, the exporter is compelled to bear the loss. Prudent exporters, when dealing with unknown customers on DP or DA payment terms, prefer to get cargo insured. Further, as a commercial practice, cargo insurance makes it possible for the exporter to get post-shipment finance from the negotiating bank because the insurance policy is one of the required documents under a CIF contract. If on the other hand, the contract is on FOB terms with payment on DP or DA basis, the negotiation bank may advance money immediately after shipment (provided the shipping documents are in order and the bank is favoured with an appropriate insurance policy).

Q14. Explain the kinds of losses. How these losses can be covered by the cargo insurance policy?

Ans. The various perils covered under marine policies may result in payment of different types of losses. These may be categorised as follows:

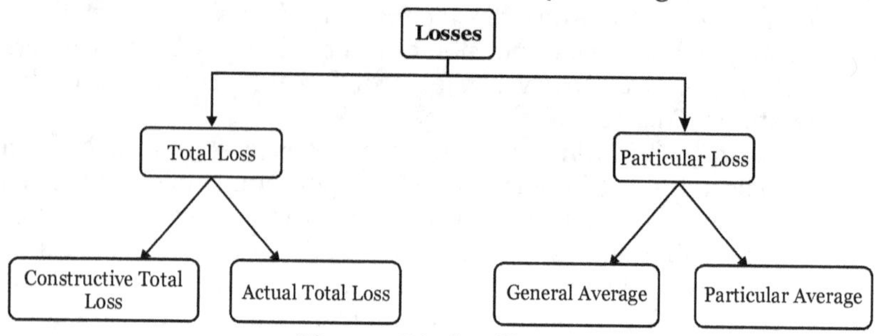

Fig. 3.1: Kinds of losses

(1) Total Loss

There are two types of total losses. These are as follows:

(a) Actual Total Loss (ATL): There is an actual total loss where the subject-matter insured is destroyed, or damaged as to cease to be a thing of the kind insured, or where the assured is irretrievably deprived. When the subject matter is destroyed, there is a clear case of actual total loss. However, the word 'destroyed' is not to be interpreted literally. If a vessel is badly damaged by fire reducing it to charred metal, absolutely beyond repair, it is deemed to be total loss. Thus, total physical destruction is not contemplated.

An actual total loss may occur in three ways. Firstly, when the insured cargo is physically destroyed when fire in the hold of the ship destroys a consignment of paper or when a ship sinks in deep water and the ship with cargo is destroyed and there is no possibility of salvage (recovery). Secondly, the insured cargo is so damaged that it ceases to be a thing insured, as in the case of cement that becomes concrete due to damage by sea water. Thirdly, actual loss also occurs when the insured cargo is irretrievably lost beyond a reasonable time period. For example, ship with cargo sinks which can be retrieved, but will take so much of time that the insured goods would cease to be of value to the insured. Similarly, when cargo is mislocated, the insured may consider it total loss if it cannot be restored to him within a reasonable time period.

(b) Constructive Total Loss (CTL): Unlike the actual total loss, CTL is not a physical loss and is not absolute. CTL may be defined as a total loss when the cost of saving, repairing or reconditioning the insured goods is more than the value of goods. For example, a machine while loading on board the carrier is damaged and the cost of repairing is so prohibitive that the insured may consider this damage as total loss. On examination of the nature of damage and the expected cost of repairing, the insurance company may also consider it as a total loss. CTL may also be claimed when an actual total loss seems unavoidable. For example, cargo in a ship while ground or ashore cannot be taken out of the ship within a reasonable cost, the assured may claim CTL.

While claiming CTL, the insured is required to abandon (or leave) his interest in the insured cargo in favour of the insurance company. This is because the insured cannot retain the goods as well as claim total loss and he has, therefore, to forego his rights in the goods.

(2) Particular Loss

There are two types of particular losses. These are as follows:

(a) General Average: Sometimes a ship-owner either sacrifices some cargo the ship is carrying or incurs some expenditure, which becomes necessary to save the journey. Such a sacrifice or expenditure will have to be shared by the interests in the saved journey. Thus, the insured will be protected from paying for the loss. Partial loss or average of this nature is known as General Average or GA and comes into being only when the ship carrying cargo arrives safely. If a ship is lost and does not, therefore, arrive at the ultimate destination, there can be no GA.

Regarding GA, an accepted principle of maritime law is that all who expose their property to maritime perils are in it together and should share in any misfortunate on an equal basis. In other words, GA sacrifices/expenditure is to be shared by all interest in the journey, i.e. the cargo owners, ship-owners and freight earners.

GA expenditure can be understood clearly from the following examples:

(i)   Some cargo is thrown into the sea to lighten the ship in rough weather;

(ii)   Water is poured on cargo (not on fire) to extinguish a fire;

(iii) Expenses are incurred to tow a ship in the danger of sinking to the safety of the port;

(iv)   A part of cargo is burnt to maintain steam in the ship's boilers when the ship runs short of fuel to delay caused by heavy weather.

The sharing of GA sacrifice or expenditure by the three parties to the adventure is done in accordance with the internationally agreed rules, known as the York-Antwarp Rules 1974.

The working out of the shares and the preparation of the GA statement is entrusted to an average adjuster who is an expert in the field. When the ship arrives at the destination port, it is declared to be on general average by the ship-owner and an average adjuster is appointed. The average adjuster will draw up the statement of percentage of GA contribution by each cargo owner and calculate the value of shares of all interests. The ship-owner then requires all these interests including cargo owners to pay a GA deposit and execute bond. Thereafter, cargo will be released to the cargo-owners. The ship-owner may, however, deliver the cargo against either an underwriter's (insurance company's) or a banker's guarantee. On completion of final adjustment, the excess, if any, is to be paid by the cargo-owner by honouring the bond.

Where the cargo-owner has an insurance policy, he will recover the GA contribution or the loss suffered by him from the insurance company. All marine policies cover GA loss and sacrifice and the insurance companies settle claims for GA contribution and normally refund GA deposits.

The loss must be directly consequential on the general average act. Demurrage and loss of market are indirect consequential losses, and are not allowed in general average.

(b) **Particular Average:** Particular average loss can be the partial loss of the subject matter insured, caused by a peril insured against, and it is not a general average loss. Particular average therefore means a fortuitous partial loss caused by a peril insured against.

Examples of particular average are— damage to the ship by stranding, running aground, collision, etc. damage to the cargo by fire, seawater, etc.

The essence of a particular average loss is that it must be accidental and, in order to be recoverable under the policy, proximately caused by a peril insured against. Any loss through ordinary wear and tear, ordinary leakage and breakage or due to the inherent nature of the subject matter insured is excluded.

It is obvious that particular average covers a very wide range of losses, and it may be damaged too, or loss of part of the subject matter insured.

Notwithstanding the vast range of perils covered under the contract of cargo insurance, insurance cover is not provided against number of perils and losses. The perils and losses which are not covered under the cargo insurance contract are covered under the Exclusion Clauses. These include the following:

(a)   General Exclusion Clauses

    (b)   War Exclusion

    (c)   Unseaworthiness and Unfitness Exclusion Clauses

An insurance company will pay expenses incurred by the insured for recovering loss for preventing it to the cargo. This is, however, subject to two conditions. Firstly, the expenses must be to prevent or minimise the loss due to the insured perils. Secondly, the liability of the insurance company will not exceed the sum insured. The recoverable charges are:

    (a)   Extra changes which include survey fees and reconditioning costs;

    (b)   Sue and labour charges, which include all expenses to prevent loss/damage to goods for which insurance company would be liable; and

    (c)   Forwarding expenses which may be incurred when voyage is terminated short of destination.

Q15. What are the responsibilities of the insured in claiming cargo insurance claims?

Or

Discuss the responsibilities of the insured in a cargo insurance claim.

Ans. It is the duty of the insured or his agents, in all cases, to take such measures as may be reasonable to avert or minimise a loss. Further, it is also his duty to protect rights of the insurer of recovery from the carriers, port authority and others. In particular, the duties of the insured or his agent are:

    (1)   Lodge claim on the carriers, port authorities and other intermediaries for any missing packages;

    (2)   If the loss or damage is apparent or visible, make an application to the agents of the carriers, port authority, customs authority and the insurer (or agent) to arrange joint survey within 3 days of discharge of cargo from the vessel (7 days in case of air consignment);

    (3)   If the loss was not apparent at the time of taking delivery of cargo, give notice in writing to the carriers and other parties within 3 days of delivery of cargo (7 days in case of air consignment);

    (4)   Lodge a proper monetary claim on carriers, port authority and customs authority;

    (5)   In case of any missing package, get a log entry made with the port authority and lodge a claim on carrier and port authority;

    (6)   If missing packages are traced subsequently, clearance may be made only after a joint survey; and

    (7)   The claims on carriers, customs and port authorities should be filed within the time limits prescribed under the relevant laws.

Q16. Enumerate the documents needed for filing the cargo insurance claims.

Ans. The claims on the insurers should be submitted duly supported by the following documents:

    (1)   Original insurance policy or certificate of insurance duly endorsed by the insured;

(2) Full set of Bill of Lading in respect of total loss claims. Otherwise non-negotiating copy of the Bill of Lading, Airway Bill, Railway, etc. as applicable;

(3) Copy of invoice with packing/weight list;

(4) Insurance survey report or other documentary evidence to substantiate cause and extent of lots;

(5) Joint ship survey discrepancy a certificate issued by the carriers;

(6) Port authority Landing Remarks certificate;

(7) Casualty report when a vessel is missing or lost;

(8) Ship Master's protest or an authenticated copy of extract from ship's Log book in case vessel encountered heavy weather or other casualty during the voyage;

(9) In case of short landing claims, a Short Landing Certificate issued by the carrier or port authority;

(10) A landed but Missing Certificate from port authority; in case where package has landed but is missing;

(11) In the event of General Average claim for refund of GA Deposit; the GA Deposit Receipt and GA Counter-Guarantee;

(12) Triplicate COG of Bill of Entry (in case of India);

(13) Copies of Letter lodging claims on the carriers, port authority, etc;

(14) Copies of correspondence exchanged with carriers to examine whether the claimant has taken necessary measures;

(15) Letter of subrogation duly stamped and signed; and

(16) Any other document as may be asked for by the insurers.

Q17. Describe various stages involved in the shipment of export cargo.

Ans. The stages of the shipment process are as follows:

(1) Filing of documents with the customs authorities for checking genuineness of the transaction and for obtaining examination order;

(2) Payment of port charges;

(3) Obtaining permission of the shipping company to bring cargo into the shipment shed;

(4) Obtaining permission from the shed superintendent for bringing the cargo into the shipment shed;

(5) Arranging for transport of cargo to move into the shipment shed through Port Gate;

(6) Permission of the Gate Inspector to move cargo into the port area;

(7) Unloading of cargo in the shipment shed;

(8) Examination of cargo by the Customs Authorities and obtaining "Let Export" Order;

(9) Obtaining "Let Ship" Order from the customs preventive officer prior to loading;

(10) Issuance of Mate's Receipt by the Master of the vessel; and

(11) Obtaining "fact of shipment" certificate from the Customs Preventive Officer.

Q18. Discuss the central excise formalities.

Or

What are the procedural formalities of excise rebate policy?

Ans. Central Excise duties on the inputs used in manufacturing export products as well as on final export products are either exempted through production under bond or are refunded after export. The Government of India has laid down procedure for either getting the duty refunded or exemption from payment of duty.

The scheme under which the Central Excise exemption or refund is provided is popularly known as Rebate of Central Excise. This scheme operates under Section 37 of the Central Excise and Salt Act, 1944, as amended from time to time as well as the relevant Excise Rules. Rule 12 of the Central Excise Rules operates for exports under claim for rebate of duty. The rebate is granted on the duty levied at finished product and on inputs for this finished product. Rule 13, 191-B and 191-BB of Central Excise Rules have been integrated into Rule 13.

Procedural Formalities

Procedural formalities of excise rebate are as follows:

Refund Procedure under Rule 12: The authorities involved in this rule are: (i) Jurisdictional Central Excise Authority known as Central Excise Range Superintendent under whose jurisdiction the manufacturing unit is located; (ii) Maritime Central Excise Authority located at the port. Rebate may be either claimed from Jurisdictional Assistant Collector of Central excise or Maritime Collector.

The documents required under Rule 12 are:

(1) Invoices to be filled in four copies; and

(2) AR4/AR5 forms to be filled in six copies.

The procedure followed is as under:

(1) The exporters prepare four copies of invoices giving all details of the consignment.

(2) The excisable goods which are to be exported under claim for rebate are to be market as export cargo in individual packages.

(3) These marks and numbers are to be specified on AR4/AR5 forms, on all the six copies.

(4) Personal Ledger Account (PLA) is to be filled in specifying the amount of duty applicable to the export consignment as debit. In PLA, the credit balance of the deposit account spent by the individual manufacturer with the Central Excise Authority is shown. Each time when goods are cleared, the amount of duty applicable to the goods to be cleared is debited and the balance is shown in the balance column.

(5) All six copies of AR4/AR5 forms are to be presented to the Range Superintendent before clearance of the cargo. Under the Self-Removal Procedure (SRP), presence of the Central Excise

Officer at the factory at the time of clearance is not necessary. But in those cases where physical examination by the Central Excise Officer is solicited before the clearance of the cargo. Six copies of AR4/AR5 forms should be presented to the Range Superintendent at least 24 hours before the goods are to be removed from the factory.

(6) After verifying the details given in the afore-mentioned documents, the Range Superintendent allows clearance of the cargo from the factory for onward transmission to the port of shipment. Following endorsements are to be given in all the six copies of AR4/AR5 forms.

"Allowed to export under claim for Central Excise Rebate".

(7) The original and duplicate copies of AR4/AR5 forms are handed over to the exporter; the triplicate copy is sent to the Maritime Central Excise Collectorate-Refund Section, having jurisdiction over the port wherefrom the goods are to be shipped; the fourth copy is sent to the Chief Accounts Officer (CAO) of the Maritime Central Excise Collectorate concerned; the 5th copy is retained by Range Superintendent for his record and future reference. The sixth copy is also to be given to the exporter or his authorised agent.

(8) The original, duplicate and sixtuplicate copies of AR4/AR5 forms are to be submitted to the Export Department of Customs House alongwith other shipping documents to prove that formal central excise clearance has been obtained from the jurisdictional Central Excise Authority.

(9) If custom officer is satisfied, he would make endorsements in the original, duplicate and sixtuplicate copies of AR4/AR5 forms. The officer returns original and sixtuplicate copies to the exporter and sends duplicate copy to the Rebate Sanctioning Authority.

(10) Rebate claim may be filed either from Maritime collector or Jurisdictional Assistant Collector of Central Excise.

(11) Following documents should be filed for claiming rebate:

(a) Application in prescribed form;

(b) Original copy of AR4/AR5 forms;

(c) Duplicate copy of AR4 in sealed cover received from Customs Officer, if required;

(d) Duly attested copy of Bill of lading;

(e) Duly attested copy of shipping Bill (Export Promotion Copy); and

(f) Disclaimer certificate in case where claimant is other exporter.

Q19. Explain the formalities of customs clearance of export cargo.

Or

Describe various stages involved in customs clearance.

Or

What are the three stages at which customs' permission for exports is granted. [June-2013, Q.No.-4(a)]

Or

What are the supporting documents to be submitted along with the Shipping Bill for getting customs' permission for exports? [June-2013, Q.No.-4(b)]

Or

What is the procedure involved in customs clearance of export cargo? Explain its various stages and the related documents. [Dec-2013, Q.No.-6]

Or

What are the objectives of custom control?

Or

Give a detailed description of procedure involved along with related documentation for seeking custom clearance of export cargo. [June-2014, Q.No.-5]

Ans. Under Section 40 of the Indian Customs Act, an overseas carries cannot permit loading of goods without permission from the customs authorities. The permission is to be obtained by the exporter, generally through his C&F agent. Various aspects of customs formalities are as follows:

Legal Framework

Under Section 50 of the Indian Customs Act requires the exporter to file a declaration in a prescribed form and submit supporting documents to enable the customs authorities to check declarations made by the exporter.

The objectives of the customs control are:

(1) To ensure that nothing goes out of the country against the laws of land and that prohibitions and restrictions regarding outward cargo are duly enforced by the customs authorities;

(2) To ensure authenticity of the value of outward cargo according to the customs valuation rules to check over and under invoicing;

(3) To assess and realise export duty/charge according to the Customs Tariff Act and any other fiscal legislation;

(4) To check that all the relevant regulatory provision enforced by various authorities in the country have been duly complied with in respect of export; and

(5) To provide export data through the customs returns.

Customs Clearance Stages

There are four stages of customs involvement. These are:

(1) Processing of documents at the Customs House, i.e. the main office. This stage involves:

    (a) checking up of documents to ensure that all relevant documents have been submitted;

    (b) verification of quantity and value of goods;

    (c)   verification and determination of rate of duty and collection of the duty amount;

    (d)   direction for the customs officer in the docks for physical examination of goods;

(2)   Physical examination of goods in the docks in accordance with the examination order given at the Customs House;

(3)   Supervision of loading be the Customs Preventive Officer; and

(4)   Post-shipment endorsements by the Customs Preventive Officer.

Documentary requirements for Customs Clearance

For movement of goods by air or by sea, the customs permission for shipment is given on a prescribed document, known as Shipping Bill. In other cases (i.e. by road/rail), the document is known as Bill of Export. There are four types of Shipping Bill/Bill of Export. These are:

(1)   Dutiable Shipping Bill/Bill of Export for those goods that attract export duty/cess;

(2)   Drawback Shipping Bill/Bill of Export for those goods which are covered by the Duty Drawback scheme;

(3)   Free Shipping Bill/Bill of Export for these goods which neither attract export duty/cess nor are covered by the Duty Drawback scheme;

(4)   Ex-bond Shipping Bill/Bill of Export for those goods which are shipped from the customs bonded warehouse.

Exporter or his agent submits the following documents to the customs department.

(1)   Shipping Bill (in duplicate, triplicate or quadruplicate) duly filled in and signed.

(2)   Declaration regarding truth of statement made in the shipping Bill.

(3)   Invoice copy

(4)   GR Form

(5)   Export Licence (wherever required)

(6)   Quality Control Inspection Certificate (wherever required)

(7)   Original Contract wherever available or correspondence leading to contract

(8)   Contract registration certificate (wherever applicable)

(9)   Letter of credit (wherever applicable)

(10)   Packing List

(11)   AR4/AR5 forms (Original and Duplicate)

(12)   Any other document

Procedural Formalities

Shipping Bill/Bill Export is the main document required by the customs authority for allowing shipment. The Shipping Bill and the other documents are submitted to the Custom House as soon as the rotation number has been given to the carrier. As soon as the documents are filed in the Custom House, the Receiving Clerk will stamp the Shipping Bills with date and time, and number them according to their category. The shipping bills involving foreign exchange will be sent to the Appraisement Section where they are allotted to appraisers and examiners for scrutiny and giving examination order. While the appraisers will examine the dutiable and drawback shipping bills and free shipping bill will be examined by the examiners.

The verification of the shipping bills be carried out with reference to value and quantity of goods, export licence/permit, compliance with other statutory requirements, rate and amount of export duty, etc.

After verification of shipping bill, the customs appraiser/examiner will give an "examination order" on the duplicate shipping bill. This "order" will enable the customs officer to carry out physical examination of goods in the docks. The "examination order" will also be counter-endorsed by the principal appraiser.

After completion of formalities at the appraisement section, the documents are given to the GR Form Clerk who puts the shipping bill number on the GR Form and detaches the original to be sent to the RBI. Further, where export duty is to be paid, the documents are given to the exporter/agent to pay it at the Cash and Accounts Department. After payment of duty, shipping bill (original) is detached and other documents are given to the exporter/agent. In other cases, shipping bill (original) is retained at the Customs House and other documents given to the exporter/agent for bringing the goods to the shipment shed and make shipment arrangement.

The second stage of customs formalities is to carry out physical examination of goods in the shed. The goods can be brought into the shed only after completing formalities. Once the goods have been brought in, the exporter/agent will present the shipping bill to the custom shed appraiser/examiner along with the shed appraiser/examiner and also along with the following documents:

    (1)   Invoice;

    (2)   Packing list;

    (3)   AR4/AR5 forms; and

    (4)   Agmark certificate (wherever applicable).

The shed appraiser/examiner would carry out physical examination according to the "examination order" given on shipping bill (duplicate). Once this activity is over, the examiner will give "Let Export order on the Shipping Bill (Duplicate)" constituting the physical examination report.

After the physical examination report, the Customs Preventive Officer at the docks givens permission for shipment on the shipping bill (duplicate) in the form of "Let Ship" order. This copy is then presented to the master of the carrier, who then in consultation with the concerned Customs Preventive Officer, commences loading operation.

The master of the carrier, after receiving consignments on board, issues "Mate's Receipt", which is obtained by the exporter or his agent through the Shed Superintendent after paying port dues. The mate's receipt provides the basis for certification of the "fact of shipment" on those documents where it is needed for claim of export incentives. These documents are AR4/AR5 forms, export promotion copy of shipping bill, GR (duplicate) and commercial invoice.

Q20. Describe the port procedure involved in the shipment of export cargo.

Ans. Export cargoes can be brought into the port only after the ship has been allotted a berth and declared for loading. Some port authorities in India require the shippers to pay port charges and have their shipping bills passed by the Customs House before bringing goods to the docks. At the Bombay Port, however, shippers have the facility of paying charges after shipment.

An exporter needs to know the following procedures:

(1) Before bringing the cargo to the shipment shed, the shipper has to obtain "carting permission: from the Shed Superintendent and also the ship's agent on the prescribed document. This document is known differently at different ports, e.g. Dock Challan at Calcutta, Port Trust Copy of the Shipping Bill at Bombay and Export Application at other ports in India. When goods are brought at the dock gate, the shipper has to present the port document and the Vehicle Ticket (in duplicate) to the Gate Inspector. At the gate, the documents are compared and checked to ensure that only such goods as have been permitted are brought to the docks for shipment. The packages, bundles, cases in each vehicle are counted to check whether their number tallies with the number mentioned in the respective vehicle ticket. Vehicles are then allowed to move to the concerned shipment shed and particulars of cargo passed through the gate recorded in a register maintained at this point.

(2) Coinciding with the arrival of the vehicle in the shipment shed, the shipper submits the vehicle ticket duly endorsed by the gate inspector, export application/dock/challan/port trust copy of shipping bill, shipping bill (duly passed by customs) and a receipt in lieu of payment of port charges, where necessary, to the Shed Superintendent. As cargo is unloaded in the shipment shed, details of the cargo received are entered in the 'Shed Export Cargo Register', which is maintained shipper-wise and shipwise.

(3) The Shipper than approaches the Customs Appraiser and the Customs Preventive Officer for Physical Examination of Goods and obtains 'Let Export/Let ship' endorsements in the Port Trust's documents also. The cargo is then allowed to be shipped. On completion of shipment, details of cargo actually shipped are recorded in the 'Shed Export Cargo Register'; form the 'Shipping Tally Sheets' which are maintained by the port trust and also the shipping lines.

(4) On receipt of cargo on board, the master of the vessel issues a document called the 'Mate's Receipt' in respect of every

shipment taken on board. At some ports, the issuance of mate's receipt is preceded by another document which has to be exchanged for the mate's receipt. The mate's receipt is subject to the terms and conditions stated in the shipping company's regular B/L. At most ports in India, the port authorities collect the mate's receipts from the Master or the Chief Officer of the vessel and pass them on the respective shippers only after ensuring receipt of all port dues. No claused mate's receipts are accepted by the port authorities, unless authorised by the shipper(s).

(5) After collecting the mate's receipt, the shipper (exporter or his agent) prepares the B/L on black forms supplied to him by the shipping company. He presents 2/3 originals and some non-negotiable copies of the document at the shipping company's office for signature of the authorised officer alongwith the mate's receipt. The mate's receipt is an important document because it is required to be exchanged for the B/L. Therefore, the shipper must collect this document from the Shed Superintendent immediately after it has been received by the latter to avoid delays and problems, which might follow if this is not collected in time.

(6) The B/L may be marked 'Freight Paid' or 'Freight to Pay'. If the freight is pre-paid, i.e. paid by the exporter, the B/L is marked or stamped to that effect and where freight is not pre-paid, the B/L is marked 'Freight to Pay': or 'Freight Collect'. The mate's receipt is retained by the shipping company. Before signing and parting with the B/L, the shipping company ensures that all the clauses appearing on the mate's receipt are reproduced on the B/L also. Read GPH books and score excellent marks.

▲ ▲ ▲

Gullybaba.com

Simply Scan QR Codes to Jump at Our Latest Products

HELP BOOKS

**TYPED
ASSIGNMENTS**

**HAND WRITTEN
ASSIGNMENTS**

**READYMADE
PROJECTS**

**CUSTOMIZED
PROJECTS**

**COMBOS OF BOOKS/
ASSIGNMENTS**

Note: The above QR Codes can be scanned and open through QR Code Scanner Application/App of your smart mobile Phone.

4 | Export Incentives and Assistance

AN OVERVIEW

Countries engaged in the task of export promotion have to establish appropriate institutional infrastructure for strengthening export marketing effort for the country as a whole. With this object in view, Government of India has established a number of specialised institutions for providing necessary services and assistance to individual corporate units from the export sector.

Export growth has become main determinant of economic growth. With the increasing requirements of imports, exports have now emerged as the only viable source of meeting the foreign exchange needs. Government of India has provided various incentives for export promotion. The scheme of financial incentives include interest subsidy on working capital and Financial Assistance Scheme for Agricultural, Horticultural and Meat Exports.

The success on the export front is crucially dependent upon the marketing of the products. Hence, special efforts have been made for improving and strengthening export marketing effort. Government of India have established a number of specialised institutions for providing necessary services and assistance to the exporters. Marketing Development Fund provides necessary financial assistance for market promotion. Exporters are required to comply various procedural formalities for fuller realisation of export incentives on a regular basis.

Q1. What is the importance of institutional infrastructure for export promotion in India?

Ans. There is a vital importance of export marketing effort for the success of export-promotion programme in any country. For undertaking international marketing operations, an exporter needs special guidance and assistance in critical areas like packaging, market promotion and publicity, quality certification, risk coverage, market intelligence, finance and credit support, etc. It is only with the support and services rendered by specialised institutions, exporter is able to successfully convert his 'production' into 'sales' in international market. Consequently, any country, including India, engaged in the task of export promotion has to establish specialised institutions for strengthening export-marketing effort for the country as a whole. This will have the way for creating an export environment and export-culture, on the foundations of which the export marketing effort at the corporate level can be effectively launched on an intensive and sustained basis. With this object in view, Government of India has established a number of specialised institutions in the country for providing the necessary services and assistance to individual corporate unit for a successful export effort. Read GPH books and score excellent marks.

Q2. Describe the role of government policy-making and consultative body in the export promotion.

Ans. The Department of Commerce, in the Ministry of Commerce has been made responsible for the external trade of India and all matters connected with the same. The main functions of the Ministry are the formulation of international commercial policy, negotiation of trade agreements, formulation of country's export-import policy and their implementation. It has created a network of commercial sections in Indian embassies and high commissions in various countries for export-import trade flows. It has set up an "Exporters Grievances Redressal Cell" to assist exporters in quick redressal of grievances.

The Department of commerce has the following bodies:

(1) Board of Trade: For ensuring a regular consultation, monitoring and review of India's foreign trade policies and operations, Government of India have set up a Board of Trade with representatives from Commerce and other important Ministers, Trade and Industry Associations, and Export Service Organisations. It is an important national platform for a regular dialogue between the Government and the trade and industry. The deliberations in the Board of Trade provide guidelines to the Government for appropriate policy measures for corrective action.

(2) Cabinet Committee on Exports: With a view to ensure regular and effective monitoring of India's foreign trade performance and related policies, Cabinet Committee on Export has also been set up.

(3) Empowered Committee of Secretaries: For speedier and quicker decision-making, an Empowered Committee of

Secretaries has also been established to assist the Cabinet Committee on Exports.

(4) **Grievances Cell:** Grievances Cell has been set up to entertain and monitor disposal of grievances and suggestions received. It is a cell meant for speedy redressal of genuine grievances. Grievances Committees headed by Director General of Foreign Trade and head of concerned Regional Licensing Authority have been constituted in the respective licensing offices. The Committee also include representatives of FIEO, concerned Export Promotion Council/Commodity Board and other departments and organisations. The grievances may be addressed to the Grievance Cell of the concerned Licensing Authority in the prescribed pro forma.

(5) **Director General of Foreign Trade (DGFT):** DGET is an important office of the Ministry of Commerce, to help the formulation of India's Export-Import Policy and implementation thereof. It has set up regional officers in almost all States and Union Territories of India. These offices are known as Regional Licensing Authorities. There is an Export Commissioner in the DGFT office, which functions as a nodal point for all export promotion schemes. The Regional Licensing offices also act as Export facilitation centres.

(6) **Director General, Commercial Intelligence & Statistics (DGCI&S):** It has been entrusted with the task of compilation and publication of data on India's Foreign Trade. It brings out various publications relating to Foreign of India. The major publications are as under:
(a)   Monthly Statistics of Foreign Trade in India;
(b)   Monthly Press Notes on Foreign Trade;
(c)   Monthly Brochure of Foreign Trade Statistics of India (Principal Commodities and Countries);
(d)   Indian Trade Classification based on Harmonised Commodity Description and Coding System; and
(e)   Indian Trade Journal.

(7) **Ministry of Textile:** Ministry of Textiles is another Ministry of Government of India, which is responsible for policy formulation, development, regulation and export promotion of textile sector including sericulture, jute and handicrafts, etc. It has a separate Export Promotion Division, offices, advisory boards, development corporations, Export Promotion Councils and Commodity Boards. The advisory boards have been constituted to advise the government in the formulation of the overall development programmes in the concerned sector. It also devises strategy for expanding markets in India and abroad. The four advisory boards are as under:
(a)   All India Handloom Board;
(b)   All India Handicrafts Board;

   (c)   All India Powerloom Board; and

   (d)   Wool Development Board.

There are Development Commissioners, Handicrafts and Handlooms, who advice on matters relating to the development and exports of these sectors. There are Textile Commissioners and Jute Commissioner who advises on the matters relating to the growth of exports of these sectors. Textile Committee has also been set up for ensuring textile machinery manufactured indigenously, especially for exports. It also issues certificates of origin and other special certificates.

(8) States Cell: The cell has been created under Ministry of Commerce. Its functions are to act as a nodal agency for interacting with State Governments or Union Territories on matters concerning export or import from the States or Union Territories. It provides guideline to State level export organisations. It assists them in the formation of export plans for each case.

(9) Development Commissioner, Small Scale Industries Organisation: The Directorate has the headquarter in New Delhi and extension centres located in almost all States and Union Territories. They provide export promotion services almost at the doorsteps of the small-scale industries and cottage units. The important functions are:

   (a)   to help the small scale industries to develop their export capacities;

   (b)   to organise export training programmes;

   (c)   to collect and disseminate information;

   (d)   to help such units in developing their export markets; and

   (e)   to take up the problems and other issues related to small industries.

Besides, there are Directorates of Industries, National Small Industries Corporation and State Corporations for the promotion of exports from small-scale industries.

Q3. Discuss the functions of export promotion councils and commodity boards.

Or

Write a short note on export promotion councils.

[June-2013, Q.No.-7(c)]

Ans. Export promotion councils and commodity boards are the key institutions in the institutional framework established in India for export promotion. These are established for servicing export-effort for specific products and/or industrial sectors. They have been entrusted with the task of promoting exports of specific products from India. The functions of the Export Promotion Councils are as follows:

   (1) Marketing Assistance: These promotional institutions are continuously involved in providing export marketing intelligence as well as guiding, assisting and advising individual corporate units in their export-plans and effort marketwise as well as productwise. The primary function of the Export Promotion Council, Commodity Board, etc. is to provide the exporters with market information on a continuous basis.

It includes market opportunities, identifying prospective importer, trade and tariff policies of importing countries, product-designs and specifications, agents and distribution channels, warehousing, publicity and promotion, pricing, packaging, shipping and transportation, buying practices, competition, Government regulations, etc. In other words, the help and assistance provided to individual exporter firms encompasses almost all the critical elements involved in export marketing effort at the corporate-unit level.

(2) **Continuous Feedback of Market Information:** Besides providing marketing service, these institutions also undertake to provide continuous feedback of market information to individual export firm in India. The council functions through their in-house bulletins, circulars and other publications including statistical information and directories of importers, etc.

For collection of such comprehensive market information, Export promotion Councils, Commodity Boards, Special Authorities, etc. have established overseas offices in all parts of the world. In addition, they also undertake market -surveys, organise specially in India, exhibitions and conferences with prospective importers, sponsor trade delegations, etc.

(3) **Mouthpiece of Industry:** Further, they also act as the mouthpiece of the industry, advising as well as seeking appropriate changes in government policies, influencing export effort of their specific areas of interest.

(4) **Product/Industry Coverage:** Complete list of Products/industries currently being looked after by different Export Promotion Councils/Commodity Board special Authorities and Industry Associations.

Commodity Boards

These statutory bodies are responsible for the development of cultivation, increased productivity, processing, research and development, and marketing. They also ensure adequate remuneration to growers by encouraging cooperative ventures, upgradation of quality and marketing the produce through auctions, etc. There are seven Commodity Boards, i.e. tea, coffee, tobacco, rubber, coir, spices and silk board. All the commodity boards, except central silk board, are the registering authority and issue Registration-cum-Membership Certificate.

Special Authorities for Some Products: There are also special authorities established for promoting exports of marine products, processed foods, cinematographic films, and khadi and khadi products.

These include (1) Marine Products Export Development Authority, (2) Agricultural and Processed Food Products Exports Development Authority, (3) National Film Development Corporation and (4) Khadi and Village Industries Commission. Similarly, for extractions of solvents, groundnut, soyabean and cotton-seed, the industry associations promoting exports of these products are as under:

(1)   The Solvent Extractors Association of India;

(2)   The Groundnut Extractors Export Development Association;

(3)   Soyabean Processors Association of India; and

(4)   All India Cottonseed Crushers Association.

Further, the office of the Jute Commissioner and Jute Manufactures Development Council look after exports of natural fibre products (other than coir) and Director of Vanaspati looks after Vanaspati.

Q4. Discuss the institutions providing technical and specialised services to the export sector in India.

Ans. Export marketing is not a one way or two-way deal in which two-three persons or organisations can complete the export-import procedures. But there is a vital need of many technical and specialised service inputs. These agencies cover important and crucial areas like packaging, quality control, risk coverage, promotion and finance. The descriptions of these agencies are as follows:

(1) Export Inspection Council and Agencies

The Export Inspection Council (EIC) was set up by the Government of India under Section 3 of the Export (Quality Control and Inspection) Act, 1963 in order to ensure sound development of export trade of India through Quality Control and Inspection and for matters connected thereof.

The export inspection agencies established by the Council, certify the quality and export-worthy aspect of the manufactured and processed products exported from India. In this way, Government of India, indirectly, assure the foreign buyers, about the quality and export-worthiness of the products, exported from India. This has been made a statutory requirement. Regular exporting units are also being declared as export-worthy units, subject to periodical inspection by the export-inspection agencies. In addition, these agencies also provide guidance and advice to individual export firms regarding technical standards and specifications required for servicing export markets world over.

Export Inspection Agencies have also been authorised to issue the GSP certificate of origin which enables exporters from India to be eligible for preferential duty concessions in the markets of developed countries from West Europe, North America, Japan, Australia and New Zealand, etc. The Export Inspection Council has set up a pilot test house at Mumbai for prompt, efficient, accurate and comprehensive testing of engineering products, particularly from small scale sector. It also offers technical support facilities to the industry. The EIC has also set up the Quality Development Centre at Madras for providing training to the inspection officers. It has also evolved procedures for assessment, evaluation and settlement of complaints from foreign buyers.

(2) The Indian Institute of Foreign Trade

The Indian Institute of Foreign Trade (IIFT) was set up in 1963 by the Government of India as an autonomous organisation to help professionalise the country's foreign trade management and increase exports by developing human resources; generating, analysing and disseminating data; and conducting research.

IIFT has, over the years, undertaken path-breaking research studies with organisations like WTO, World Bank, UNCTAD and the Ministry of Commerce & Industry, Government of India. The Institute has also trained more than 40,000 business professionals across 30 countries in various facets of international business and trade policy via its Management Development Programmes. **IIFT** performs the following functions:

(a) **Store-house of Market Information:** It functions as a store-house of export marketing information, product-wise as well as market-wise. It has conducted market surveys in every part of the world, identifying export opportunities for the entire export sector as a whole.

(b) **Provides International Business Management Training:** In addition, the IIFT has been the pioneer and premier institution offering international business management education programme including basic programmes as well as in service education.

Being a government institution, it also offers training programmes for Government of India service personnel from Indian Foreign Service, Indian Administrative Service, Central Trade Service, and Indian Economic and Statistical Service.

(c) **Advises Government On-trade Policies:** An important function of the Institute has been to advice Government of India on all aspects of foreign trade policies, strategies and operations. Being a premier institution, it is frequently approached for necessary advice and guidance by other export service organisations including export promotion councils as well as individual export corporate units.

(3) Export Credit Guarantee Corporation

Export Credit Guarantee Corporation of India Limited was established in the year 1957 by the Government of India to strengthen the export promotion drive by covering the risk of exporting on credit. Being essentially an export promotion organisation, it functions under the administrative control of the Ministry of Commerce & Industry, Department of Commerce, GOI. It is managed by Board of Directors comprising representatives of the Government, Reserve Bank of India, banking, insurance and exporting community.

It provides a range of credit risk insurance covers to exporters against loss in export of goods and services. For example, it offers guarantees to banks and financial institutions to enable exporters to obtain better facilities from them and provides Overseas Investment Insurance to Indian companies investing in joint ventures abroad in the form of equity or loan.

ECGC help exporters in the following ways:

(a)   Offers insurance protection to exporters against payment risks;
(b)   Provides guidance in export-related activities;
(c)   Makes available information on different countries with its own credit ratings;
(d)   Makes it easy to obtain export finance from banks/financial institutions;
(e)   Assists exporters in recovering bad debts; and
(f)   Provides information on credit-worthiness of overseas buyers.

(4) EXIM Bank

Export-Import Bank of India is the premier export finance institution in India, established in 1982 under the Export-Import Bank of India Act 1981. EXIM bank is set up on the recommendations of several committee and study groups such as the Alexander Committee, on Export-Import (1977) and Tandon committee on Exports (1980). Its headquarters is at Bombay and its branches are at import centres in India and abroad. The Bank was carved out of the International Wing of IDBI.

Export-Import Bank of India provides:

(a)   Financial assistance to promote Indian Exports through direct financial assistance;
(b)   Overseas Investment Finance;
(c)   Term finance for export production and export development;
(d)   Pre-shipment Credit;
(e)   Line of Credit;
(f)   Buyers Credit;
(g)   Relending facility;
(h)   Export Bills Rediscounting;
(i)   Refinance to Commercial Banks;
(j)   Finance for Computer Software Export;
(k)   Finance for Export marketing & Bulk import finance to Commercial Banks;
(l)   EXIM Bank also extends non-funded facility to Indian Exporters in the form of guarantee;
(m)   Diversified lending programme of the EXIM bank now covers various stages of Exports, i.e. from the development of Export market to the expansion of production capacity for exports, production for exports and post-shipment financing; and
(n)   The EXIM bank also focus on export of manufactured goods, project exports, exports of technology, services and export of computer software.

(5) Indian Council of Arbitration

The Government of India established the Indian council of Arbitration in 1965 at the national level. The Council provides for arbitration facilities with respect to both domestic and foreign trade. Even when both parties are foreign, they may submit their dispute to arbitration under the rules of the Council. Its membership includes representatives of public, private undertakings and many commercial organisations and institutions apart from experts from various professions like engineers, chartered accountants, lawyers, judges and technocrats. Between 1995 and 2006, the membership of the Council steadily increased. At present, the Indian Council of Arbitration has about 5000 members. During the year 2005-2006, there was increase in the number of cases with the Indian Council of Arbitration. It is expected that the international caseload of the Indian Council of Arbitration will increase considerably as many international contracts actually contain an arbitral clause referring to the arbitration rules of the Council. The main objective of the Indian Council of Arbitration is to promote amicable, quick and inexpensive settlement of commercial disputes by means of conciliation/arbitration. It maintains a panel of arbitrators, which include eminent and expert persons from various lines of trade and professions. The names of suitable persons of foreign nationals are also included in the panel to provide a wide choice to the foreign parties in regard to selection of arbitrators.

(6) Federation of Indian Export Organisations (FIEO)

The Federation of Indian Export Organisations (FIEO) functions as the coordinating body for various Export Promotion Councils and other service institutions established by the Government for trade promotion purposes. The Federation is the primary servicing agency to provide integrated assistance to government recognised export houses. It emphasises on intra and inter-regional cooperation in trade and economic matters with a view to promoting harmony and understanding through economic, and trade and technical ties. In addition, the national-level trade and industry associations like Federation of Indian Chambers of Commerce and Industry (FICCI), Associated Chamber of Commerce (ASSOCHAM) and Confederation of Engineering Industries (CEI) also play the coordinating role for advocating the viewpoint and promoting the interests of the sectors they represent.

(7) India Trade Promotion Organisation (ITPO)

India Trade Promotion Organisation has been formed by merging Trade Fair Authority of India and Trade Development Authority. This is the premier trade promotion agency of the Government of India with the headquarter in New Delhi. It has also set up offices abroad in New York, Frankfurt, Tokyo and Dubai. ITPO is a service organisation, which maintains close interaction with the trade, industry and the Government. The organisation serves the industry by providing marketing information and support for participation in fairs. It also helps in developing exports of new items and uses its network of offices in India and abroad for improved trade-related services. It has set up a Trade Information Centre at New Delhi. In specific term, the objectives of ITPO are:

    (a)   to organise trade fairs in India and abroad;

    (b)   to organise trade development and promotion through specialised programmes such as buyer-seller meets, contact promotion, promotion through departmental stores, exchange of business delegations, etc.

(c)   to assist technically competent units in product development and adaptation;

(d)   to encourage and involve medium scale and small-scale industrial units in export promotion efforts,

(e)   to conduct in-house and need-based research on trade and export promotion; and

(f)   to enlist the involvement and support of the State Governments in the promotion of India's foreign trade.

(8) National Institute of Fashion Technology (NIFT)

National Institute of Fashion Technology, New Delhi has been established for human resource development for the garment industry. It conducts professional programmes in the disciplines of Apparel Merchandising and marketing, fashion design and garment manufacturing technology. It offers training through workshops and consultancy services. It has entered into technical agreement with the Fashion Institute of Technology, New York and the Nottingham Polytechnic, UK.

Q5. Write a note on commercial wing of Indian Embassies abroad.

Ans. The commercial wing of Indian Embassies abroad provides assistance in export marketing effort. There are 65 formal Commercial Wings functioning in the Indian Missions/Posts abroad, which are funded from the Budget of Department of Commerce. These Commercial Offices, working as units are attached to the Indian Missions. These include the office of the Ambassador of India to WTO in Geneva. In addition, about 20 other Indian Missions have also been provided with commercial budget either to employ local Marketing Assistants for undertaking commercial and economic job or to carry out trade promotional activities.

The Commercial Offices abroad provide the institutional framework and are meant to promote India's trade and economic exchanges with the world. The primary task of these wings is to assist the Government in formulation of its trade and economic policies through regular feedback on the prevailing global market trends, trade activities, etc. Individual export-unit as well as export promotion and service institutions can equally utilise the services of commercial wing of Indian Embassies abroad for various purposes such as specific market information, importers and or import-agents' names and addresses, arranging meetings with prospective importers during the visits of foreign markets by Indian exporters. Further, specific information about various tenders, as well as supply of tender documents, and other project information including market assessment, marketing practices, technical standards and specifications, etc. can also be attained through this channel. Advise the guidance regarding visits of trade delegations, trade fairs and exhibitions, development plans, market-studies, etc. is also given by these offices on specific requests.

In keeping with the requirement of quick dissemination of information, data and bilateral/multilateral exchanges, a computer database report system was introduced in the Department for monitoring the activities of the Commercial Offices abroad. The Commercial Representatives posted abroad are kept informed of the important developments in the Indian Economy and Quarterly Newsletters are issued to the Commercial Wings. Most of the Commercial Wings are now provided with modern IT equipment.

Q6. Briefly discuss Government participation in foreign trade.

Ans. The GOI played a supplementary role in private sector at the corporate level for export efforts. Besides playing a supplementary role in export promotion, the Government Corporation have also been functioning as major exporters of minerals and other canalised items of exports besides developing India's exports to Eastern Europe. State Trading Corporation of India as well as Minerals and Metals Trading Corporation of India have emerged as the largest trading houses in India's export sector. They have also provided the small and medium manufacturers, with an effective export outlet. Over the recent past, they have also developed 'counter trading' for augmenting India's exports. Other Government Corporations functioning in the export sector include the Spices Trading Corporation, Handloom and Handicrafts Export Corporation (HHEC), Metal Scarp Trading Corporation, Projects and Equipment Corporation of India Limited, Mica Trading Corporation of India Limited, Tea Trading Corporation of India Limited and Cashew Corporation of India Limited.

Q7. Discuss the need and importance of export incentives.

Ans. Export incentives have become a universal practice cannot be denied as the Doha round of World Trade Organisation has failed on the issue of incentives and subsidies provided universally for most of export commodities especially the agriculture produce. While the developed countries continue to subsidies, their exports these countries want the developing nations to withdraw subsidies and incentives to their exporters and none of the participating country is willing to concede.

Both developed as well as developing countries follow the practice of providing incentives to let the exports grow. The export incentives are in the form of tax-concessions or fiscal incentives and financial incentives including various other subsidies. The competition in the international market is very intensive that without specific and liberal export incentives, it is rather impossible to compete. The reason of this situation is that almost every nation has list their monopoly position and the export of traditional goods have either been challenged by new entrants as in the case of India, especially the spice, tea, iron ore, etc. Similarly, to get a share of the export market, the countries provide incentives for the growth of its economy or for the consumption of surplus production of certain commodities as soya bean and maize in case of USA and wheat in case of Australia.

The incentives also help a country to expand the export to boost industrial and agricultural production, which in turn give a major input to the growth of employment, revenue generation and growth of foreign exchange earnings and the total economic growth of a country.

    Export Procedures and Documentation [AED-01]

Export incentives play an important role in International Trade. As these incentives impart cost competitiveness to exports, thereby facilitating greater market penetration. In order to promote exports and to obtain foreign exchange, the Government of India had framed several schemes. These schemes grant incentive and other benefits. Under schemes, raw material and other components can be imported without payment of customs duty for use in goods to be exported.

Export incentives take the form of cash assistance or cash compensatory support on exports of certain items; duty drawback, i.e., a refund of central excise and customs duties levied on raw materials and components used in the manufacture of exports; import replenishment to replace imported raw materials and components used in the manufacture of exports; airfreight subsidy on the export of certain products; special treatment for export-oriented units for import of raw materials; and credit facilities from approved financial institutions at pre-shipment and post-shipment stages.

Q8. Explain the facilities/concessions for increasing the production base for exports from India.

Ans. In India, there is export promotion policy to ensure larger exportable surpluses. In other words, if a country wants to export more, it must have more to export. It will have more to export only if more and more is produced for export. Hence, it calls for increasing flow of production and investment resources into the export sector. The facilities under export promotion policy are as follows:

(1) Relaxations in Industrial Licensing Policy/MRTP/FERA/ Foreign Collaborations

For easier facilitation in creation/expansion of production capacities for increasing export potential of Indian economy, necessary relaxations have been provided for in the policies for industrial licensing, MRTP (Monopolies and Restrictive Trade Practices Act), FERA (Foreign Exchange Regulations Act), etc. The Foreign Exchange Regulation Act has been liberalised and rupee has been made fully convertible for all approved external transactions. As a result, exporters of goods and services and those who are in receipt of remittances are able to sell their foreign exchange at market determined rates. The importer and foreign travellers are also able to buy foreign exchange at market determined rates. Exporters have also been allowed to maintain foreign currency accounts. There is a general liberalisation of remittance of foreign exchange for visits abroad, agency commission, export claims, reduction in export value, reimbursement of expenses incurred on dishonoured export bills, consular fees, etc. Consequently, creation of additions of production capabilities for export is liberally allowed, both in the large-scale as well as small-scale sectors. Foreign collaboration and foreign capital investment is also liberally permitted for the export sector.

(2) Liberal Import of Capital Goods

Import policy of India allowed imports of machinery and equipment without import Licence. In addition, special provisions have been made for import of capital goods at a concessional rate of import duty.

Export Promotion Capital Goods (EPCG) Scheme has been introduced for liberal import of capital goods. Under this scheme, capital goods for the manufacture of goods and for providing services can be imported at zero duty or 10 per cent duty against an obligation to export four times of CIF value over 5 years and six times of CIF value over 8 years respectively. Computers systems can also be imported under this scheme. Import of Capital goods for farm sector may be allowed at zero duty against obligation to export six times the CIF value on FOB basis over six years, if the import of capital goods is of ₹5 crores or more.

(3) Establishment of Export Processing Zones (EPZ), Export-Oriented Units (EOU), Electronic Hardware Technology Parks (EHTP) and Software Technology Park Units (STP)

Export promotion policy established many units according to the need of sector. Units undertaking to export their entire production of goods may be set up under Export Processing Zones (EPZ) Scheme, Export Oriented Units (EOU) Scheme, Electronic Hardware Technology Park (EHTP) Scheme or Software Technology Park (STP) scheme. Such units may be engaged in manufacture, production of software, agriculture, aquaculture, animal husbandry, floriculture, horticulture, pisciculture, viticulture, poultry farming and sericulture. Units engaged in service activities may also be considered.

These units may import all types of goods. Including capital goods for manufacture, production or processing, provided, they are not prohibited items. Second hand capital goods may also be imported in accordance with the provisions of the policy. These units are permitted to sell 25 per cent of the production in value terms in the Domestic Tariff Area subject to payment of applicable duties. Rejects upto 5 per cent of the value of production may also be sold in the DTA. Supplies from DTA to these units will be regarded as deemed exports. Foreign equity upto 100 per cent is permissible to these units. These units shall be exempted from payment of corporate income tax for a block of five years in the first eight years of their operation.

(4) Assured Supply of Raw-material Imports

For making available the supplies of imported raw materials to the export sector, the import policy provides the scheme of Duty Free Licence. Import of raw materials, intermediates, components, consumables, parts, accessories, mandatory spares and packing materials may be permitted against a duty free licence. Duty Free Licence includes Advance Licence, Advance Intermediate Licence and Special Imprest Licence.

An advance licence is granted to a merchant-exporter or manufacturer-exporter for the import of inputs required for the manufacture of goods without payment of basic customs duty. An Advance Intermediate Licence is granted to a manufacturer-exporter for the import of inputs required in the manufacture of goods to be supplied to the ultimate exporter holding an Advance Licence/Special Imprest Licence. A Special Licence is granted to a manufacturer-exporter for the import of inputs required in the manufacture of goods to be supplied to the categories mentioned in the policy.

Q9. Discuss about export houses and trading houses. Which criteria have to be measured for checking the eligibility for Export House, Trading house, Star Trading House and Super Star Trading House?

Or

Write a short note on export houses and trading houses.

[Dec-2013, Q.No.-7(c)]

Ans. From the beginning of the Second Five Year Plan, the foreign exchange problem began to assume serious proportions, and the government began to realise the need for vigourous export promotion. It was very clear the concentrated efforts should be made for the promotion of export of non-traditional items. It was also realised that unless positive steps were taken to build up a number of merchant houses, concentrating almost exclusively on exports and capable of undertaking trade on a sustained basis, it would be impossible to compete successfully against the highly experienced and resourceful trading houses of other countries. The importance of promoting merchant houses was further underlined by the need for providing channels for the export of the products of the small-scale sector.

An export house is defined as a registered exporter holding a valid Export House Certificate issued by the Director General of Foreign Trade. The objective of the scheme is to recognise established exporters as Export House, Trading House, Star Trading House and Superstar Trading House with a view to build marketing infrastructure and expertise required for promotion. Such houses should operate as highly professional and dynamic institutions and act as important instruments of export growth.

Export/Trading/Star Trading/Super Star Trading Houses have been accorded special status. When exporters achieve the specified level of exports over a period, they may be recognised as EH/TH/STH/SSTH. The exporters, registered with FIEO or EPC are eligible for this purpose. The export performance criteria may be based on either f.o.b. value of exports or net foreign exchange earnings.

(1) FOB Criteria

This criteria is used for the recognition of an exporter in one of these categories. FOB can be measured as an average value earned through physical exports during the three preceding years or during the preceding year whichever is opted for by the exporters. However, recognition as a Super Star Trading House requires exports in a minimum of at least three product groups. In addition to physical exports, other specified exports and services for which payment is received in free foreign exchange also qualify for the purpose of the eligibility criteria. The level of export performance for the purpose of recognition shall be as per the table below:

Table 4.1: FOB Criteria

Category	Average FOB value during the preceding three licensing years (in `)	FOB value during the preceding three licensing years (in `)
Export House	15 crores	22 crores
Trading House	75 crores	112 crores
Star Trading House	375 crores	560 crores
Super Star Trading House	1125 crores	1680 crores

The status conferred under these categories is generally valid for three years from April of the licensing year during which the application is made.

(2) Net Foreign Exchange Earnings

Special weightages are given to certain categories of exports in calculating the NFE earned and assessing the export performance of a company in deciding its classification. Exporters have an option for obtaining the status of Export and other Houses based on the following Net Foreign Exchange Earnings. Look at Table for these criteria:

Table 4.2: Net Foreign Exchange Criteria

Category of Houses	Average Net Foreign Exchange Value of eligible exports during the preceding three licensing years	Net Foreign Exchange Value of exports made during the preceding licensing years
Export House	`12 Crores	`18 Crores
Trading House	`62 Crores	`90 Crores
Star Trading House	`312 Crores	`450 Crores
Super Star Trading House	`937 Crores	`1350 Crores

Q10. Describe the various incentives provided for the expansion of production base for export.

Or

Analyse the different price support measures introduced in India for rendering Indian exports more competitive.

[June-2013, Q.No.-5]

Ans. Under the Export Promotion Policy of India, various types of incentives have been provided for a price support measures. These include (1) Fiscal Incentives and (2) Financial Incentives.

(1) Fiscal Incentives

Fiscal incentives include the following for export promotion:

    (a) Duty Drawback: In the manufacturing of many export products, imported or indigenous raw materials and components are used on which customs or central excise duty has been paid. When the finished products are exported in which duty paid inputs are used, a part or whole of the amount of such duty is allowed to be drawn back by the exporter or it is refunded to him. This results in substantial reduction in the cost of material inputs for export production. In other words, import duties and central excise duties on material inputs for export activity are allowed to be drawback by the exporters under the incentives policy for duty drawback.

The scheme of Duty Drawback has been formulated by the Drawback Director under the Central Board of Revenue and Customs from the Ministry of Finance. Details regarding Drawback Scheme can be from 'Drawback Rules' as notified by the office of Drawback Director. Refund of Duty Drawback is granted on post export basis. The benefit of duty drawback has been provided on the basis of (i) all industry rates or (ii) brand rates separately fixed for individual manufacturers of the export products. The incentive of duty drawback helps to reduce significantly the material cost of export products. It is very important for countries like India, which have simple manufactures to offer for exports, which are very much influenced by the material cost.

(b) **Central Excise Rebate:** Under this scheme, the Central Excise Duties on the inputs and final product or on the output proposed for export are refunded to the exporter. It helps in further reduction in the overall cost of production for exports. The scheme also provides for a Bond System under which outright exemption from Central Excise Duties can be claimed by the exporter. The scheme is operated as per Central Excise Rules notified by the Central Excise department.

(c) **Income-Tax Exemption:** Export incentives in the form of income-tax concessions have also been provided for exporters. Export profits are totally exempted from income-tax. However, for assessment purposes total taxable profits of the company/firm are calculated on the basis of the entire sales turnover including domestic as well as export sales. From the taxable profits so arrived at, that portion is exempted from income-tax, which represents the ratio of export-sales to total sales turnover. For instance, if export sales are 25 per cent of the total sales turnover of the firm, then 25 per cent of the taxable profits will be exempted from income-tax.

(d) **Sales Tax Exemption:** There is no tax on sales made for export purpose. The exporter need not pay sales tax either on the goods purchased from manufacturers or traders.

(2) Financial Incentives

The major scheme of financial incentives include interest subsidy, financial assistance scheme for agricultural, horticultural and meat exports.

(a) **Interest Subsidy:** In India, export sector has also been given interest subsidy under which the working capital is made available by the banks to the export sector at a concessional or subsidised rates of interest. Under this scheme, working capital required for pre-shipment credit as well as post-shipment credit is provided to the export sector at concessional rates of interest. This measure helps Indian exporters to reduce the working capital cost of export operation.

(b) Financial Assistance Scheme for Agricultural, Horticultural and Meat Exports: In order to promote the exports, of agricultural, horticultural and meat products, Agricultural and Processed food products Export Development Authority (APEDA) provides financial assistance for the following purposes:

(i) Feasibility studies, surveys, consultancy and data base up gradation;

(ii) Development of infrastructure;

(iii) Export promotion and market development;

(iv) Packaging development;

(v) Quality control;

(vi) Upgradation of meat plants;

(vii) Organisation building and Human Resource Development;

(viii) Air freight assistance for export of horticultural products export by air; and

(ix) Generation of relevant research and development through research institutions.

Thus, export incentives in the form of tax-concessions or fiscal incentives, as well as financial incentives, play a major role in rendering Indian exports, competitive in the international market. However, in view of the highly competitive nature of international market, every country in the world makes an all out effort to increase her exports, for which various types of different fiscal and financial incentives are provided. Thus, the practice of incentives has almost become universal, covering both developed as well as developing countries.

Q11. Describe the measures taken by the Government of India for strengthening the export marketing effort.

Ans. Production can be converted into 'sale' only through the marketing effort. In other words, "marketing effort" provides the necessary link or channel between production and sales. Hence, success on the export front is dependent upon the marketing effort. Export promotion policy in India therefore, pays special attention to the need for improving and strengthening export marketing effort.

With this objective, the Government of India has established a very comprehensive network of institutions for servicing the export sector. In other words, an effort has been made to provide the necessary infrastructure for servicing the export sector, particularly to improve the export marketing effort. With this object in view, Government of India has established a number of specialised institutions for providing necessary services and assistance to individual corporate units from the export sector. Institutions established for strengthening export marketing effort include Export Promotion Council, Commodity Boards, Special Authorities and Industry Associations. These are the key institutions servicing export effort at individual corporate level product wise.

The primary function of these institutions is to provide the exporter with export marketing guidance and advice as well as complete information and details covering almost all the critical elements involved in export marketing effort at the individual corporate unit level on a continuous basis.

In addition, separate institutions have also been established for providing technical and specialised services to the export-sector in India. These institutions provide necessary guidance, help and assistance to individual corporate units, especially in the field of packaging, quality control, risk coverage, long-term credit, trade fairs and exhibitions, settlement of disputes, package service and market information. For supplementing the export-effort by the private sector, Government of India has also established a number of Corporations in the Government sector for directly undertaking export-import activity.

Various State Governments have also established Export Corporations-for promoting exports from different states respectively.

- **Market Development Assistance:** This assistance is provided for overall development of overseas markets. It is provided for sponsoring, inviting trade delegations within and outside the country, market studies, publicity, setting up of warehouses/showrooms, research and development, quality control, etc. It is largely available to Approved Organisations, Export Houses/Consortia of Small Scale Industries, Individual exporters or other sponsored persons. The assistance is given for air fare, daily allowance, participation in fairs and exhibitions, etc. The assistance is disbursed by the FIEO and Ministry of Commerce.

- **External Marketing Assistance Scheme for Jute:** The External Marketing Scheme provides grant of market assistance at the rate of 5 per cent and 10 per cent of FOB value on export of specified diversified products. The benefit is available to both manufacturer-exporters and merchant exporters.

Q12. What do you mean by Duty Drawback Scheme? Discuss the types of drawback rates.

Or

Explain the procedures and related documentation required for fixation of brand-rate for duty drawback.

[June-2013, Q.No.-6(a)]

Or

Write a short note on duty drawback scheme.

[June-2014, Q.No.-7(d)]

Or

Explain the procedure for fixation of brand rate for duty drawback. **[Dec-2014, Q.No.-6(a)]**

Ans. Duty Drawback Scheme is meant for the relief of Customs and Central Excise Duties on the inputs used in the manufacture of export product. The admissible duty drawback amount is paid to exporters by depositing it into their nominated bank account. Section 75 of the Customs Act, 1962 and Section 37 of the Central Excise Act, 1944, empower the Central Government to grant such duty drawback. Customs and Central Excise Duties Drawback Rules, 1995 have been framed outlining the procedure to be followed for the purpose of grant of duty drawback (for both kinds of duties suffered) by the Customs Authorities processing export documentation.

Drawback Rates: There are two types of drawback rates. These are:

(1) **All Industry Rate:** It refers to an average rate based on the average quantity and value of inputs and duties (both Excise and Customs) borne by them and Service Tax suffered by a particular export product. The All Industry Rates are notified by the Government in the form of a Drawback Schedule every year and the present Schedule covers 2837 entries. The legal framework in this regard is provided under Sections 75 and 76 of the Customs Act, 1962 and the Customs and Central Excise Duties and Service Tax Drawback Rules, 1995.

(2) **Brand Rates or Special Brand Rates**: The Brand Rates of Duty Drawback are fixed on the individual request of an exporter/manufacturer. It is allowed in cases where the export product does not have any AIR of Duty Drawback or the same neutralises less than 4/5th of the duties paid on materials used in the manufacture of export goods. This work is handled by the jurisdictional Commissioners of Customs and Central Excise. Exporters who wish to avail of the Brand Rate of Duty Drawback need to apply for fixation of the rate for their export goods to the jurisdictional Central Excise Commissionerate. The Brand Rate of Duty Drawback is granted in terms of Rules 6 and 7 of the Drawback Rules, 1995.

The rates at which the incentive of duty drawback will be granted to individual exporter have been specified product-wise in the drawback schedule specified under the drawback rules. Sometimes the amount or rate of drawback are not determined in respect of export goods. In such cases, the manufacturer or exporter of such goods may apply in the prescribed form "Application for Fixation of Drawbacks Rates". The application should be submitted to the Department of Revenue, Ministry of Finance or with the Customs House/Central Excise Collector ate in whose jurisdiction their manufacturing unit is located. The application must be submitted within 60 days from the date of export.

The documents prescribed for such application are as follows:

(1) Application for Fixation of Drawback Rates;

(2) DBK Statement I;

(3)   DBK Statement II;

(4)   DBK Statement III; and

(5)   Relevant facts including the proportion in which the material or components are used in the production or manufacture of goods and duties paid on such material or components.

A copy of such application should be sent directly to the Director (Drawback), Ministry of Finance, New Delhi. On receipt of the application, the customs/central excise officer will verify the application and forward to the Director (Drawback), Ministry of Finance, Government of India, New Delhi for fixation of Brand Rate. If satisfied, he will determine the amount or rate of drawback in respect of such goods. The Government has also provided simplified procedure of brand rate fixation without insisting on pre-verification of data by the Drawback Department.

Q13. Explain the procedure for claiming duty drawback. Which documents are required for claiming drawback?

Or

Write a short note on formalities for claiming Duty drawback.   **[Dec-2012, Q.No.-7(a)]**

Or

Explain the procedures and related documentation required for making a claim for duty drawback.
[June-2013, Q.No.-6(b)]

Or

Explain the procedure for making a claim of duty drawback on export.   **[Dec-2014, Q.No.-6(b)]**

Or

What is Duty Drawback Credit Scheme? Explain briefly.

Or

Write a short note on procedure for exports by post.
[Dec-2014, Q.No.-7(d)]

Ans. Exporters have to make sure that no separate claim is being made for rebate of central excise duties under the Central Excise Rules. The Shipping Bills and other documents are scrutinised and examined by the concerned Customs Officer. Duplicate and Triplicate copies of the Shipping Bills with suitable examination order are returned to the exporters for presenting them to the Docks Appraising Officer. The Custom Officer gives examination report on both the copies of shipping bills and returns duplicate and triplicate copies to the exporters and original copy is retained.

Exporters present duplicate and triplicate copy of shipping bills duly examined by the customs office to the Docks Appraising Officer alongwith the export goods. If the officer finds it in order, he endorses 'Let Export' order on both copies of the Shipping Bills.

Triplicate copy of the Shipping Bill is deemed to be a claim for the drawback. If claims are found admissible and in order, are sanctioned. The amount is credited in the ledger account of the exporter maintained in the Drawback section.

Documents

The claim for duty drawback is filed alongwith the following documents:

(1) Copy of export contract or letter of credit, as the case may be;

(2) Copy of packing list;

(3) Copy of AR4 form, wherever applicable;

(4) Insurance certificate whenever necessary;

(5) Copy of communication regarding rate of drawback (if applicable);

(6) Copy of Test Report (if required);

(7) Declarations (if required);

(8) Declaration regarding not availing MODVAT;

(9) Certificate from the Jurisdictional Excise Superintendent (if applicable); and

(10) Any other documents.

Where an exporter desires that he may be granted the incentives of drawback provisionally, he may, after making the application, apply in writing to the Drawback Directorate. He may request that a provisional amount be granted to him towards on export of such goods, pending determination of the amount or rate of drawback. However, for making provisional claims of duty drawback, an exporter may be required to execute a general bond for the amount of drawback claim, with the Collector of Customs at the port from which, the said goods are exported.

Duty Drawback Credit Scheme

As an export promotional measure, the Government of India have authorised the Reserve Bank of India to instruct the commercial banks (Authorised Dealers in Foreign Exchange) to grant interest-free credit to the exporters. The credit is given against their duty drawback entitlements pending scrutiny, sanction and payment by the Custom House. Such interest-free credit is being made available to exporters in India for a period of 90 days. However, the scheme is applicable only for export of such products for which drawback rates have already been determined either on all industry rate basis or on brand-rate basis.

Drawback on Export by Post

Where goods are to be exported by post under a claim of drawback, the outer surface of the packing must be marked as 'DRAWBACK- EXPORT'.

In such cases, the exporters will submit to the postal authorities a 'Drawback Claim Form' instead of a shipping bill giving details regarding drawback schedule number, product description, drawback rate and amount.

Q14. What is the importance of refund of central excise in promoting export? List the documents required for refund of central excise.

Ans. It is essential for refunding of central excise, as exports should not bear the burden of indirect taxes. For the export promotion, refund of central excise is an important fiscal incentive. Hence, exportable goods are either exempted from such taxes or these taxes are refunded, if exemption is not possible. In India, excisable goods are free from the incidence of excise duty levied by the Central Government, both on finished product and raw materials. The scheme is governed by the section-37 of the Central Excise and Salt Act, 1944 as amended from time to time. Manufacturers of export products are required to register their factories with the local Central Excise Authorities, by opening Personal Ledger Account (PLA). In PLA, the credit balance of the deposit account opened by individual manufacturers with the Central Excise Authority is shown. At the time of removal of a consignment, the amount of duty actually levied on the consignment is shown as debit entry. After the proof of exportation, the equivalent amount is again entered on the credit side. PLA is not needed in case of exporters under bond because the duty has not been actually paid.

Documents required for refund of central excise

The major excise documents are as follows:

(1) ***Invoices***: Invoices are prepared in four copies. The original copy is for the buyer, duplicate for the transporter, triplicate for the Central Excise Officer and fourth copy for manufacturer's record.

(2) ***AR4/AR5 Forms:*** These are prepared in sixtuplicate. Both AR4/AR5 forms can be used for export in Bond or under Rebate of Central Excise duty. AR4 form is to be used where either finished stage duty is not paid or its rebate is to be claimed later on. It can be elaborated as under:

(a) Form AR4 is to be used in case of exports in Bond, of all goods without payment of duty on finished item (not on inputs).

(b) AR4 Form is also used where finished stage duty is paid and a rebate thereof is to be claimed after export.

Form AR5 is used where goods are manufactured/ exported without the payment of duty or inputs (input stage duty). It can be elaborated as under:

(a) AR5 form is used where no duty is paid on production inputs and the finished stage duty is also not paid on account of their export being made in bond.

(b) AR5 form is also used where inputs stage duty is not paid but duty on finished goods is paid and the rebate thereof is to be claimed after export.

(3) **Form C:** It is an application for refund of excise duty. It contains details like AR4 Form No. and date of Shipping bill, name and address of the factory and its licence number, tariff classification of the goods exported and shipment details.

Note: ARE-1 is introduced in place of earlier AR-4 and AR-5 forms.

Q15. Discuss the formalities prescribed under Central Excise Rules for:

(a) Export Under Claim of Rebate Under Rule 12 (i) (a)

Ans. Under the Central Excise Rule 12(i) (a), rebate of duty paid on export of duty paid goods shall be granted. The rule permits to grant rebate on all excisable goods except mineral oil and goods supplied as ship stores. The facility is available on export of goods to all countries other than Nepal and Bhutan. The procedure can be discussed as follows:

Removal of Goods without Examination: Exporters are allowed to remove the goods for export without getting the goods examined by the Central Excise Officers. AR4 Form is prepared in sixtuplicate. The exporter retains the original and duplicate copies of AR4 Form for presenting alongwith the consignment to the customs officer. The exporter delivers triplicate, quadruplicate, quintuplicate and sixtuplicate copies to Superintendents of Central Excise having jurisdiction over the factory or the warehouse. These forms should be delivered within 24 hours of the removal of the consignment.

The jurisdictional superintendent shall examine the information and variety the facts of payment of duty. If he is satisfied with the information, he will sign and put stamp on AR4 Form. He sends the triplicate copy to the rebate sanctioning authority, quadruplicate to the chief accounts officer in the collectorate headquarters, the quintuplicate to the office copy, retained by the central excise officer and sixtuplicate to the exporter.

Exporter under Central Excise Seal (After Examination): Exporters are allowed to remove the goods for export in a seal. The sealing of goods is done by the Central Excise Officers. The sealed exportable goods are not examined by the customs officers at port. For this purpose, exporters are required to submit six copies of AR4 form to the superintendent of central excise having jurisdiction over the factory or warehouse. These forms should be submitted at least 24 hours before the removal of the exportable goods. The Superintendent of Central Excise or his inspector may go for sealing of goods. He examines the goods, relevant information and verifies the factors of payment of duty. He may also draw samples, if necessary, in triplicate. Two sets of the sealed samples are handed over to the exporters for delivering to the customs officer at the port. The officer retains third set for his record.

If the officer is satisfied with the details of exportable goods, he would sign on all six copies of AR4 form and allow the clearance of goods. He returns original, duplicate and sixtuplicate copies to the exporter for presenting to the customs officer at the port. The officer sends triplicate copy to the rebate sanctioning authority, quadruplicate to the chief accounts officer at his collectorate headquarters and retains the quintuplicate copy for records. The exporter shall use the sixtuplicate copy for the purposes of claiming drawback.

Submission of Forms at the Customs Office: The exporters present the original, duplicate and sixtuplicate copies of AR4 form to the customs officer at the port alongwith the consignment. The custom officer examines and verifies the goods and other relevant facts. In case of export under seal, he ensures that it is not broken. If he is satisfied, he allows the export of the goods.

The custom officer makes endorsement on the original, duplicate and sixtuplicate copies of AR4 form. He returns original and sixtuplicate copies to the exporter, and sends duplicate copy to the rebate sanctioning authority.

Filing Claim for Rebate: Exporters have been granted option of claiming rebate either from Maritime Collector or Jurisdictional Assistant Collector of Central Excise. The exporters are required to file the claim within six months from the date of export. The claim should be filed in the prescribed form alongwith original copy of the AR4 form duly endorsed by the customs officer certifying the exporter of the goods. Maritime Collector of Central Excise or Jurisdictional Assistant Collector will compare the original AR4 form with the triplicate copy of the form received from the Superintendent, Central Excise. If he is satisfied, he shall sanction the rebate either in whole or in part as the case may be.

Documents: Following documents are required to be filed for claiming rebate:

    (1)   Application in prescribed form;

    (2)   Original copy of AR4 form;

    (3)   Duplicate copy of AR4 form in sealed cover received from Customs Officer, if required;

    (4)   Duly attested copy of Bill Lading;

    (5)   Duly attested copy of Shipping Bill (Export Promotion Copy); and

    (6)   Disclaimer Certificate in case claimant is other than Exporter.

(b) Export Under Claim for Rebate of Duty on Excisable Materials used in the Manufacture of Export Goods (Rule 12 (1) (b))

Ans. Under Central Excise Rule 12(1)(b), rebate has been granted on the duty paid on raw materials/inputs used in the manufacture of the finished goods exported from India except to Nepal or Bhutan. Rebate may be granted on any excisable materials used in the manufacture and packing of the goods exported. The rebate of input stage may be claimed on the export of all finished goods whether excisable or not. In order to claim this rebate on the input stage, the export must be in the name of the exporter. The rebate may be granted on the duty paid on raw materials, consumables, components, semi-finished goods, assemblies, sub-assemblies, intermediate goods, accessories, parts and packing materials required for manufacture of export goods.

    The rebate on input stage cannot be claimed where:

    (1)   the finished goods are exported under claim for Duty Drawback;

    (2)   the finished goods are exported in discharge of export obligation under a Value Based Advance Licence or a Quantity Based Advanced Licence issued before 31 March 1995; and

    (3)   the facility of input stage credit is availed under MODVAT provisions under Chapter VAA of Central Excise Rules, 1944.

    The manufacturers of finished goods are required to file a declaration in quintuplicate to the Collector of Central Excise having jurisdiction over the factory. The declaration shall contain details of finished goods to be exported, the details of materials required and their consumption ratios.

The Collector of Central Excise may nominate suitable officer for verifying the declaration. The officer shall examine and verify the information furnished by the manufacturer. If the officer is satisfied, he may grant permission to the applicant for manufacture and export of finished goods under claim for Rebate of Central Excise duties paid on materials/inputs used in the manufacture of finished goods.

Procedural Formalities: The manufacturers are required to prepare AR5 Form in Sixtuplicate. He shall submit them to the Jurisdictional Superintendent of Central Excise atleast 24 hours before the removal of the goods for export from the factory. Where export goods are dutiable, the manufacturer may avail the facility of export, without payment of Central Excise duty on finished goods under Central Excise Bond [Rule 13(1)(a)]. Finished goods may also be exported after payment of Central Excise duty leviable on finished goods under claim of Rebate [Rule 12(1)(a)].

The exportable goods under AR5 form will be moved directly from the place of manufacture to the place of export. The packages are required to be marked legibly in ink or oil colour in a durable manner with progressive number. The Superintendent of Central Excise shall verify the information contained in AR5 form. The Superintendent of Central Excise shall examine and verify the facts, certificates and declaration made by the manufacturer. If the Superintendent is satisfied, he will allow the clearances for exports by singing and putting stamp on AR5 forms. The Superintendent shall draw samples wherever feasible in triplicate. He would handover two sealed samples to the manufacturer or his authorised agent for delivering to the Customs Officer at the point of export. He would retain the third set for record. The export consignment shall be sealed by the Superintendent of Central Excise before permitting clearances. The Superintendent of Central Excise will handover original, duplicate and sixtuplicate copies of AR5 form to the exporter. Triplicate copy will be sent to the Jurisdictional Assistant Collector of Excise. Quadruplicate copy is to be given to Chief Accounts Officer at the Collectorate headquarter.

The original, duplicate and sixtuplicate copies of the AR5 form shall be presented by the exporter or his agent to the customs officer at the point of export alongwith the goods, shipping bill and sealed samples. The customs officer shall examine them carefully. If he is satisfied, he may clear the goods for shipment. After the shipment of the goods, the customs officer would make endorsements in the original, duplicate and sixtuplicate copies of the AR5 form by putting his signature and stamp. He would give the original and sixtuplicate copies to the exporter. The duplicate copy will be sent to the Assistant Collector of Central Excise. The exporter will use the original copy of AR5 form for claiming rebate from the Jurisdictional Assistant Collector of Central Excise. Sixtuplicate copy will be presented in the customs house for record.

Claiming of Rebate: The application for rebate is made to the Jurisdictional Assistant Collector of Central Excise. Where exports are under claim for rebate under Rule 12(1)(a), the same should be claimed in the combined application for rebate.

Documents: Following documents should be submitted for filling claims:

    (1)   original copy of AR5 form duly endorsed by the customs officer;

    (2)   duly attested copy of Shipping Bill (Export Promotion Copy);

    (3)   duly attested copy of Bill of Lading/Airway Bill;

    (4)   duplicate copy of Central Excise Invoice [where rebate under Rule 12(1)(a) is also being claimed]; and

    (5)   duplicate copy of the AR5 form received from the customs officer in a sealed cover (if obtained).

If the Assistant Collector is satisfied, he will sanction the rebate.

(c)   Exporter of Goods Under Bond Under Rule 13

Ans. The exporters have been permitted to export the excisable goods without the payment of Central Excise duty. Exporters are required to execute a bond with the Central Excise Authority equivalent to the amount of excise duty on the basis of their estimate. All the excisable items and the raw materials required for their production are covered under this scheme.

There are also provisions for export under bond on a regular basis. This is covered under Rule 14. For this purpose, Running Bond Account is maintained. In this case, the amount of bond is determined on the basis of the excise duty involved in export transaction over a period of time, generally regarded as transit period. Exporters are required to maintain a bond account of requisite value with the Central Excise Authority of the region, whenever any block transfer are made in favour of other central excise authority, debit shall be made in the account. Suitable debit shall also be made whenever exports are allowed against the bond.

On acceptance of the proof of export, the bond account shall be credited to the extent the debit was made while permitting the exports. The running bond account shall be credited after the block transfer is returned by the other authority.

There are six types of bonds. These are:

- B1 (Surety)
- B1 (Security)
- B1 (General Surety)
- B1 (General Security)
- B16 (General Surety)
- B16 (General Security)

B1 (Surety) and B1 (Security) bonds are to be executed for an individual excisable consignment. The exporters can execute a consolidated B1 general bond to cover a series of export from his factory or B16 bonds with the prescribed excise authority. Manufacturer exporters who have executed B16 bonds are not required to execute separate bond to cover duty on goods exported without payment of duty.

Manufacturer-exporters other than those registered with EPCs and Central Excise, Export Houses, etc. are required to execute B-1/B16 bond with 100 per cent security/bank guarantee. Merchant exporters other than registered exporters shall execute B1 bond with 25 per cent security/bank guarantee.

Procedure: Packages in which goods to be exported are packed, shall be legibly marked in ink or oil colour or in such other durable manner as the Commissioner of Central Excise may allow. Exporters shall prepare Invoices, AR4/AR5 forms and execute the relevant bond for this purpose.

Removal of Goods without the Examination of Central Excise Authority: Exporters are allowed to remove the goods without the examination of Central Excise Authority. Exporters shall prepare AR4/AR5 Forms in sixtuplicate. They will deliver triplicate, quadruplicate, quintuplicate and sixtuplicate copies of AR4/AR5 forms to the Jurisdictional Superintendent of Central Excise. The forms should be submitted within 24 hours of the removal of goods. The exporters shall retain the original and duplicate copies for presenting to the customs officer at the point of export alongwith the consignment. The Jurisdictional Superintendent of Central Excise shall examine the consignment and relevant information. If he is satisfied, he would allow the clearance of goods. He would send the triplicate copy of the authority before whom the bond is executed. He would send quadruplicate copy to the Chief Accounts Officer and retain the quintuplicate copy for his record. Sixtuplicate copy will be returned to the exporter.

Removal of Goods after the Examination of Central Excise Authority: In this case, the exporter shall submit AR4/AR5 forms in sixtuplicate to the Jurisdictional Superintendent of Central Excise. Exporters are required to submit the application forms 24 hours before the removal of goods. The Excise Authority shall examine the goods and relevant information. He may draw the samples in triplicate wherever necessary. Two sets of sealed sample will be returned to the exporter for delivering to the customs officer at the point of export. The third set will be retained for his record. If the Excise Officer is satisfied, he would allow the clearance of goods. He shall return original and duplicate copies of AR4/AR5 forms to the exporter for presenting to the Customs Officer at the point of export. The sixtuplicate copy shall be given to the exporter in a sealed cover for handling over to the Customs Officer. The triplicate copy shall be sent to the authority with whom the exporters have signed the bond. Quadruplicate copy will be sent to the Chief Accounts Officer at the headquarter. Quintuplicate copy shall be retained for records.

The exporters shall present original, duplicate and sixtuplicate copies of AR4/AR5 forms to the customs authority at the point of export alongwith the consignment. The customs officer will check the consignment and verify the relevant information. If he is satisfied, he would clear the goods for shipment. After the shipment of the goods, the customs officer would make endorsements on original, duplicate and sixtuplicate copies of AR4/AR5 forms. He would return original and sixtuplicate copies to exporters. The duplicate copy will be sent to the authority before whom the bond was executed.

Documents: Following documents shall be filed by the exporter as a proof of export of goods:

    (1)   Original copy of AR4/AR5 forms;

    (2)   Duplicate copy of AR4/AR5 forms in a sealed cover received from Customs Officer;

    (3)   Duly attested copy of Bill of Lading; and

    (4)   Duly attested copy of Shipping Bill (Export Promotion Copy).

Q16. Describe various facilities of Duty Exemption Scheme.

Ans. Registered exporters are eligible for the facility of duty free import of raw materials, components, packing materials, etc. required for manufacture of the product for executing export orders. Duty Exemption Scheme consists of Duty Free Licence and Duty Entitlement Pass Book. These are discussed as follows:

(1) Duty Free Licence

Import of raw materials, intermediaries, components, consumables, parts, accessories and packing materials may be permitted against a Duty Free Licence. It includes advance licence, advance intermediate licence and special imprest licence, which are as follows:

    (a) Advance Licence: An advance licence is granted to a merchant exporter or manufacturer exporter for the import of inputs required for the manufacture of goods without payment of basic customs duty. Raw materials, components, intermediates, consumables, parts, spares (not exceeding 5 per cent of the CIF value of the duty free licence), packing materials and computer software may be imported under this scheme. However, such inputs shall be subjected to the payment of additional customs duty equal to the excise duty at the time of import. Exemption from payment of additional customs duty shall be allowed, if the advance licence is issued with actual user condition to the manufacturer exporter or merchant exporter. Advance licences shall be issued in accordance with the policy and procedure in force on the date of issue of licence. It shall be subjected to the fulfilment of a time bound export obligation and value addition as may be specified.

    (b) Advance Intermediate Licence: An advance intermediate licence is granted to a manufacturer exporter for the import of inputs required in the manufacture of goods to be supplied to the ultimate exporter or eligible deemed exporter holding an advance licence/special imprest licence.

    (c) Special Imprest Licence: A special imprest licence is granted to a manufacturer exporter for the import of inputs required in the manufacture of goods to be supplied to the following categories:

        (i)   Supplied to units in Export Processing Zones, Exports Oriented Units, Technology Parks, etc.

        (ii)   Supply of capital goods to holders of licences under zero duty Export Promotion Capital Goods Scheme.

        (iii) Supply made to projects financed by multilateral or bilateral agencies.

    (iv) Can be availed by the subcontractor of the main contractor to the project.

    (v) Supplies made to United Nations Organisation or under the aid programme of the United Nations or multilateral agencies and paid for in foreign exchange.

Other Schemes, besides the above mentioned schemes, are Advance Release Orders and Back to Back Inland Letter of Credit.

    (a) **Advance Release Orders:** A duty free licence holder has the option either to import items allowed under the licence directly or to obtain them from indigenous sources or canalising agencies. This option may be availed against Advance Release Orders denominated in foreign exchange or Indian Rupees. An Advance Release Order may be granted by the Licensing Authority which issued the duty free licence.

    (b) **Back to Back Inland Letter of Credit:** Instead of an Advance Release Order, the exporter may avail the facility of Back to Back Inland Letter of Credit. Such exporter may approach to a bank for opening an Inland of Credit in favour of an indigenous supplier.

Conditions

In order to avail duty exemption licence scheme, the exporters are required to follow the conditions of the export obligations, Input-Output norms, value additions, etc. These are discussed as under:

    (a) **Exporter Obligations:** The export obligations shall be fulfilled within a period of 18 months. In case of supplies under Special Imprest Licence to the projects, the export obligation must be fulfilled during the contracted duration of execution of the project. The period shall commence from the date of issuance of the licence.

    (b) **Input-Output Norms:** The standard input-output norms for the imports and exports for the grant of a duty free licence shall be in accordance with the norms published by the Director General of Foreign Trade. In respect of goods for which such standard input-output norms have not been published, the norms will be as specified by the competent authority.

    (c) **Value Addition:** Unless otherwise specified the duty free licence shall be subject to the achievement of a minimum value addition of 33 per cent.

    (d) **Third Party Exports:** The advance licence holder may export directly or through their party. In this case, shipping bills relating to the export shall show the names of both the licence holder and the third party.

Procedure to obtain Licence

Any merchant exporter or manufacturer exporter who holds an Import-Export Code No., Registration-cum-Membership Certificate, a specific order or letter of credit or project authority, may apply for duty free licence. In case of exporters working under production programme and exports to warehouse by FIEO in Dubai made by Export Houses or Public Sector Undertaking on consignment basis, application may be filed without export order or letter of credit. An application for a duty free licence may be made in duplicate to the concerned Licensing Authority having jurisdiction under the Duty Exemption Scheme. The Licensing Authorities are Regional Licensing Authority, Advance Licensing Committee and Zonal Advance Licensing Committee. The application is sent alongwith the following documents:

    (a)   Profile of Exporter-Importer;
    (b)   Bank receipt or demand draft in duplicate towards the payment of application fee;
    (c)   Export order or Letter of credit, if any;
    (d)   Self certified copy of valid RCMC; and
    (e)   Any other documents if required.

(2) Duty Entitlement Pass Book (DEPB) Scheme

The objective of Duty Entitlement Pass Book Scheme is to neutralise the incidence of Customs duty on the import content of the export product. The neutralisation shall be provided by way of grant of duty credit against the export product.

The DEPB scheme will continue to be operative until it is replaced by a new scheme which will be drawn up in consultation with exporters. Under this scheme, an exporter may apply for credit, as a specified percentage of FOB value of exports, made in freely convertible currency.

The credit shall be available against such export products and at such rates as may be specified by the Director General of Foreign Trade by way of public notice issued in this behalf, for import of raw materials, intermediates, components, parts, packaging material, etc. The holder of DEPB will have the option to pay additional customs duty, if any, in cash as well. The DEPB will be valid for a period of 24 months from the date of issue. The DEPB and the items imported against it are freely transferable. The transfer of DEPB will however be for import at the port specified in the DEPB, which shall be the port from where exports have been made.

Imports from a port other than the port of export shall be allowed under TRA facility as per the terms and conditions of the notification issued by Department of Revenue.

Normally, the exports made under the DEPB Scheme should not be entitled for drawback. However, the additional customs duty or excise duty paid in cash or through debit under DEPB should be adjusted as CENVAT Credit or Duty Drawback as per rules framed by the Department of Revenue.

Q17. Describe the procedure of exemption under income tax and sales tax.

Ans. For the promotion of export, various taxes and duties have been exempted. Not only this even all profits from exports are exempted from income tax. Types of tax exemptions are as follows:

(1) Income Tax Exemption

Under the Income Tax Act, tax incentives are granted in order to promote exports. These major incentives are as follows:

(a)   All export profits derived from export of goods or merchandise outside India, except mineral oil and minerals; and ores and services are exempted from the income-tax. The benefit is also available to supporting manufacturers/processors, selling goods or merchandise to an Export/Trading House for export.

(b)   Tax relief is provided on export of computer software and for import of system.

(c)   A deduction of 50 per cent of the profits from project exports is granted to an Indian company or resident tax payer.

(d)   Five years tax holiday is provided to the units in Free Trade Zones/Exports Processing Zones and 100 per cent Export Oriented Units.

The exporters or manufacturers are required to enclose with their tax return a report in the prescribed form duly signed by a Chartered Accountant.

(2) Sales Tax Exemption

Purchase of goods meant for exports are exempted from sales tax. However, the purchaser of goods has to be a registered dealer for the class of goods meant for exports: He is allowed to furnish a satisfactory proof of export of goods to the seller of goods, along with Form-H. Proof of export can be in the form of export-invoice and Bill of Lading (non-negotiable copy) or Airways Bill or postal receipt, etc.

The seller will then submit the proof of export along with Form-H to the sales tax authorities. The exporter has to fill-in Form-H in triplicate and issue original and duplicate copies to the supplier and retain the triplicate copy for his own record. The supplier submits original of Form-H and proof of export to the Sales Tax Authority.

Thus, for availing the benefit of sales tax exemption, the exporter should first get the items concerned covered under his local sales tax registration certificate and apply for issuance of Form-H.

The exporter should enclose the following documents for issuance of Form-H.

(a)   Copy of shipping bill, duly certified by the customs authority;

(b)   Copy of Invoice duly certified;

(c)   Copy of letter of credit; and

(d)   Copy of confirmed export order.

Question Papers

Export Procedures and Documentation: AED-01
December, 2012

Note: *Attempt any four questions, including question no. 7 which is compulsory.*

Q1. Discuss the formalities prescribed under Central Excise Rules for:

(a) Claiming rebate of central excise rule 12

Ans. Refer to Chapter-4, Q.No.-15 (a) (b)

(b) Export under central excise bond under rule 13

Ans. Refer to Chapter-4, Q.No.-15 (c)

Q2. Explain the rationale for price-support measures for export promotion in India. Also describe the institutions set-up for government policy-making and consultation for export promotion in India.

Ans. Refer to Chapter-4, Q.No.-10 and Q.No.-2

Q3. What are the objectives of customs control? Discuss the responsibilities of the insured in a cargo insurance claims.

Ans. Refer to Chapter-3, Q.No.-19 and Q.No.-15

Q4. What are the advantages of containerisation? Explain various methods to deal with the foreign exchange risks.

Ans. Advantages of Containerisation: Containerisation has following advantages:

- They offer a means of consolidating cartons, boxes, etc. into a manageable unit load.
- Providing due care is taken in loading and unloading a container, the product packaging need not be as robust as would be required for un-containerised transit.
- A container whose capacity is fully utilised provides an economic transport solution.
- Containers offer the opportunity to optimise the capacity of the carrying medium, be it road, rail or ship.
- They are secure and considerably reduce the risk of theft and pilferage of goods.
- They provide an opportunity to offer, through the use of different transport modes, an end-to-end service from supplier to customer.

Now, Refer to Chapter-2, Q.No.-27

Q5. (a) Describe the different kinds of policies and financial guarantees issued by ECGC.

Ans. Refer to Chapter-2, Q.No.-20

(b) Discuss the role of export import Bank of India.

Ans. Refer to Chapter-2, Q.No.-16

Q6. Discuss the provisions of foreign exchange regulations concerning exports under exchange control regulations.

Ans. Refer to Chapter-2, Q.No.-10

Q7. Write short notes on any two of the following:

(a) Formalities for claiming Duty Drawback

Ans. Refer to Chapter-4, Q.No.-13

(b) Export Documents

Ans. Refer to Chapter-1, Q.No.-18

(c) Duties of an exporter under FOB and CIF contracts

Ans. Refer to Chapter-1, Q.No.-12 and Q.No.-13

(d) Consignment wise pre-shipment inspection

Ans. Refer to Chapter-3, Q.No.-7

▲ ▲ ▲

The art of being wise is the art of knowing what to overlook.

Export Procedures and Documentation: AED-01
June, 2013

Note: Answer any four questions, including question no. 7 which is compulsory.

Q1. What are the important items in India's export trade? What are the important destinations for exports from India? What are the changes that have taken place in recent years?

Ans. Refer to Chapter-1, Q.No.-3 and Q.No.-4

Q2. "All parties in documentary credit deal only in documents". Discuss.

Ans. Refer to Chapter-2, Q.No. 6

Q3. Distinguish between 'Received for shipment B/L' and 'On board ship B/L' as also between 'clean B/L and 'claused B/L'.

Ans. Refer to Chapter-1, Q.No.-22

Q4. (a) What are the three stages at which customs' permission for exports is granted?

Ans. Refer to Chapter-3, Q.No.-19

(b) What are the supporting documents to be submitted along with the shipping Bill for getting customs' permission for exports?

Ans. Refer to Chapter-3, Q.No.-19

Q5. Analyse the different price support measures introduced in India for rendering Indian exports more competitive.

Ans. Refer to Chapter-4, Q.No.-10

Q6. Explain the procedures and related documentation required for:

(a) fixation of brand - rate for duty drawback, and

Ans. Refer to Chapter-4, Q.No.-12

(b) making a claim for duty drawback.

Ans. Refer to Chapter-4, Q.No.-13

Q7. Write short notes on any two of the following:

(a) Export - Import Bank of India

Ans. Refer to Chapter-2, Q.No.-16

(b) 'Self certification system of quality control and inspection of export cargo.

Ans. Refer to Chapter-3, Q.No.-7

(c) Export Promotion Councils

Ans. Refer to Chapter-4, Q.No.-3

(d) Central Excise Rules for claiming rebate of central excise under Rule, 12

Ans. Refer to Chapter-4, Q.No.-15 (a) (b)

(e) Packing credit

Ans. Refer to Chapter-2, Q.No.-13

▲ ▲ ▲

> **A teacher who is attempting to teach without inspiring the pupil with a desire to learn, is hammering on a cold iron.**
>
> **-Horace Mann**

Export Procedures and Documentation: AED-01
December, 2013

Q1. Discuss the broad objectives and contents of India's export import policy highlighting some of the recent developments that have taken place in this context.

Ans. Refer to Chapter-1, Q.No.-7 and Q.No.-8

Q2. Discuss the need for documents in international trade. Substantiate your answer with suitable illustrations.

Ans. Refer to Chapter-1, Q.No.-18

Q3. Discuss the mechanism of realising payments under documentary credit. Enumerate the advantages of the system from the view points of both exporter and importer.

Ans. Refer to Chapter-2, Q.No.-4

The advantages of payment using documentary credit to the seller clearly include an assurance of payment irrespective of the solvency of the buyer; an assurance of payment irrespective of any disputes with the buyer concerning the underlying goods (under the principle of autonomy of credit); if the credit is transferable, the seller can use it to finance his own acquisition of goods; and not have to pursue the buyer in a different country, with all the risks and cost that this carriers.

The system has fewer obvious advantages for the buyer. However, without the credit system, the transaction would possible never come about at all, as the seller might not be willing to trade with foreign buyer unless he was assured of payment. Moreover, the doctrine of strict compliance benefits the buyer considerably in that he can insist on a perfect tender of documents if payment is to be made. In the light of a very high percentage non-complaint/defective tenders, the buyer effectively has a right to call off the transaction should the market have moved against it.

Q4. What are the various systems of quality control in our export trade? Discuss.

Ans. Refer to Chapter-3, Q.No.-7

Q5. Explain the salient features of liner and tramp shipping services. What method would you recommend for exports of Air conditioners and why?

Ans. Refer to Chapter-3, Q.No.-3

We would recommend liner shipping for export of air conditioners because it provides regular and scheduled shipping services to carry heterogeneous cargo suiting the marketing requirements of General Cargo. A liner ship is built and run to satisfy the transport demand of a variety of cargo. The designs of the holds and number of decks will be different from those of a tramp shipping services.

Liner shipping connects countries, markets, businesses and people, allowing them to buy and sell goods on a scale not previously possible. Today, the liner shipping industry transports goods representing approximately one-third of the total value of global trade.

Q6. What is the procedure involved in customs clearance of export cargo? Explain its various stages and the related documents.

Ans. Refer to Chapter-3, Q.No.-19

Q7. Write short notes on any two of the following:

(a) Financial Guarantees of ECGC

Ans. Refer to Chapter-2, Q.No.-20

(b) Indian Trade Promotion Organisation

Ans. Refer to Chapter-1, Q.No.-6

(c) Export Houses and Trading Houses

Ans. Refer to Chapter-4, Q.No.-9

(d) Commercial Invoice

Ans. Refer to Chapter-1, Q.No.-20

Export Procedures and Documentation: AED-01
June, 2014

Note: Answer any four questions, including question no. 7 which is compulsory.

Q1. What are the salient features of Indian Export Import policy 1997-2002? Suggest necessary changes in the policy to restore equilibrium in the country balance of payments.

Ans. Refer to Chapter-1, Q.No.-8

Q2. Discuss the role of Export Credit and Guarantee Corporation of India (ECGC) in promoting exports from India. Illustrate your answer with some of the ECGC schemes.

Ans. Refer to Chapter-2, Q.No.-19 and Q.No.-20

Q3. Discuss the significance of quality control and preshipment inspection in exports. What are the different system of preshipment inspection and give a detailed account of procedure involved in any one of them.

Ans. Refer to Chapter-3, Q.No.-7

Q4. What are the various methods permitted under RBI regulations for realising export proceeds? Which in your opinion is safest from exporter view point and why?

Ans. Refer to Chapter-2, Q.No.-14

Q5. Give a detailed description of procedure involved along with related documentation for seeking custom clearance of export cargo.

Ans. Refer to Chapter-3, Q.No.-19

Q6. Write an explanatory note on financing of exports under deferred payment highlighting the role of Export Import Bank of India.

Ans. Refer to Chapter-2, Q.No.-15 and Q.No.-16

Q7. Write short notes on any two of the following:

(a) Procedure for export under claim for excise duty Refund/Rebate.

Ans. Refer to Chapter-4, Q.No.-15 (a) (b)

(b) Post-shipment finance for export

Ans. Refer to Chapter-2, Q.No.14

(c) Procedure for export by air

Ans. Refer to Chapter-3, Q.No.-6

(d) Duty draw back scheme

Ans. Refer to Chapter-4, Q.No.-12

▲ ▲ ▲

Note: Answer any four questions, including question no. 7 which is compulsory.

Q1. **Discuss the broad trends in Indian exports, commodity wise and destination wise, and state the various methods of promoting products abroad.**
Ans. Refer to Chapter-1, Q.No.-3, Q.No.-4 and Q.No.-5

Q2. **What is the role of Export Import Bank in financing exports from India? Explain, and state its service programmes for commercial banks.**
Ans. Refer to Chapter-2, Q.No.-16

Q3. **(a) Distinguish between liner and tramp shipping services.**
Ans. Refer to Chapter-3, Q.No.-3

(b) **Briefly explain the various forms of chartering the shipping services.**
Ans. Refer to Chapter-3, Q.No.-5

Q4. **What do you mean by FOB and CIF contracts? Describe the obligations of exporters under these two contracts.**
Ans. Refer to Chapter-1, Q.No.-11, Q.No.-12 and Q.No.-13

Q5. **Explain the various methods used for dealing with foreign exchange risks.**
Ans. Refer to Chapter-2, Q.No.-27

Q6. **Explain the procedures for:**
(a) **fixation of brand rate for duty drawback.**
Ans. Refer to Chapter-4, Q.No.-12

(b) **making a claim of duty drawback on exports.**
Ans. Refer to Chapter-4, Q.No.-13

Q7. **Write short notes on any two of the following:**
(a) **Parties in Documentary Credits**
Ans. Refer to Chapter-2, Q.No.-2

(b) **Self Certification Schemes for Quality inspection**
Ans. Refer to Chapter-3, Q.No.-7

(c) **Shipping Bill**
Ans. Refer to Chapter-1, Q.No.-26

(d) **Procedure for exports by post**
Ans. Refer to Chapter-4, Q.No.-13

▲ ▲ ▲

Export Procedures and Documentation: AED-01
June, 2015

Q1. **Write a detailed note on Institutional Infrastructure for Promoting exports from India. Give a detailed account of the working of any one organisation.**

Ans. Refer to Chapter-4, Q.No.-1 and Q.No.-3

Q2. **What are the various steps involved in processing of an Export Order? Explain in detail any two steps along with the documentation required.**

Ans. Steps that need to be followed in processing an export order are as follows:

Step 1: Scrutinise the order with reference to the terms and conditions of the contract. The export order must specify the mode of payment in unmistakable terms such as the latter of credit, documents on payment, documents against acceptance. The most important documents required by an importer are:

- Bill of exchange
- Commercial invoice
- On board clean bill of lading
- Marine insurance policy
- Packing list and
- Certificate of origin. These should be given to the negotiating bank.

Step 2: For a manufacturer-exporter, after the export order has been confirmed, a "delivery note" should be sent to the works manager. This note should contain all relevant details pertaining to the specifications/requirements or the importer. Nothing should be left at the discretion of the works/factory manager. A merchant-exporter, who purchases the required goods from the market or gets them produced by other manufacturers, also has to provide the necessary specifications/requirements/instructions to the supplier of the goods to be exported.

Step 3: After the goods have been manufactured/procured, the followings are to be done:

- Clearance from the Central Excise authorities by obtaining the Gate Pass (GP)-1 form if goods are to be removed under claim for rebate of duty, GP-2 form if goods are to be removed under a bond, i.e., as per the terms and conditions of the Collector of Customs; or

- AR-4/AR-4A form if the exporter wishes to avail the services of the Central Excise Officer for the purpose of having a physical verification at the factory and thereafter sealing of packages:
- The concerned export inspection:
- A railway receipt has to be obtained if the goods are dispatched by train to the port of shipment.

Step 4: Once the goods have been dispatched to the port, the works/factory manager is supposed to send a 'dispatch advice' to the firm's export department. Then marine insurance cover is solicited. At this stage, formalities regarding floor price regulations, canalisation, certificate of origin ECGC (Export Credit Gnarantee Commission) cover need to be completed. Thereafter, the export department sends the following documents to its clearing and forwarding agent (henceforth called the agent):

- Commercial invoice
- Original export order
- Original letter of credit
- GR form showing RBI code number of the exporter
- AR-4A/AR-4 form
- Excise gate pass
- Packing and weight lists
- Certificate of inspection
- Declaration form
- Invoice
- Export licence where necessary
- Purchase memo
- Railway receipt

Step 5: After the agent has taken control of the consignment; a shipping bill is prepared by him. Three kinds of shipping bills are to be prepared depending on the category of export goods. These are free, dutiable and drawback shipping bills.

Step 6: Once the shipping bill has been cleared by customs, the agent forwards a copy of the shipping bill to the Shed Superintendent of the concerned Port Trust and thereafter a Dock Challan is made, which is then released to the agent after debiting the exporter's account with the concerned Port Commissioner.

Step 7: A Mate's Receipt is prepared by the ship's export clerk and is given to the agent once port charges have been paid. The agent then forwards the relevant documents to the exporter.

Step 8: After receiving the above documents from the agent, the exporter files a claim with the Maritime Collector of Central Excise for drawback of excise duty. In the meantime, a shipment advice should be sent to the importer. Documents are then presented to the negotiating bank.

Thereafter, the documents are transmitted to the banker of the importer, after which the importer would take custody of the consignment once the goods reach their destination and other relevant formalities are completed at that end.

Q3. What is meant by Packing Credit? What are the conditions of eligibility for availing the facilities? What is the procedure adopted? Has the ECGC any role in such loans?

Ans. Refer to Chapter-2, Q.No.-13

Q4. What are the obligations of export under CIF contract? Are they different from those under FOB contract?

Ans. Refer to Chapter-1, Q.No.-13 and Q.No.-12

Q5. Why are the documents essential in any export transaction? Explain the rationale of any two documents.

Ans. Refer to Chapter-1, Q.No.-18, Q.No.-20 and Q.No.-22

Q6. Discuss the formalities prescribed under Central Excise rules 12 and rule 13.

Ans. Refer to Chapter-4, Q.No.-15

Q7. Write short notes on any two of the following:

(a) EPCG Scheme

Ans. Refer to Chapter-1, Q.No.-8

(b) Export Processing Zones

Ans. An Export Processing Zone (EPZ) is a Customs area where one is allowed to import plant, machinery, equipment and material for the manufacture of export goods under security, without payment of duty. The imported goods are subject to customs control at importation, through the manufacturing process, to the time of sale/export, or duty payment for home consumption.

In other words, Export processing zones (EPZs) are areas within developing countries that offer incentives and a barrier-free environment to promote economic growth by attracting foreign investment for export-oriented production. The number of zones internationally, countries hosting EPZs, and firms operating in them, and the business volume they handle, are all growing rapidly, suggesting their importance. Yet, business research on EPZs is virtually nonexistent, leading to poor understanding of their role in international marketing.

The export processing zones in India came into existence soon after the political independence, when India proclaimed the first Industrial Policy Revolution in the year 1948. It was from then that the actual industrial growth begun in India, which resulted in the constitution of the export processing zones later. Export promotion has always been the chief concern of the government of India and it strictly follows the ISI policy while carrying out all its activities.

Some of the significant features of the Export Processing Zones in India have been enumerated as under:

- The activities that are carried out in the EPZ in India are not liable to be licenced apart from the IT enabled sectors.

- The units set up in the export processing zones in India can select their desired locations by following certain parameters as prescribed by the state governments.
- The export processing zones in India religiously follows the active export-import policy.
- The units in EPZ in India are totally custom bonded.
- The proposals for the units in Export processing zones in India are entitled to follow the automatic route for approval as enforced by the state governments.
- The proposals, which do not fall under the procedure of automatic route system, are governed or approved by the FIPB.
- The activities in EPZ in India belonging to the Domestic Tariff Area sector are converted into Export oriented units to meet the parameters set for the export production by the government.
- 100 per cent FDI is granted to these zones.

(c) Institute Cargo Clause

Ans. Institute cargo clauses are attached to a type of marine insurance that covers cargo in transit. These clauses are to specify what items in the cargo are covered should there be damage or loss to the shipment. Institute cargo clauses can cover everything from the cargo itself to the container that holds it to the mode of transportation used to ship it.

There are three basic sets of institute cargo clauses; A, B, C. Just like we are able to get insurance on smaller, domestic packages; bulk freight is insured too.

These clauses were developed by the International Chamber of Commerce as a means of insurance for cargo while it is being shipped from the original location to its final destination.

Just like auto insurance, the higher premium we pay the more coverage we get. The three clauses are as follows:

- Institute Cargo Clause A is considered the widest insurance coverage.
- Institute Cargo Clause B is considered a more restrictive coverage.
- Institute Cargo Clause C is considered the most restrictive coverage.

Each of the *institute cargo clauses* are reserved for *goods in transit*. The items being shipped are considered *goods in transit* when they have departed the original location and are in transit to the final destination.

When goods are *insured* during transport, whether it be by land, air or sea; it means that if the cargo is damaged or lost during transit it will be refunded or replaced to whichever party held the "technical" ownership.

(d) Clearing and Forwarding Agents

Ans. Refer to Chapter-1, Q.No.-31

Export Procedures and Documentation: AED-01
December, 2015

Note: Answer any four questions, including question no. 7 which is compulsory.

Q1. Why do the companies sell their goods abroad? What are the advantages a firm can derive thereby? Discuss giving suitable illustration in support of your answer.

Q2. What do you understand by exchange control? Explain the broad rationale for these controls.

Q3. Distinguish between:

(a) Insurance Policy and Insurance Contracts

(b) Consular Invoice and Customers Invoice

(c) Received for shipment Bill of Lading and On board shipped bill of lading

Q4. What are the various forms of chartering of shipping services? Explain briefly.

Q5. Describe the various types of perils in cargo against which insurance can be obtained. Enumerate the documents needed for filing a claim under a cargo insurance policy.

Q6. What is a letter of credit? What are the various partie's involved therein? Explain its mechanism as a trade financing tool.

Q7. Write short notes on any two of the following:

(a) ECGC Guarantees

(b) C and F Agent

(c) Procedure for fixation of brand rate under duty drawback scheme

(d) Bill of entry

Note: Answer any four questions, including question no. 7 which is compulsory.

Q1. Describe the institutional framework for export promotion in India.

Ans. Refer to Chapter-4, Q.No.-1 and Q.No.-2

Q2. What is the rationale of Export trade control? Describe the procedure of obtaining an export license.

Ans. Export Trade Control: Exports may be made freely except to the extent they are regulated by the provisions of Import-Export policy, 1997-2002 or any other law for the time being in force. Government continuously make effort to promote exports by providing various assistance and facilities. At the same time, control is exercised on exports of such commodities and services which are vital to the economy. The primary object of the Government is to promote exports to the maximum extent but in such a manner that the economy of the country is not affected by unregulated exports of items essentially needed within the country. Hence, export control is exercised to a very limited extent in respect of minimum number of items.

India's foreign trade (exports and imports) is regulated under the provisions of the Foreign Trade (Development and Regulation Act, 1992 and Foreign Trade (Regulation) Rules, 1993. This act provides for the development and regulation of foreign trade by facilitating imports into, and augmenting exports from India. Besides, exports are also regulated by the following major acts:

(1)   Ancient Monument Preservation Act, 1904

(2)   Indian Coffee Act, 1942

(3)   Tea Act, 1953

(4)   Foreign Exchange Regulation Act, 1973

(5)   Coir Industry Act, 1942

(6)   Dangerous Drugs (Import, Export and Transhipment Rules), 1957

(7)   Arms Act, 1959 and Arms Rules, 1962

(8)   Antiquities and Art Treasures Act, 1972

(9)   Dangerous Drugs Act, 1953

(10) Indian Post Office Act, 1898

(11) Drug and Magic Remedies (Objectionable Advertisements) Act, 1954

(12) Motor vehicle International Circular Rules

(13) Wild Life Protection Act

Gold can be exported with the sanction of Reserve Bank of India. Exports of a. few products are canalised through specified agencies like STC, MMTC, etc. Despite various laws and regulations relating to exports, the restrictions or regulation on exports has been minimum. The new Export-Import Policy, 1997-2002 has further liberalised the list of items under export control. Negative list contains only a few items which are banned or prohibited. Presently there are 10 items in the Negative list. There are 32 items subject to licensing and 6 items are canalised for export. The items in the Negative lists may vary from time to time. Besides, exports of some items are permitted with minimum regulation and without licence.

Procedure to obtain Export Licence: An application for grant of export licence in respect of items mentioned in the EXIM policy may be made in the prescribed form to the Director General of Foreign Trade or its Regional Licensing Authority. The application shall be accompanied by the documents prescribed therein. The Export Licensing committee at the Headquarters may consider such applications on merits for issue of export licences. A special High powered licensing committee shall consider applications for the export of dual purpose chemicals and for special materials, equipments and technologies as specified in the policy.

The procedures for making an application for other items are described below:

(1) An application for export of canalised items may be made to the canalising agency concerned in accordance with the procedure prescribed by such agency.

(2) An application for the export of samples or exhibits in excess of the ceiling may be made to the Director General of Foreign Trade.

(3) An application for export of items included in the Negative List of exports (excluding Prohibited items) for projects abroad undertaken by an Indian contractor or subcontractor or consultancy organisation may be made to the Director General of Foreign Trade. The application is accompanied by a copy of the project approval by the concerned, authority. The project approval provides the details of quantities, specifications and value of the individual items required to be exported.

(4) The application for export of gifts, indigenous or imported spares and replacement goods in excess of the ceiling or period prescribed may be made to the Director General of Foreign Trade.

Applications for export licences are to be made on prescribed forms. There is no application fee on export licences/permits. An export licence shall ordinarily be issued with a validity period of 12 months or such shorter period as the licensing authority may specify. The licence may be revalidated on merits for such period as the licensing authority may deem fit.

Other Provisions: Importer-Exporter Code Number: No export or import shall be made by any person without an Importer-Exporter Code (IEC) number unless specifically exempted. An application for grant of IEC number shall be made by the Registered/Head office of the applicant to the concerned Licensing Authority. The Licensing Authority shall issue an IEC number in the prescribed format.

RBI Code Number: This code number is a requirement under the Foreign Exchange Regulation Act (FERA). For obtaining the code number, the firm has to apply to the Divisional Office of the Reserve Bank having jurisdiction over the area where the firm is located. There is a prescribed form of application for this purpose which is to be submitted in duplicate along with the report from the bank where the firm has opened a current account. The firm is also required to furnish the permanent income-tax account number. If the application is in order, the Reserve Bank will allot the RBI Code Number. This Code Number is permanent and there is no need to renew it.

Registration-cum-Membership Certificate: Any person, applying for a licence to import or export or for any other benefit or concession under this policy shall be required to furnish Registration-cum-Membership Certificate (RCMC). RCMC may be obtained from any one of the Export promotion Councils/Commodity Boards/Special Agencies relating to his main line of business.

Compliance with Laws: Every exporter or importer shall comply with the provisions of the Foreign Trade (Development and Regulation) Act, 1992. They will comply with the provisions of this act and the terms and conditions of any licence granted to them, as well as provisions of any other law for the time being in force.

Q3. Describe the major documents needed by the importing country. Explain their relevance in Import Trade.

Ans. Refer to Chapter-1, Q.No.-26

Q4. What is post shipment finance? Explain various methods of post shipment finance.

Ans. Refer to Chapter-2, Q.No.-14

Q5. Distinguish between:

(a) Deemed exports and actual exports

Ans. The term 'export authorizations' refers to export licences or permits that may have been granted or confirmed by the exporting state, regardless of whether shipment or delivery of the arms have taken place. The term was introduced in recognition of the fact that the authorization to export arms or items may be granted well in advance of delivery and the fact the sometimes authorizations are not used in full especially, for instance, if they involve multiple deliveries of arms or items over a number of years. A similar phrase appears in other provisions of the treaty, including Article 8(3), according to which an importing state party may request information concerning a 'pending or actual export authorization'. The term 'export authorizations' refers to actual export authorizations, not pending ones.

The term 'actual exports' refers to exports of defence equipment that have been authorized by the exporting state and have in fact been physically shipped or delivered to the importing state or end user.

Deemed Exports: It refers to those transactions in which the goods supplied do not leave the country and the payment for such goods are made in India. The supply of goods shall be regarded as deemed exports provided the goods are manufactured in India. The categories of supply include: Supply of goods against duty free licences issued under the Duty Exemption scheme, supply of goods to Export Oriented units, Export processing zones, Software Technology Parks, Electronic Hardware Technology parks, etc. Supply of capital goods to holders of licences under the Export Promotion Capital Goods Scheme (subject to eligible benefits), Supply of goods to projects financed by multilateral or bilateral agencies/funds as notified by the Ministry of Finance. Supply of goods to any project or purpose in respect of which the Ministry of Finance permits the import of such goods at zero customs duty. Supply of goods to power, oil and gas sectors in case of notification duty approved by Ministry of Finance.

Deemed exports shall be eligible for the following benefits in respect of manufacture and supply of goods qualifying as deemed exports.

(i) Advance Intermediate Licence

(ii) Deemed Exports Drawback Scheme

(iii) Refund of Terminal Excise Duty, and

(iv) Special Import Licence at the rate of 6% of the FOR value (excluding all taxes and levies).

(b) Financial and fiscal incentives

Ans. Refer to Chapter-4, Q.No.-10

Q6. Explain the procedure and related documentation for obtaining Advance license under Duty Exemption scheme.

Ans. Refer to Chapter-4, Q.No.-16

Q7. Write short notes on any two of the following:

(a) INCOTERMS

Ans. Refer to Chapter-1, Q.No.-11

(b) Self Certification Scheme

Ans. Refer to Chapter-3, Q.No.-7

(c) Containerisation

Ans. Containerisation is a system of satandardised transport, that uses a common size of steel container to transport goods. These containers can easily be transferred between different models of transport – container ships to Lorries and trains. This makes transport and trade of goods cheaper and more efficient.

In international trade, containerisation has become a predominant form of unitised transport. I: enables the transportation of cargo from the warehouse of the exporter to that of the importers directly.

Now, Refer to December-12, Q.No.-4

(d) Shipping Bill

Ans. Refer to Chapter-1, Q.No.-26

▲ ▲ ▲

Export Procedures and Documentation: AED-01
December, 2016

Note: Answer any four questions, including question no. 7 which is compulsory.

Q1. What are the specific advantages from exports to (a) the exporting country and (b) the individual exporter? Explain clearly.

Q2. Discuss the mechanism of realising payments under letter of credit arrangements. Enumerate its advantages from the point of view of both exporter and importer.

Q3. Discuss the duties of an exporter under FOB and CIF Contract. Which Term of Contract is beneficial for exporter?

Q4. What is the need for documents under export import business? Enumerate the various documents which an exporter has to submit to various organizations. Explain briefly the relevance of these documents.

Q5. Why is Cargo Insurance needed? Describe the various types of perils against which insurance cover can be obtained and also state the different covers under insurance policy.

Q6. Describe the procedure and related documentation involved in claiming:

(a) duty drawback on exports.

(b) rebate of central excise under rules 12 and 13.

OR

(c) customs clearance of export cargo.

Q7. Write short notes on any two of the following:

(a) Indian Trade Promotion Organisation

(b) Export Houses and Trading Houses

(c) Various forms of chartering of shipping services

(d) Uniform Customs and Practices under Documentary Credit (UCPDC)

▲ ▲ ▲

Export Procedures and Documentation: AED-01
June, 2017

Q1. Explain the provisions regarding exports under the Foreign Trade Policy of Government of India.

Q2. What do you mean by export sales contract? Describe the general conditions in export sales contract with suitable examples.

Q3. (a) Describe the basic principles of ECGC operation.
(b) Discuss the procedure for making a claim from ECGC along with the documentation formalities.

Q4. State the various methods of receiving payments from the buyers. What are the various steps involved in realising payments under the letter of credit arrangement? Discuss with suitable examples.

Q5. Distinguish between pre-shipment finance and post-shipment finance. Discuss the various pre-shipment finance available to Indian exporters.

Q6. Explain the various forms of chartering of the shipping services.

Q7. (a) Describe the responsibilities of the insured under the cargo insurance.
(b) Discuss the procedure for filing claims under cargo insurance along with the documentation formalities.

Q8. Write short notes on any two of the following:
(a) Deemed exports
(b) Arbitration
(c) India Trade Promotion Organisation
(d) Strengthening export marketing effort

Export Procedures and Documentation: AED-01
December, 2017

Note: *Answer any four questions, including question no. 7 which is compulsory.*

Q1. **Why is international trade important for a country? Discuss with examples and state the sources of information for international trade.**
Ans. Refer to Chapter-1, Q.No.-1 and Q.No.-6
Q2. **Distinguish between:**
(a) **Domestic sales contract and export sales contract**
Ans. Refer to Chapter-1, Q.No.-10
(b) **Documents against Payment and Documents against Acceptance**
Ans. Refer to Chapter-2, Q.No.-1
Q3. **Describe the foreign exchange regulation concerning exports under the exchange control regulation.**
Ans. Refer to Chapter-2, Q.No.-10
Q4. **Distinguish between spot rate and forward rate. Discuss the methods of dealing with foreign exchange risks.**
Ans. Refer to Chapter-2, Q.No.-24 and Q.No.-27
Q5. **Explain various kinds of perils with suitable examples under the cargo insurance.**
Ans. Refer to Chapter-3, Q.No.-12
Q6. **Explain the procedure of customs clearance formalities, along with the documentation required at each step.**
Ans. Refer to Chapter-3, Q.No.-19
Q7. **What is duty drawback scheme? Explain the procedure for claiming duty drawback along with the documentation requirements and formalities.**
Ans. Refer to Chapter-4, Q.No.-12 and Q.No.-13
Q8. **Write short notes on any two:**
(a) **Promoting Products abroad**
Ans. Refer to Chapter-1, Q.No.-5
(b) **Legal Documents in Importing Countries**
Ans. Refer to Chapter-1, Q.No.-26
(c) **Tramp shipping services**
Ans. Refer to Chapter-3, Q.No.-3
(d) **Open cover**
Ans. Refer to Chapter-3, Q.No.-11

▲ ▲ ▲

Export Procedures and Documentation: AED-01
June, 2018

Note: Answer any four questions, including question no. 7 which is compulsory.

Q1. **Discuss the general provisions relating to imports.**
Ans. Refer to Chapter-1, Q.No.-9 (Pg. No.-15)

Q2. **(a) Distinguish between liner and tramp shipping services.**
Ans. Refer to Chapter-3, Q.No.-3 (Pg. No.-111)

(b) **Distinguish between financial and fiscal incentives.**
Ans. Refer to Chapter-4, Q.No.-10 (Pg. No.-155)

Q3. **Describe the different kinds of policies and financial guarantees issued by ECGC.**
Ans. Refer to Chapter-2, Q.No.-20 (Pg. No.-91)

Q4. **Discuss the methods of dealing with foreign exchange risks.**
Ans. Refer to Chapter-2, Q.No.-27 (Pg. No.-101)

Q5. **What are different kinds of losses related to cargo insurance? How these losses can be covered by the cargo insurance policy?**
Ans. Refer to Chapter-3, Q.No.-14 (Pg. No.-128)

Q6. **Explain the procedure and related documentation required for:**

(a) **Fixation of brand rate for duty drawback**
Ans. Refer to Chapter-4, Q.No.-12 (Pg. No.-158)

(b) **Making a claim for duty drawback**
Ans. Refer to Chapter-4, Q.No.-13 (Pg. No.-160)

Q7. **Write short notes on any two of the following:**

(a) **Duty Entitlement Pass Book**
Ans. Refer to Chapter-4, Q.No.-16(2) (Pg. No.-170)

(b) **Role of clearing and forwarding agent**
Ans. Refer to Chapter-3, Q.No.-10 (Pg. No.-121)

(c) **Self certification system of quality control and inspection of export cargo**
Ans. Refer to Chapter-3, Q.No.-7 (Pg. No.-118)

Export Procedures and Documentation: AED-01
December, 2018

Note: Answer any four questions, including question no. 7 which is compulsory.

Q1. Describe the general provisions related to exports under the Foreign Trade Policy of Government of India.

Q2. State the steps involved in the processing of an export order. Discuss any four steps in detail.

Q3. Explain the foreign exchange regulations concerning exports under the Exchange Control Regulations.

Q4. Describe the methods of quality control and pre-shipment inspection of the export cargo.

Q5. "Insurance contract is in the nature of indemnity." Discuss and explain various kinds of perils under cargo insurance, with suitable examples.

Q6. Distinguish between:

(a) Domestic sales contract and export sales contract

(b) Spot rate and forward rate of exchange rate

Q7. Write short notes on any two of the following:

(a) Sources of information for foreign trade

(b) Methods of dispute settlement

(c) India Trade Promotion Organisation

(d) General conditions in export contracts

Export Procedures and Documentation: AED-01
June, 2019

Note: Answer any four questions, including question no. 7 which is compulsory.

Q1. You are a manager in an export firm and planning to export engineering goods to USA. State the documents required under CIF contract. Explain them briefly.

Q2. What is letter of credit? Explain the mechanism of realising payment under the letter of credit arrangements.

Q3. What do you mean by Post-Shipment finance? Explain various types of Post-Shipment finance available to Indian exporters.

Q4. Explain the types of standard policy issued by ECGC along with the areas of risks covered as well as risks not covered.

Q5. (a) Describe the features of Liner Shipping Services.

(b) Discuss the role of Clearing and Forwarding Agents.

Q6. What do you mean by duty drawback? Explain the procedures for claiming duty drawback along with the documentation formalities.

Q7. Write short notes on any two of the following:

(a) Methods of promoting products abroad

(b) Standardised Pre-Shipment export documents

(c) Export Promotion Councils

(d) Air freighting

Export Procedures and Documentation: AED-01
December, 2019

Q1. A Letter of Credit reconciles the conflicting interests of buyer and seller in an export contract. Explain the mechanism of Letter of Credit.

Ans. Refer to Chapter-2, Q.No.-4 (Pg. No.-66)

Where an exporter is unable to procure order with advance payment, the next best alternative is the documentary credit method. In this method at the instance of importer, bank usually in the importing country sends a letter to the exporter giving an assurance or an undertaking that the payment will be made soon after shipment. In order to ensure that the exporter complies with the agreed terms and conditions of sales contract, the letter from the bank stipulates submission of certain documents. As credit is given to the exporter on the basis of documents, the methods is referred to as a system of payments through documentary credits.

According to the Uniform Customs and Practices relating to Documentary Credits (UCP), documentary credit has been defined as 'any arrangement whereby a bank acting at the request and in accordance with the instructions of a customer (the importer) undertakes to make payment to or to the order of a third party (the exporter) against stipulated documents and compliance with stipulated terms and conditions.' Payment through documentary credits have become popular because the mechanism therein reconciles the conflicting interest of buyers and sellers. In this method, a bank gives an undertaking to the importer that he will make payment to the exporter only after he has ensured compliance with stipulated terms and conditions. At the same time, he also gives an undertaking to the exporter that payment will be made as soon as documents evidencing compliance with stipulated terms and conditions are submitted.

Q2. "In export-import trade, people deal in documents and not in goods." Critically examine this statement.

Ans. Refer to Chapter-2, Q.No.-6 (Pg. No.-70)

Q3. Discuss the role of Export Credit Guarantee Corporation (ECGC) of Indian in promoting exports. Also describe the various risk cover policies issued by ECGC.

Ans. Refer to Chapter-2, Q.No.-19 and Q.No.-20 (Pg. No.-91)

Q4. Describe in detail, various stages involved in the shipment of export cargo.

Ans. Refer to Chapter-3, Q.No.-17 (Pg. No.-132)

Q5. **"Export incentives have become a universal practice." Discuss.**

Ans. Refer to Chapter-4, Q.No.-7 (Pg. No.-151)

Q6. **Identify the institutions providing technical and specialised services to the export sector in India and specify their roles.**

Ans. Refer to Chapter-4, Q.No.-4 (Pg. No.-146)

Q7. **Write short notes on any two of the following:**

(a) **Bill of Lading**

Ans. Refer to Chapter-4, Q.No.-22 (Pg. No.-162)

(b) **Value Added Network Services (VANS)**

Ans. A value-added network (VAN) is a private, hosted service that provides companies with a secure way to send and share data with its counterparties. Value-added networks were a common way to facilitate electronic data interchange (EDI) between companies. As the Internet created competition for this service with the advent of secure email, VANs responded by expanding their service offerings to include things like message encryption, secure email, and management reporting.

A value-added network simplifies the communications process by reducing the number of parties with which a company needs to communicate. The VAN accomplishes this by acting as an intermediary between business partners that share standards-based or proprietary data. VANs are set up with audit capabilities so that the data being exchanged is formatted correctly and validated before it is transferred to the next party. VANs are sometimes referred to as added-value networks or turnkey communications lines.

(c) **Inter-modal Transportation**

Ans. Intermodal transportation is the movement of cargo from one location to another location via more than one mode of transportation (i.e. rail, road, river/ocean). Unitisation, in general terms, may be defined as consolidation of a number of bags, boxes, packs, etc. in a single cargo unit, the most important of which is the container. The purpose of unitisation is to assist the process of cargo handling through reducing the handling frequency of each cargo unit. Unitisation has particular relevance to the making up of a number of "small sized" items into one unit of standard size.

In international trade, containerisation has become a predominant form of unitised transport. It enables the transportation of cargo from the warehouse of the exporter to that of the importers directly. Containerisation offers many advantages including the following:

(i) Speed and economy of handling

(ii) Safety both with regard to breakage and pilferage

(iii) Greater efficiency due to less re-handling of individual packages

(iv) Less packaging cost

(v) Less cost of insurance and handling

(vi) Door-to-door transport service.

(d) **Documents against Payment**

Ans. Refer to Chapter-2, Q.No.-1 (Pg. No.-62)

▲ ▲ ▲

Export Procedures and Documentation: AED-01
June, 2020

Note: Answer any four questions, including question no. 7 which is compulsory.

Q1. State the major trends of India's exports? Do you agree with the view that India's exports are concentrated in a few markets? Explain with examples.

Q2. What is the method of realising payments under Documents against Payment (DP)? How does it differ from that of Documents against Acceptance (DA)?

Q3. What do you mean by Post-shipment Finance? Explain the various methods of Post-shipment finance.

Q4. Describe in detail the various stages involved in Custom Clearance.

Q5. Explain the framework of export incentives in India and analyse as to how far it provides a total approach to export promotion.

Q6. Discuss the procedure for obtaining Advance License under Duty Exemption Scheme.

Q7. Write short notes on any two of the following:

(a) Pre-shipment Export Finance

(b) ISO 9000

(c) Linear and Tramp Shipping Services

(d) CIF Contract

Export Procedures and Documentation: AED-01
December, 2020

Note: Answer any four questions, including question no. 7 which is compulsory.

Q1. Do you think that "The basis of international trade is to be found in the diversity of economic resources in different countries"? Discuss and describe the importance of international trade with suitable examples.

Q2. Explain the foreign exchange rules concerning exports under exchange control regulations.

Q3. Describe the methods of quality control and pre-shipment inspection for the export of goods.

Q4. (a) Describe the procedure for taking a policy from ECGC along with the obligations of policyholders.

(b) Discuss the procedure for making a claim from ECGC along with the documentation formalities involved.

Q5. Describe the customs clearance formalities relating to export of goods along with the documentation formalities involved.

Q6. Describe various government policy making and consultations related to institutional set up involved in promoting exports from India.

Q7. Write short notes on any two of the following:

(i)   General conditions in export contracts

(ii) Financial guarantees of ECGC

(iii) India's Trade Promotion Organization

(iv) Exports under central excise seal.

Export Procedures and Documentation: AED-01
June, 2021

Note: Answer any four questions, including question no. 7 which is compulsory.

Q1. Enumerate the steps involved in the processing of an export order and explain any three steps in detail.

Q2. (a) You are a manager in an Export-Import organisation. How is your organisation exposed to the risk as an exporter as well as an importer during the export-import transactions?

(b) Describe the 'spot rate' and 'forward rate' with suitable examples.

Q3. Explain various types of losses under 'cargo insurance' with suitable examples.

Q4. Describe the principal features and legal implications of 'FOB contract' and 'CIF contract'.

Q5. Explain various legal documents required for exports from India and the procedural formalities involved therein.

Q6. What do you mean by 'Duty Drawback Scheme'? Discuss the procedure for claiming duty drawback along with the documentation formalities.

Q7. Write short notes on any two of the following:

(a) Sources of Information for Exports

(b) Rationale of Export Documents

(c) Pre-Shipment Finance

(d) Export Houses

Export Procedures and Documentation: AED-01
December, 2021

Note: *Answer any four questions, including question no. 7 which is compulsory.*

Q1. What do you mean by FOB contract? What are the legal implications of FOB contract? Discuss the general conditions in export contracts.

Q2. List out the steps involved in the processing of an export order. Describe any three processes in detail.

Q3. What is Pre-Shipment Finance? Explain various pre-shipment finance available to Indian exporters.

Q4. Distinguish between spot rate and forward rate. Discuss the foreign exchange risks faced by an exporter and importer with suitable examples.

Q5. What is Chartering? Explain various forms of engagement of the carrier.

Q6. Why is Institutional infrastructure required for the promotion of export? Describe the government policy making and consultations for the promotion of export.

Q7. Write notes on any two of the following:

(i) Need and rationale of documentation

(ii) Role of Export-Import Bank of India

(iii) Port procedure for exportable goods

(iv) Fiscal incentives for export promotion

Export Procedures and Documentation: AED-01
June, 2022

Note: *Answer any four questions, including question no. 7 which is compulsory.*

Q1. What is Bill of Lading? Describe various types of Bill of Lading. How can you create transferability in the Bill of Lading?

Q2. Explain the general provisions regarding imports under the foreign trade policy.

Q3. What do you mean by letter of credit? Describe various types of letter of credit.

Q4. What are various types of standard policy provided by ECGC? Describe the risks covered and not covered under the standard policy.

Q5. Why should exportable goods be insured? Describe the features of open cover policy and open policy under cargo insurance.

Q6. What are the objectives of customs control? State the stages of customs clearance of export cargo and also discuss the documentary requirement along with the procedural formalities.

Q7. Write notes on any two of the following:

(i)   Importance of International Trade

(ii) Pre-shipment and post-shipment credit in foreign currency

(iii) Role of clearing and forwarding agents

(iv) Export of goods under bond for central excise duty clearance.